GOVERNMENT
MUST NOT DO
ANYTHING FOR ANYBODY

"You cannot help men permanently by doing for them what they could and should do for themselves." Abraham Lincoln

A sequel to the book entitled "There is No Demo At All in Government by Political Party Representatives" also by the same author

Dr Cleopas Sibanda

GOVERNMENT
MUST NOT DO
ANYTHING FOR ANYBODY

Dr Cleopas Sibanda

African Occupational Health Doctors (AFROHD)

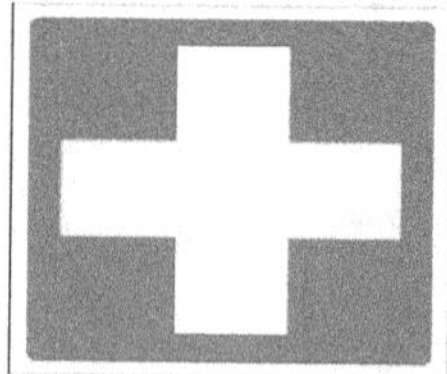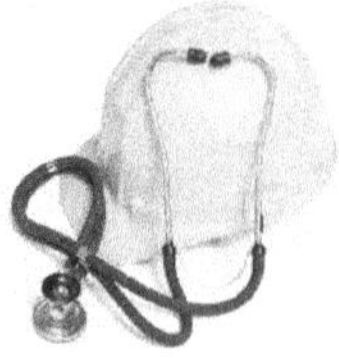

Publications

About the author

Dr Cleopas Sibanda is a well travelled occupational health specialist physician originally from Zimbabwe. He has more than twenty eight years of experience in the field. This is his third book. His first book is entitled "The Management of HIV and AIDS in the Workplace Made Easy." The book was published in 2009 and is freely available online. His second book of which this one is a sequel is entitled "There is No Democracy At All in Government by Political Party Representatives." It was published in 2017 and can be bought online or from any bookshop which happens to sell it. Dr Sibanda says that his many years of service in various health delivery and other public and private service delivery systems have exposed him to both the root cause of and the global solution to most of the challenges which every country and every people face on this earth. He says that government is the cause and also the solution at the same time to most of the challenges which are experienced by people here on earth in general and in their own respective countries in particular. It all boils down to government and governance, he says. And this is the reason why he wrote both his previous and also this book. Dr Sibanda does not rule out writing more such books about happenings in other walks of life of which he may be experienced. Dr Sibanda is a consultant on occupational health, workers compensation and social protection issues.

To my Mom and Dad – I miss you guys!

Published, Marketed and Distributed

By

African Occupational Health Doctors (AFROHD) Publications

An NGO registered under the Swaziland Companies Act No. 8 of 2009
Certificate No. 178 of 2013
Company ID: 201302083001785. Company No. R7/37832
MBABANE, Swaziland.

Cell: +268 7683 3180.   Email: afrohd9@gmail.com

ISBN 978-0-7978-0508-8

This edition printed by:

Table of contents

Page

Quotable quotes about governance

1. Government's first duty is to protect the people, not run their lives. *Ronald Reagan.*

2. The care of human life and happiness, and not their destruction is the first and only object of good government. *Thomas Jefferson*

3. The government's job is good governance for everybody. *Narendra Modi.*

4. Democracy, good governance and modernity cannot be imported or imposed from outside a country. *Emile Lahoud.*

5. The speed of decision making is the essence of good governance. *Piyush Goyal.*

6. I have embrace crying mothers who have lost their children because our politicians put their personal agendas before the national good. I have no patience for injustice, no tolerance for government incompetence, no sympathy for leaders who fail their citizens. *Donald Trump.*

7. I don't make jokes. I just watch the government and report the facts. *Will Rogers.*

8. Giving money and power to government is like giving whiskey and car keys to teenage boys. *P.J. O'Rourke.*

9. One of the key problems today is that politics is such a disgrace; good people don't go into government. *Donald Trump.*

10. The impersonal hand of government can never replace the helping hand of a neighbour. *Hubert H. Humphrey.*

Introduction

If there is one public institution whose existence is known by almost everyone in the world, it is government. And if there is one public institution which is not very much liked by almost everyone in the world, it is government again. People are always patriotic by nature. They love their countries, cities, hometowns and villages, but they usually do not have many kind words for government institutions which govern these places.

The points of contention are usually always the same. All over the world, governments are accused of fermenting unnecessary, self-centred and self-serving socio-political and socioeconomic conflicts, being corrupt and fraudulent in their dealings and generally apt to lie about anything and everything most of the time. And most of the time these accusations actually hold some water.

Governments are prone to keep on increasing taxes year after year, especially the so called sin taxes on tobacco and alcohol. And yet at the same time that governments continue to collect more and more taxes from people, they usually continue to deliver less and less public services every year. What is worse, government public service quality also continues to decrease year after year. Such being the case, casual conversation on buses, in cars, kombis, trains, bars, restaurants, hotels and everywhere is always full of complaints about governments.

What is wrong with government? Frank Kingdom once said that questions are the creative acts of intelligence. On the other hand, Albert Einstein once quipped that the formulation of a problem is far more essential than its solution, while Thaddeus Galas said that what happens is not as important as your reaction to what happens. Medical doctors know that all these wise sayings and the original question which generated them – what is wrong with government - are good and relevant to the solution to the government problem. There is definitely something wrong with governments all over the world if everyone is always complaining about their own government. The question is just what the hell is wrong with governments?

Without the correct diagnosis there may not be the correct solution or treatment to any problem. The good question of what is wrong with government is an intelligent request for the correct diagnosis as alluded to by the wise sayings quoted above. Immediately after arriving at the correct diagnosis, the next good question must be pathogenesis or how and why things are wrong because it is the meticulous formulation of the problem which will give rise to the solution to that problem like what Albert Einstein said as quoted above. And as is the case with all challenges, setbacks, or problems, all these things matter less than our own responses to them. Our own responses to problems must never make problems more problematic than they already are. In medicine the dictum is "first, do no harm."

So, what exactly is wrong with government? Is the problem in the making, i.e., the processes and mechanisms by which governments are installed? Or is the problem in the structure of government, i.e. that almost rigid supportive framework which is made up of all government institutions? Or is it in the ways in which government functions, i.e., those physiological processes which keep government alive and kicking as a vital organ of the state. Or is the problem in the character of government itself, i.e., in the blood which runs through all governments and their various institutions? Or is it just about almost everything which is wrong with government? Where exactly is the pathology in the whole government system and what exactly is that pathology?

Most if not all people who just complain about government everyday and everywhere in this world have never taken time to ask themselves all these pertinent questions, let alone try to answer them. And yet without asking all these questions and also without providing correct answers to them, there would not be any solution to the ubiquitous challenge of bad government. Such a passive reaction to this challenge is not helpful at all as alluded to by Thaddeus Galas in the quote above. Governments are not myths or mysterious animals of which we as the governed people have absolutely no clue. People are not government creations but governments are creations of the people. Governments may sometimes fail to understand their own people because they did not create them, and consequently they may also fail to serve these people well, but people must always be able to understand their own governments because they are the ones who created them. Such being the case, people must not just demand that their own governments serve them well, but they must also make these governments serve them well. This is what this book is all about. Serving people well does not necessarily mean governments actually doing things for anybody. It just means that governments must ensure or make sure that all people under their jurisdiction have access to all the basic services which they want or need at all times, everywhere and anywhere. The question here will only be about the physiology of it or how government must work or function in order to ensure high quality public service delivery.

The approach which this book takes in trying to answer the question as to what is wrong with government is very systematic. You may realise that the question of wrong or right is a very subjective one. Essentially, it is a matter of opinion, perception, thoughts or expectations. And this is where this book starts from. Are our own opinions and expectations of government as individuals, communities, societies, countries and nations good, right and correct, or are they bad, wrong and incorrect? What exactly is the universally correct mandate, purpose, duty, responsibility or obligation of government? And how must government deliver on its mandate in terms of what it must do and how it must work or function as it does it? What is the best structural outlook or framework of government in terms of fitness for purpose or function? All in all, what is the best strategy which would cure government from there being something wrong with it as everyone else seems to think that there in fact is something wrong with government? All these pertinent questions and much more are answered in this book. Just keep on reading.

Chapter 1: Our expectations of government are wrong

Is anything and everything possible with government?

In generally what do most people anywhere in this world expect of their governments? It is not an exaggeration to say that most people expect their own government to be friendly, fatherly, motherly, brotherly, sisterly, kind, understanding, sympathetic and even very, very generous towards them. They also expect it to be powerful, merciful and beneficent in a Godly kind of way. Such being the case, most people expect their government to always be there for them and provide them with everything which they cannot provide for themselves either as individuals, communities or nations. For example, many people expect government to provide them with things like food, housing, shelter, health, hygiene, education, training, transport, communication, justice, safety, security, peace, freedom, joy, happiness, human dignity, personal identity, and socioeconomic growth and development whenever they may not be able to provide themselves with these things.

Proof that such expectations about government exist in every general population in this world, if ever proof was needed in the first place, is amply provided by politicians and governments themselves. During election campaigns, politicians and their governments try to outdo rival contestants in promising to do anything and everything for the electorate once in power. They promise not only good, responsible and accountable governance, but plenty of service delivery too. They promise people that once in power, they would deliver all sorts of services including cheap food, affordable energy, affordable or even free housing, free healthcare, free education, affordable transport and communication, safety, security and many more other basic human needs or basic necessities of life. The electorate usually cheers, dances and ululates to all these tasty promises without even thinking about whether or not it is actually possible for any government to be able to practically do that in the first place. After all, people seem to believe that government is the nearest thing to God there is on earth so anything and everything must be possible with government, they seem to surmise.

Our collective political heartbreak

Yes, it is very heartbreaking that politicians everywhere in this world routinely win elections by making false promises and telling clear blue lies to the electorate. Yet in this regard, all politicians must be forgiven. It is not entirely their fault. They must be forgiven because they make the false promises and tell the clear blue lies which the electorate itself actually wants and expects them to say during election campaigns. This fact was clearly pointed out and actually demonstrated in my previous book entitled "There is No Democracy At All in Government by Political Party Representatives."[1] If politicians did not tell such clear blue lies or make such false promises during election campaign times, even when they themselves as politicians know these things to be false, the chances of them winning would be very slim. The electorate would not vote for them but for those who tell such clear blue lies or make such patently false promises to them. Unfortunately, this is just the way it is. This phenomenon is quite paradoxical. The biggest mystery of all this is that most of the time, the electorate itself also knows that it is being taken for a ride, but they still want to go on and take the ride anyway! Apparently, the thing is that the electorate would be pinning their hopes on the false belief that a change of guard or a change of political leadership, may bring about real changes in the way government works or delivers public services to them.

New cast, same old story

But only changing the cast or just changing the players would not at all change the end results or the tragedy which the politics of public government actually is all over the world today, especially in sub-Saharan Africa and other developing countries. There must also be a change of the basic storyline first and foremost if the electorate wants to end up differently from the comic tragedy of false hope and false promises year in and year out. But apparently, at every election time we just keep the same old storyline, change the players and continue to be heartbroken from one political term of office to another. As the electorate, we never seem learn at all.

The tragedy which public government politics is today

Currently, our public government politics is actually a tragic comedy of dodgy political caricatures who routinely win elections by emptying stinky buckets of muck over the heads of opponents and then loudly foul-mouthing these opponents to largely clueless, ignorant and misguided, but enthusiastically cheering mobs of purchased supporters. Besides energetically, dramatically and rather comically trying to show how very bad their opponents are, our winning politicians cannot at all say or prove how very good they themselves are. And neither do they have any substantially different, good or better plans for the future for our various politically beleaguered countries. What is worse is that the general electorate itself just blindly buys into this crap, hook, line and sinker, year in and year out. Politically speaking, this is really tragic!

Politics must be about substance and not rhetoric

Unfortunately, many people have come to the assumption, belief and conclusion that politics is a complete waste of time. After watching fresh and new politicians exchanging power from one election to another over decades but witnessing no substantial changes in their lives or the state of their nations, no one must blame such fatalistically despondent people. It is only natural.

People say that kids say the damnedest things, but no one says the damnedest things like a politician who is vying to be elected. In a small twelve-council-seat town somewhere in Africa, one politician who was vigorously campaigning for a town council seat once promised his audience that if they elected him as their ward councillor, he would build dams, bridges and airports for them! His constituency was just a small town ward with absolutely no river or stream and no major road passing through it, let alone space for an airport or even a helipad! But the biggest surprise was that the crowd cheered this lying and false promising politician on, ululated, stomped their feet and clapped hands for him all the way through his Shakespearian campaign speech which was full of sound and fury but signifying nothing. Needless to say, the false promising politician went on to win the ward council seat hands down!

Politicians routinely claim that once elected they would create thousands, hundreds of thousands and sometimes even millions of jobs for the people who would have elected them into power and also for everyone else. And yet most of the people who vie for elected political positions are usually not even employers by themselves, and neither would they have any capacity whatsoever to create even just one job at their own homesteads, let alone in the whole country. But they just brazenly bluff their way through like that anyway. And people still clap hands, stomps their feet in apparent appreciation and vote them into power regardless. Currently, most of our national politics are comical tragedies brimming with such mesmerism, flirtation and deception as must boggle the sane mind.

False first world political promises

One political contestant who wanted to be in there for the long haul once promised his audience that once elected he would, within a ten year period of time, turn around the fortunes of his country so that it would instantaneously become a first world country. And yet his very small country, small both in terms of population and land surface area, was not only the poorest country in its part of the world, but probably in the whole world as well. On a scale between one and five, it probably fitted squarely into the fourth or fifth world status, but that did not prevent this enterprising politician from having such utopian dreams about its next socioeconomic growth and development trajectory and destination! Or was he just taking his chances and goofing through it all? Regardless of hard facts on the ground which indicated the impossibility of the promised miraculous turn around in the fortunes of this small country, our false promising politician was cheered on and supported all the way through. And yet seventy-five percent of the country's population was rural based and also extremely poor, living on less than one United States (US) dollars per day each. The country was highly riddled with tuberculosis, HIV (Human immunodeficiency virus) and all other imaginable diseases of poverty. School attendance rates were as low as thirty percent and morbidity and mortality rates were sky high. Just how on earth could such a country be transformed by a single individual from being a fourth world country to becoming a first world country within just ten year flat would have been a mystery to any correct minded person? But then on that fat promise alone, he won the lections! As much as we may want to say that politicians are not entirely correct minded people, perhaps we should also say the same thing about the electorate itself as well. If we are sane, how come we always end up with crazy politicians in our governments all the time?

We need to change our political fortunes

There is absolutely no question about the fact that we desperately need to change our political fortunes. Our whole world and individual nations are definitely hurtling towards some very, very serious disaster of one kind or another because of mismanagement by our governments and politicians. We could be heading towards something bigger than the last world war if we are not careful. We must urgently take stock of where we stand politically ourselves as individuals and also do the same about our countries. Politics is everywhere and politics is what governs and runs our lives every day. If we think or believe that politics is a waste of time and refuse to be involved in it, we will only be cheating ourselves because whether we are actively involved in it or not, politics still determines our destinies as individuals, communities or societies. In fact politics determines everything which we do and which happens to us on a daily basis. There is no denying this fact. Such being the case, we must all stop being smart Alecs about our political involvement and go out there and get actively involved in politics in one way or the other in order to shape the future we want for ourselves, our countries and our future generations. Anything less than this would just be crooked and fallacious thinking.

We have misguided political expectations

As we take stock of our current situations as individual nations and also of our current positions as individual people in the field of politics, me must agree that most of us have poor, wrong or misguided political expectations of ourselves, our governments and our politicians. The evidence is there everywhere for everyone to see. Here is some of the evidence: Most eligible people have given up on politics. They no longer want to listen to, hear, see, think, talk or do anything related to politics. Of course, this is a very big mistake on their part as has already been pointed out above because politics is always coming back to bite these people where it really hurts most, and it is actually biting them every day as we speak. Evidence of this is provided by their daily complaining about shoddy public service delivery systems, skyrocketing commodity price inflation, ever rising unemployment rates, rampant crime and so forth and so on. These people who have abdicated on politics are misguided in the sense that they believe that someone somewhere is going to sort this political mess out for them without themselves as individuals being actively involved or helping out somehow or in any way whatsoever. Unfortunately, there is nothing as unhelpful and further from the truth than that. The fact of the matter is that a man's head cannot be shaved in his absence. For that to happen, the man must be physically present in person together with his head. Political battles are not won for you by anyone but you have to win them for yourself.

More evidence of our misguided expectations come from the fact that politicians and their governments lie and make false promises in our faces year in and year out, but still year in and year out we continue to vote for them. We all vote for these lying politicians one way or the other. Usually, a very vociferous but misguided few or minority amongst us actively votes for these liars at the ballot box, while the quiet but enlightened majority of us do so by passively boycotting the polls erroneously believing that we would be fixing someone or something and yet we would only be fixing ourselves through our political abstinence. Remember that silence means consent. And of course, the biggest evidence of our misguided political expectations comes from our belief that government is some sort of earthly God, father or mother who is there to look after, feed, clothe, house, secure and protect us all from all sorts of evil as already alluded to at the very beginning of this chapter. This is very tragic indeed!

The biggest question is why are we so misguided about political issues today? What is wrong with us? Where did we lose it? In the following few paragraphs, I shall try to humbly show you the things which are wrong with us and which have caused us to be so misguided and so wrong about ourselves, politics, politicians and our governments. I really do not know if this disease can be treated or not, but it is deeply rooted in all of us and very widespread too. The disease is called ignorance, the good same old ignorance!

Today, most people do not know much

If people continue to win elections based on trivialities, lies and false promises, then what hope is there for this world in terms of national politics and socioeconomic growth and development? Where has the real substance gone in our national and global politics? One would think that in this so called information age and knowledge based economy, people would know better than to listen to the lies and false promises which politicians everywhere in this world routinely tell us every day, but the answer is no. In politics, we do not seem to know any better than during the good old days of underdevelopment. Maybe those good old days were even better because the people of that time usually wanted concrete proof before they believed anything they were told. Today, it seems like people do not need any proof at all in order for them to believe anything. They just need to see it, hear or read about it in the newspapers, on the internet, on social media, on radio or on television and that's it, they believe! To make matters worse, the recent advent of internet based false news has created even more confusion. There is false news now, but then there is also false, false news! No one knows what to believe anymore.

Unfortunately, it is not very far away from the truth to say that today's highly revered knowledge and information based superhighways and the internet have bred a rather amusing generation of people who do not know anything and who also do not think or reason on their own or for themselves! This is really tragic indeed. Despite what they think or want to believe, today's kids and their wannabe quasi-middle-class egocentric and highly pompous parents actually know and understand much less real substance about the world around them, the world in which they live, than their olden days counterparts. This paradox is aptly demonstrated by Cambridge University North Korean Professor Ha-Joon Chang in Chapter 17 (Thing 17: More education in itself is not going to make a country richer) of his book entitled "23 Things they don't tell you about capitalism" pp 178 - 189 (Penguin Books, 2011) [2]. In that masterful book, the professor credibly argues that because of today's rampant and extreme technological innovations and advancements, today's information, knowledge and technological age industrial general workers, for example, possess much less productivity relevant information, knowledge and practical job skills relevant to their own jobs than their industrial age counterparts did way back then in the 1850s to early 1900s. For example, because of automation, many industrial workers have been relegated from being skilled artisans who could actually do amazing things with both their hands and their heads (brains) down to mere manual labourers who just pick up finished boxes of goods from machines and stack them up on shelves ready for dispatch. This is really unfortunate and such a big waste of both viable and valuable human brains.

Shopkeepers who are illiterate and innumerate

Even today's shopkeepers no longer need to know much about how to count, add and subtract as they used to do in the industrial age past. Today everything, sometimes even including counting out the change, is done for them by the computerised and bar-coded vending machine-like tills which shopkeepers sit around and operate. And to say that they actually operate the tills is a histrionic, big and boastful exaggeration because in reality, the till machines actually operate themselves while the shopkeepers just sit there and punch a few buttons without as much as even thinking about what they would be doing or knowing what would be happening inside the till machines as they do so! All they know is that at the end of the transaction, they must receive the change and the till slip from the machine and courteously hand both over to the customer with an urbanely polite smile, and their job is done!

If working has become so much robotic, how much of the brain is actually being used to do the work? Perhaps none at all or just very little of it! Inevitably, this work-related mental idleness is then transferred to everything else in life, including to the game of public government politics. This is the main reason why politicians can today get away with murder as far as telling clear blue lies and making false promises is concerned. No one asks them the real tough questions or demands that they speak real commonsense or stop telling lies or making false promises because the generality of their audiences also knows nothing about anything, let alone the politics of public governance. All that we seem to know and understand today is to Google things up on the internet and believe everything which we get from there. And what is worse is that while we are on the internet, we seem to be interested in trivialities rather than really substantive issues. Really substantial and important issues never take centre stage on the internet as compared to what can be called rubbish. This is very tragic indeed!

Educated people who seem to know nothing

Even when we put the massive technological advancement and the technology based industry aside and strictly consider the good old knowledge and skills based industry, there is actually not that much difference in terms of the paucity of or the diminishing individual job knowledge and job skills which are now required there too as compared to the little knowledge and skills which are needed in today's productive and tertiary industry as already demonstrated by the issue of the shopkeepers and till operators above. Because of the availability of too much knowledge and information and the advent of super-specialisation, today's professionals as individuals actually know and can do much less than their industrial age counterparts. For example, old time medical practitioners (doctors) were indeed total and complete medical practitioners as individuals because they could practically diagnose and treat almost all illnesses from medical, surgical to psychiatric, and also in all human beings from pregnant women, newborns, children, adults to the elderly. They could also do post mortems as a matter of routine. But today's medical practitioners are individually nowhere near like that! Today's doctors have become high-end individual specialists who can treat only particular given specific illnesses, only in one particular part of the body, and also only in a given specific and particular age group or population! Someone once cheekily defined a medical doctor specialist as someone who knows more and more about less and less so that in the end he or she knows everything about nothing! To be very honest, a medical practitioner who knows anything and everything there is to know, say, about dermatological malignancy (cancer of the skin) and pretty nothing much about anything else as far as human diseases and aliments are concerned cannot be said to be a very useful or knowledgeable medical practitioner in terms of the politics of public health services delivery! The above cheek in tongue definition of a specialist is today not very far away from the truth as far as it describes not only the various and specific professional groups such as medical doctors, but also as far as it describes even the general population as a whole. However, as far as medical doctors go, one wonders if we still got any real and complete medical practitioners left out there in this world anymore? Indeed, today's world seems to be full of educated people who do not know much about the world that they live in, especially when it comes to government politics.

We are the educated fools of politics

If our day to day professional lives and perhaps also our daily lives in general, have inadvertently become so highly specialised, trivialised and compartmentalised, ditto goes for our political and social lives as well. That is the inevitable result of such a situation. Is it any wonder then that even today's highly educated people are routinely and repeatedly taken for a ride by our false promising and lying politicians? That is to say if we can refer to less (in terms of quantity) but high-grade (in terms of quality) information, knowledge and job skills in one particular individual person as being highly educated in the first place! The answer to this question is definitely nope. In today's high-grade cutting edge technology, knowledge and information based socioeconomic super-highways, the fact is that individual people as individuals actually possess far much less knowledge, information, technical skills and understanding about the world around them or what they do and how they do it than the people of the industrial age era. And yet the pool of community and societal information, knowledge and job skills, and the rate at which these things can be shared within and between our communities is much, much greater than before. What an unfortunate paradox this is. It looks like the more educated we get as society, the more ignorant we become, or is it the more stupid we become, as individual members of that society? Or maybe today we are not exactly getting educated in the true sense, meaning and functional nature of the word education, but we are just getting learned the bookish way? Perhaps we are just learned and not educated people after all, or we are just educated fools? Take your pick, but we definitely need some serious improvement as far as our functional political, government and general knowledge are concerned, or else we shall continue to be used and abused by wannabe politicians who lie and make false promises to us every day.

In the politics of life, academic excellence is overrated

The above tragic state of affairs in our communities, societies and social lives today as far as our diminishing individual capabilities are concerned is well illustrated by the real life observations in some of our own neighbourhoods everywhere in this world, but especially in black Africa. The general observation is that those among us who are highly intellectually gifted, the intelligencia or intellectual *cream de la cream* of our societies, usually end up with first-class university academic and professional degrees and doctorates. These people become super-high class academics and professionals and then get employed as innovative industrial researchers and developers who then give birth to the high-grade and cutting-edge industrial technologies, ideas, theories and concepts which have undeniably transformed our world into the touch-button extra-automated technological world it is today.

The second best grade of our intelligent people end up with second grade university or college degrees and usually go back to join the ones they left behind in colleges to become the usual day to day professionals such as teachers, nurses and artisans among others. These are the people who actually work, do things and sustain us every day in this world. As already alluded to above, the third best intelligent group of people amongst us end up with college diplomas and degrees and working as the usual professionals (teachers, nurses and artisans) who everyone takes for granted until they withdraw their services one day. These chaps spend the rest of their lives in employment or just working for somebody else. Rarely do they ever get to work for themselves. Maybe the reason for this is that they just got too much work on their hands to even start thinking of how they can profitably work for themselves. But ain't we grateful that we have such dedicated professionals in this world! Without teachers, this world would probably grind to a proper halt, and that is the truth.

Anyway, the famous high school dropouts or the fourth best (if they can be called best at anything) intelligent amongst us usually end up among the piles of garbage that litter our streets today. But a few of them, a very few of them one must emphasize, usually ends up pulling up amazing stunts and miracles. As soon as they drop out of high school, these people face the harsh realities of life head-on. Maybe for the exact same reason that they drop out of high school, they usually also simultaneously drop out of home and end up living on the streets. Out there on the streets, they get broke for prolonged periods of time, thereby forcing them to step out of their scholastic dreams and comfort zones and to embrace the real and unforgiving world out there with both outstretched hands. They would really not have much choice but to do just that. Out there on the streets, high school dropouts have some hungry and sleepless nights which force them to quickly learn to believe in and depend on themselves. After failing to make it through formal education, these high school dropouts quickly realise that they cannot limit themselves to the rules of the classroom. They have to somehow try to make it in life, and make it differently too in terms of doing it without that much of a formal education. They quickly learn the hard way that in real life, things do not always logically and rationally add up. Four and four is not always equal to eight. In real life, sometimes four and four is equal to zero, other times it is equal to eight, and sometimes it may be equal to sixteen. It all depends. These high school dropouts also deliberately and quickly lose the people who do not believe in them, these usually being their "successful" high school friends and all the detractors who think that they are failures in life just because they dropped out of high school. They then, out of necessity, start to do some very practical stuff and other things to help themselves out of their own bad situations. Sometimes they start or join social clubs, start or join informal businesses and start or join political parties. They contest elections and lose again and again. They start businesses and dismally fail many times. But they keep picking themselves up and trying again and again and again all the time. They keep on doing so until one day, boom, they hit the jackpot! Call it just being lucky or anything that you want, but eventually, some of these initially despised and so called high school dropouts have become highly successful politicians, presidents and prime ministers, or even highly successful industrialists, investors, business tycoons or business magnates of one variety or another! Today these high school dropouts are the world movers and shakers. They are the people who drive our national and world industrial and political economies. These are the people we today beg to lead us into the Promised Land and deliver us from the combined evils of poverty, diseases, corruption and crime. And these are the very same people who employ all of us today from our first class Virgin Airliners and Silicon Valley computer geeks, down to our lowest class back street and ground floor intelligencia!

The now obscenely successful high school dropouts are the people who refused to make the classroom be their world but made the world their classroom [3]. These are the people who are really educated about the way the world works and functions and how to get your fair share out of it. And these are the really educated people and not the pretenders to the throne whom all of us seem to be today. For of what real and practical use or value is a high class university degree, doctorate, college diploma or school leavers certificate if without getting a job or being employed by another person, you could starve to death despite having such very high sounding academic and professional qualifications? The answer to this rhetorical question is pretty obvious. An educated person is the one who can independently survive in any situation he or she may find himself or herself in. There is indeed a very big difference between being educated and being learned. Thus in real life politics, academic excellence is indeed overrated! And this is the reason why politicians make fools of us every day.

The entrepreneurial spirit always carries the day

Anyway, to continue with our real life observations, fifth level intelligencia (actually the not so intelligent amongst us) usually drop out of school at primary school grade level. The only thing which they walk out of school with is what they brought along with them in the first place. This would be the usual traditional, cultural, social, religious and moral education, or the things which they learnt while they were still at home before they even came to school. From a very early, young and tender age in life, these primary school dropouts also learn the hard way in exactly the same way as the group just above them, their high school dropout counterparts whom we discussed in the paragraphs immediately above this one. Primary school dropouts also quickly learn that they have to use whatever little education they have and depend on themselves if they are going to survive in this harsh, cruel and unforgiving world. And yet by the time their more "successful" counterparts graduate from universities and colleges, some of these primary school dropouts would also have long made it in life just like some of their high school dropout counterparts described above. They would have long made it as high level and high profile amazing miracles performing prophets, preachers and practitioners of the traditional, cultural and western religious varieties. Some of them would be commanding full and overflowing churches every Sunday or even several times in one week as evangelical Bishops, Pastors, Prophets or Preachers. Others would be having day and night fully loaded consultation rooms as traditional healers, black and white magic man, fortune tellers and clairvoyants of all descriptions. Never mind what the holier-than-though and pretentious people amongst us would say during the day about these preachers, prophets, traditional healers and magic men, some of these people will actually be rolling them in big time, really big bucks, just like their more successful businessman and politician high school dropout counterparts discussed above. And guess what? Who would be spending their hard earned bucks purchasing the services of all these spiritual and miracle men? It would be just about all of us! From the first class super intelligent Silicon Valley destined whiz kids down to the dullest of the dull, we all converge at the doorsteps of preachermen, prophets and traditional healers trying to heal ourselves of unknown ailments and also trying to purchase a little bit of luck so that we can also make it rich in our different life endeavours just like them! In the meantime, just like what politicians and businessmen do, it would be the pastors and the traditional healers who would actually make it out of our stupid, desperate and befuddled benevolence. What a bizarre world we live in today! Such being the case as described above, politicians can continue to lie to us and make all the false promises which they can make, and they shall continue to get our blind votes, year in and year out. What a pity really, and what a shameful and heartbreaking tragic comedy has our naivety laden participation in public government politics become today. Even educated people are hopelessly fooled by the simple and lying politicians who they continue to vote for!

School rewards caution while life rewards daring

What the above observations about our different destinies in life tell us or indicate is that academic excellence may actually be overrated if it is not in fact actually overrated. Top academic achievers are not necessarily guaranteed to become top achievers in real life. It looks like real life situations require more than just "the ability to understand a concept, memorise it and reproduce it in an exam. School rewards people for their memory while life rewards people for their imagination. School rewards caution while life rewards daring. School hails those who live by the rules while life exalts those who break the rules and set new ones." These words of wisdom are supposed to have been uttered by one Jack Ma from China some time ago. Thus, the major problem with the way we practice politics today is that we are very academic about it. We are full of bookish attitudes and bookish expectations about politics, politicians and government. We must all come down from our high tables and sit flat on the ground if we want real change in the way we are governed by our politicians.

Our political storylines must change for the better

In order for our political storyline to change from the current tragic comedy to romantic comedy, the electorate must force politicians to first of all write correct storylines if they want to be voted into government. For example, instead of being fed clear blue lies and false promises, the electorate must somehow force aspirant government politicians to write storylines of comprehensive, holistic and sustainable national and global socioeconomic growth and development systems, guaranteed national food security systems, proactive national housing development systems, flexible national health services delivery systems, outcome or results oriented national education and training systems, dynamic national transport and communication systems and universal national social protection systems before they can be voted into government. Such would be the kind of politics which would positively and significantly change the outcome or end results as far as public government is concerned. And yet this is the kind of politics which is extremely rare in this world today, especially in African. What a very sad, sad, sad situation this is indeed! Today's electorate seems to just want to hear clear blue lies and false promises and more clear blue lies and false promises year in and year out! One day this has to change and it shall change. Just keep on reading this book and then do your own part as a responsible member of society and also as part of the electorate in your own country and you will see what would happen. Things would definitely and really change for the better I promise!

A political paradigm shift is needed

In order for the political storyline to change from the current tragic comedy of clear blue lies and false hope to perhaps a romantic comedy of socioeconomic growth and development for example, the governed public must take stock of what they really want or need from their government and what government can actually do in practice and what it cannot do. They must also take stock of what government must of should do and what it must not or should not do. It cannot be that government must or should do anything and everything for the public. There are things which governments must do for the people and then there are things which the people must do for themselves. The electorate must first of all take serious stock of these things and then change their expectations of government accordingly. In other words, the public itself must first of all change its own attitude towards politics and politicians in general and get real in order for politics to get better.

The public must seriously ask itself if it is feasible or even desirable for government to do anything or everything for everybody or anybody. For example, can government provide everyone with affordable food, free housing, free health services, free education and affordable transport and communication services? Does any government anywhere in this world have the capacity to do that? Does it have the necessary resources required of such a onerous task even if it might have the desire to do so? Does government have the knowledge, technical skills, financial, human, material and many other resources which are required for such a task? Obviously there is no government on this planet which has the capacity to play God with its people like that. And yet the electorate apparently still expects government to play fusty with them like that and most governments still continue to promise the same fusty stuff every time before being elected into power! For us to end up differently in terms of our own personal, community and national political and socioeconomic fortunes, we have to individually and collectively change our perceptions and expectations of our governments to more realistic and more practical ones than the current unrealistic and altruistic views which we seem to tenaciously hold on to. A political paradigm shift is really needed here.

Chapter 2: The actual mandate of government

The basic mandate of government

Broadly speaking, there are only two natural or God given mandates, duties, responsibilities or obligations of government. First and foremost, the major purpose of government is to be the main custodian of national existence and national identity (i.e. national sovereignty) in addition to being the chief custodian of the national purse and all of the country's natural resources. As chief custodian of the whole country, all of its natural resources and its entire population, government must then ensure that everyone contributes to and benefits from all of these things in its custody, from each according to his or her capacity to contribute, and to each according to his or her basic human needs. This is the first major, most important and most basic mandate of any government anywhere and everywhere in this world.

The second most important basic mandate, obligation, duty or responsibility of government is not to do anything for anybody as many people routinely and erroneously suppose, but to just ensure and insure that everyone under its jurisdiction has access to and actually enjoys all their basic human rights. What this means is that government must just make sure that all of the people under its jurisdiction have access to all the basic human rights which they are naturally entitled to. And that in the event that these people, for one reason or another, cannot access these basic rights, then government itself must insure, guarantee or see to it that they do so without fail.

Government must do without doing

Ensuring or making sure that someone has access to something is not exactly the same thing as physically providing that person with the thing in question. However, insuring that someone has access is actually guaranteeing that it shall happen, and that may mean practically providing that person with the thing in question or paying for it to be provided and then seeing to it that that person actually gets that thing. In the case of government obligations, duties and responsibilities towards people accessing their basic human needs and human rights, insuring access is the last resort while ensuring access is the first option and not vice versa. This means that more often than not, government must not directly do anything for anybody, but must just ensure that it is done. It is very important for people to know and appreciate the difference between these two similar and yet very different modes of operation as far as government mandates, obligations, duties and responsibilities to ensure that people under its jurisdiction access their basic human rights are concerned. Government must and shall practically do things for its people by itself only as a last resort and not as a first point of call. This is because practically doing things for people is actually not government's natural or God given mandate. The reasons for this shall be explained and laid bare in this and all the other subsequent chapters of this book. And this in fact is the major reasons why this book was written. We need to make that vital paradigm shift from being fixated with government doing things for us to doing things for ourselves with the help of government. And this is the paradigm shift which would make our public politics much better politics, devoid of lies and false promises.

Human rights

Human rights are intrinsic or natural entitlements which people, either as individuals or as part of humanity, communities or societies, are naturally born with. Human rights are God given entitlements or rights. All human beings, without exception and without discrimination, are naturally entitled to the whole full range of basic human rights and they must be allowed and assisted to enjoy all of them and fully so too. That is what the laws of nature and the laws of natural justice demand of all of us as individuals and even more so as governments to assist and ensure that such happens everywhere in this world.

The United Nations (UN) Universal Declaration of Human Rights (UDHR) of 1948, and many other UN treaties and conventions as well, have tried to enumerate some of the more important basic human rights which people must be allowed to access and enjoy anywhere and everywhere in this world. Some of these UN and other UN agencies human rights conventions are briefly enumerated below as follows: The International Convention on the Elimination of All Forms of Racial Discrimination (ICERD, 1956); the International Convention on Civil and Political Rights (ICCPR, 1966); the International Covenant on Economic, Social and Cultural Rights (ICESCR, 1966); the Convention on the Elimination of All Forms of Discrimination Against Women (CEDAW, 1979); the Convention Against Torture and Other Cruel, Inhuman or Degrading Treatment or Punishment (CAT, 1984); the Convention on the rights of the Child (CRC, 1989) and the International Convention on the Protection of the Rights of All Migrant Workers and Members of Their Families (UN ICRMW, 1990).

The International Labour Organisation (ILO), the World Health Organisation (WHO) and many other UN Agencies as well also have very important internationally recognised human rights conventions which deal with issues which are closely related to their own field of work. All those other international human rights conventions and not just the UN ones listed above, are also very important and must be observed as well. That is the way it must be with all world governments and their respective countries.

Such being the case as it is, some of the more common basic human rights are as follows: the right to life, liberty, freedom and happiness, the right to personal independence, self-esteem, self-actualisation and self-determination, the right to social protection (i.e. food, housing, shelter, clothing, health, hygiene, water, sanitation, education, training, transport, communication, safety, security, peace), the right to justice, human dignity and personal identity, and the right to socioeconomic growth and development (i.e. the right to own wealth or to be wealthy). All these basic human rights must be protected and accessed by everyone without exception.

Ensuring access to basic human rights

When one studies the contents of all the international conventions and treaties of the United Nations and all its Agencies with the view that national governments are mandatorily obliged to actually (i.e. practically or physically) do all the things which are listed therein, one might be overwhelmed by the enormity of it all to the extent that one might think that it is practically impossible for any national government to do that or achieve it. And yet that is not the case at all. National governments do not have to actually do any of these things by themselves in terms of practical implementation. They just have to ensure that these things happen and thus that all people under their jurisdiction have access to all their basic human rights.

How can national governments ensure that all their people access their basic human rights? All what national governments must do is to just put in place operating systems and mechanism, legal and otherwise, which would ensure that universal access to all basic human rights actually happens and then just monitor, evaluate, review and continuously improve such operating systems and other enabling mechanisms as and when necessary. For example, the fact that people have the right to life does not mean that government must go around impregnating women by itself or forcing men to do so and thus ensuring that children are born. No, not at all, because such would be criminal, ridiculous and unheard of! In this case, government must just put in place legal and other operating systems and mechanisms which would allow people to have children if and when they want to do so.

For example, many countries have legislated legal ages of sexual consent and marriage at which people could legally have sex, thus also implying that they could also now have children or get married if they want to. Countries have also legislated legal ages of majority or of being "a major" or an adult at which time a person can independently do anything which they want including getting married, but of course, always within the confines of the law. Such legal mechanisms ensure and enable there to be life. It would be a blatant quadruple denial of basic human rights if national governments were to completely ban sex or pregnancy or tell people how many children they could or could not have, and yet such has actually happened in some countries of this world! The right to have sex, to be pregnant and to have children are already three separate basic human rights by themselves. Having sex, being pregnant and having children can separately be sources of great joy and happiness, and being happy is another very solid and accepted basic human right on its own. And that makes four of them in just one sexual scoop. Anyway, the detailed discussions of each one of the more common basic human rights, what they mean and how government can ensure and insure that people have access to them and so forth and so on are found in Chapter 7 of this book. In this chapter we concentrate more on what the actual mandate of government is or should be.

What government must do and not do

Now that we have established what the basic mandate of government is, the next most important question which must be answered is that what must government do in order to deliver on its mandate? And subsequent to this question, how must government do what it must do in order to deliver on its mandate? The flipside of the first question is very important as well: What must government not do as it tries to deliver on its mandate? In this chapter, we are going to answer the first question and its flipside. The question of how government must do what it must do in order to deliver on its mandate is answered in chapter 4 and also in many of the other subsequent chapters of this book. In subsequent chapters of this book, each one of the basic human rights which were enumerated in some paragraphs above is discussed in detail in terms of how government must ensure and insure that people under its jurisdiction have access to and actually access each one of the basic human rights in question. Some of the basic human rights which are discussed further like this are the right to life, liberty, freedom and happiness; the right to personal independence, self-esteem, self-actualisation and self-determination; the right to social protection (i.e. food, housing, shelter, clothing, health, hygiene, water, sanitation, education, training, transport, communication, safety, security, peace); the right to justice, human dignity and personal identity; and the right to socioeconomic growth and development. In this chapter, the discussion is now going to be centred on what government must actually do or how government must fulfil its responsibility, duty, mandate and obligation to be the custodian of national identity and national existence (i.e. national sovereignty) and the national purse, and also to ensure that all the people under its jurisdiction access and enjoy all their basic human rights. The above referenced matter is pretty simple really. If one looks very careful at all the basic human rights with the eye to find important commonalities therein, one would see that in summary, government is just obliged to govern, legislate, serve, listen, work, deliver, empower, compete and protect. And that, in general, is exactly what government must do! That's all. Yes, government has the duty or obligation to govern, legislate, serve, listen, work, deliver, empower, compete and protect and pretty much nothing else. It is as simple as all that. Below, we are going to discuss what each one of these duties, responsibilities and obligations of government really mean in practice, while in chapter 4 we shall discuss the how part or component of it.

Government has the duty and obligation to govern [1]

Government has the duty and obligation to govern people, communities and countries. However, this does not mean that it has the duty and obligation to actually do things for people, communities and countries. The definition of to govern is to regulate or control. When one regulates or controls something, one does not get intimately involved in whatever that something is all about or is actually doing. For example, when a flow meter regulates flow, the flow meter does not flow with the flow. It just controls the rate and amount of flow which passes through.

One of the most important governing responsibility, duty and obligation of government is to steer or control the national vehicle or the country as a whole in a given direction and towards a given station or destination as chosen by its people. This steering role does not in any way imply that government must then row the country in that direction and towards that given station or destination. It just implies that government must position and stabilise the country for a journey towards a people chosen direction and destination. The rowing part of it can and must in fact be left to the passengers themselves, the people who want to go in that direction and arrive at that destination. The reason for this is because rowing is not part of the original mandate of government. Rowing the country forward is not the principal mandate, duty, responsibility or obligation of any government. It is the natural duty and responsibility of the governed people themselves. The other reason why government must not row the country forward is that government is not naturally equipped for rowing as shall be seen later on in the next chapter (Chapter 3) of this book.

What the above implies is that government must largely confine itself to steering rather than rowing duties. It must confine itself to the role of planning, organising and catalysing national socioeconomic growth and development rather than getting intimately involved in the reaction process itself as if it were also a substrate. As to how government can just plan, organise and catalyse things to move in the right direction at national level while enabling and allowing people to do the rest of the job, Chapter 3 of this book is there just for that.

Government has the duty and obligation to legislate

In order for government to be able to govern, control or regulate, it must of necessity legislate. This means that it must develop, examine, debate, pass, enact and finally enforce governing legislation. Legislation refers to the laws, rules and regulations which government uses to govern, control or regulate society on a daily basis. Contrary to what many people think or believe, the second most important mission or function of government is not to legislate as what the order in which these issues are discussed in this book might imply, but to accomplish certain specific government duties and responsibilities for and on behalf of the governed people through legislation. It is just that legislation is needed first and foremost before any other government mission or function can be accomplished. This is the reason why legislation must be discussed first before any other government duties which are dependent on it can be discussed. When developing and passing legislation, government must be driven by the function, mission or objective of the legislation and not just by the legislation in itself as a piece of legislation. What this means that when passing any legislation government must be mission oriented or mission driven rather than rule driven. Rules must be there to serve the mission because the mission is naturally more important than the rules. The mission is not there to serve the rules. Many governments get lost in this regard when they prioritise the rules instead of the mission. The dictum is that if the rules prevent the mission from being accomplished then the rules must give way to the mission and not for the mission to succumb to the rules.

Government has the duty and obligation to serve

Government is there to serve its people and not the other way round. It is as simple as all that. Government has the duty and obligation to be the servant of the people and not to be their master. Naturally, people have the right and capacity to do things for themselves and to determine their own destiny with or without government. Such being the case, government has the responsibility, duty and obligation to be customer oriented or customer driven. And it is people who are customers here and not government. As such, government must aim to satisfy the needs of its people first and foremost, instead of aiming to satisfy its own needs or the needs of its own bureaucracy. For example, many governments routinely pursue white elephant, short term but very expensive national projects which they believe would win them votes in the next general elections at the expense of long term and realistic national socioeconomic growth and development issues which the country and the people actually need and which may even cost far less than the white elephant projects. Such is very unfortunate, sad and tragic but it happens all the time in all our countries. Such government behaviour would not be in the service of the people and the country but it would be in the service of government alone. And yet government has the duty and obligation to serve the country and its people and not just to serve its own interests or to be served by the country and its people.

Government has the duty and obligation to listen

Government has the duty and obligation to listen to its people. People are the government and government is the people. Without people there is no government. People were there first before government was there. This is a fact. This is not like a chicken and egg question. Present day national governments are a very recent phenomenon compared to cultural, traditional and customary law based local community governments. Individual families, clans and tribes have always governed themselves in their own communities and in their own good ways without present day national governments. In fact, present day national governments are actually guilty of interfering with cultural and traditional norms, values and communal government systems. This is one of the most important sources of the political conflicts which we see all over the world today. For these reasons, government must know that even though it has the right to govern and legislate, it cannot do so without listening to its people, without their consent and without their participation. As part of its duty and obligation to listen to its people, government must not be arrogant. Government must know, accept and understand the fact that it may have plenty of brilliant ideas of its own, but actually it does not know anything about what its people really want or need [1]. It also does not know much about how the people want what they want or need to be delivered to them. Such being the case, government cannot do anything on its own or by itself. It needs a lot of information, assistance, expert advice and help, financial support and many other such things from the people themselves. Arrogance would not help government to go anywhere or to get the assistance or help which it needs from its people in order for it to be able to govern them correctly, properly, efficiently and effectively.

Very close to not being arrogant, government must also be very far sighted, broadminded, thorough, comprehensive and holistic in its approach to tacking its intrinsic duties, obligations and responsibilities. It must see the bigger picture and how things are intertwined and interact, and then together with the people, determine the most appropriate course or action to take in order to give people what they want or need. Government must know and understand the fact that it cannot govern people if it cannot listen to them because government is actually by common consensus. Without common consensus between people and government, then government cannot govern them. People would always resist and fight the authority of any government which they do not agree with until the end. This is the main reason why dictatorships and some such other tyrannical and autocratic governments never last. Successful governments have always listened to much more than they ordered their people around.

Government has the duty and obligation to work

Government has the duty and obligation to work or function and to make things work or function. It has the duty to make government work or to be functional instead of not working or not being functional. The right to a functional as opposed to a dysfunctional government is an intrinsic and basic human right too. This brings to the fore the question of how government can and must be made to work or become functional and how it actually works or functions. These two go hand in hand. A functional or working government is a government which is delivering efficiently and effectively on its entire core mandate. In this case, efficiency speaks to the unit cost per given output in terms quantity of public services. Efficiency ensures that people getting real value for the money which government spends on delivering public services. People must get real bang for their bucks or so they say. On the other hand, effectiveness speaks to the quality of delivered public services in terms of their usefulness or being fit for purpose at the highest level. A government which does not deliver efficiently and cost effectively on its entire core mandate is a dysfunctional government. It is a government which is not working. People do not deserve dysfunctional government. They do not need such government, and they have the right to something better than that. Such being the case, no one must stop people from getting rid of any dysfunctional government and getting a new functional government in its place because such would be their basic human right too.

How can government position itself to be a functional or working government instead of being a dysfunctional one? First of all, government must understand that the business of governing is real business and not the political manifesto based dreams and imaginations which people are usually promised by prospective government politicians at election times. Such being the case, government must be business minded in its approach to governing or to public service delivery, its core business mandate. Being business minded means that government must focus on earning rather than just spending. It must become entrepreneurial, innovative and business savvy instead of just conducting its business in the same old, same old fashioned bureaucratic way [2]. For example, instead of cutting budgets or retrenching in order to save money during hard financial times, government must be innovative and start funding results, outputs and outcomes instead of just funding activities or inputs which do not produce any tangible results. Government budgets must not just be about expenditure alone but also about, and in fact mostly about income generation just as it is in the private corporate business world! As far as investment, productivity and socioeconomic growth and development are concerned, government must become innovative and enterprising not by becoming the major investor, producer and socioeconomic driving force of the country all by itself. In this regard, government must promote investment, productivity and socioeconomic growth and development by wisely and cleverly nudging, hedging and leveraging on the free markets and free market forces through subtle market manipulation, stimulation and re-positioning in order to achieve the long term results or outcomes which its people want. However, government or state intervention in the free market must be controlled and calculated instead of being brazen and reckless. And there are many way of doing this without raising any eyebrows. For example without taking its eyes off ensuring functionality, government can regulate, deregulate and sanction as and when necessary in order to steer the economy in a certain preferred direction. After that, it can then just legally monitor, investigate, evaluate, review and continuously improve both service delivery and the governing or regulatory service environment thereof in order to improve the chances of arriving at the desired destination.

In terms of empowering a particular group of people or encouraging (or even discouraging) activity or economic growth and development in a particular industry or economic sector, government can adopt many enterprising initiatives in order to achieve a desired outcome or end result. Legal licensing, taxes, grants, subsidies, loans, loan guarantees, franchising, contracting in or out, public-private partnerships, public-public partnerships, public enterprises and private public enterprises are just a few of some of the methods which can be employed as government takes on a business approach to public service delivery. Government can also strategically use preferential procurement i.e. buying from businesses or enterprises which it wants to promote in the national economy, in order to achieve its public service delivery goals. Government guarantees, insurance, rewards, awards and bounties have all been successfully employed to attain desired public objectives.

Government is one of the biggest if not actually the biggest investor in any country. Such being the case, government investment policy in terms of where it puts its investment money can greatly influence the direction, rate and final destination of aggregate national socioeconomic growth and development. The collection and publication by government of useful and accurate national statistics, social and economic data alone can also catalyse the national economy in unimaginable ways. Armed with relevant and useful business information in terms of market forces, demand and supply situations, both the private and public investors can then come in to invest their hard earned monies with the hope of making more. Technical assistance, vouchers, seed money, naming and shaming detractors and quid pro quos have also been successfully and entrepreneurially used by many national governments to achieve certain desired public service deliver objectives. In fact, the list of business-like enterprising approaches, methods and mechanisms which governments can employ is almost limitless. At the end of the day the bottom line is that one way or the other, government must work or function and it must be seen to be working or functioning. No government must ever be allowed not to work or to be dysfunctional because a dysfunctional government is a recipe for national disaster! Where there is no functional government there is social conflict, war, hunger, poverty, disease, misery, no observation of human rights and everything else which is bad and ugly about human nature!

Government has the duty and obligation to deliver

Right on the heels of its duty and obligation to be functional or to work, government also has the duty and obligation to deliver. This means that it has the duty and obligation to meet and satisfy the legitimate expectations of the people it governs. Since government is by unwritten but common public consensus, there is in fact an implicit instead of explicit but all the same valid psychological contract between government and those whom it governs in terms of expectations. A psychological contract is an implicit as opposed to explicit, and unilateral and opposed to bilateral but mutually shared unwritten and unsigned mental belief or conviction of being owed certain favours in return for certain obligations which one believes they owe the other person. It is like an unwritten and unsigned job contract or understanding between the employer and the employee. Psychological contracts actually exist in every interpersonal human relationship from basic family relationships through employer-employee relationships up to government-governed people relationships. In return for accepting or conceding to be governed by their government, people expect certain quid pro quos from government such as access to basic human rights, public service delivery and social protection. What this means is that people have the right to legitimate public service delivery expectations as far as their government is concerned. For example, people have the right to expect their government to preserve the existence of their country, its defining identity and its people (i.e. national sovereignty). They also have the right to expect their government to be the chief custodian of the country's natural resources, public purse and public image. The right of people to expect their government to govern, legislate, serve, listen, work, deliver, empower, compete and protect are thus all a given. These are all legitimate expectations to which people are entitled. Legitimate expectations are thus human rights too. Such being the case as it may, government has a duty and obligation to deliver on the legitimate expectations of its people. No one must tell people not to expect government to do those things which they legitimately are entitled to expect it to do. In fact, the main job of government is to meet the legitimate expectations of the people. If it cannot meet the legitimate expectations of the people in terms of public service delivery, then government would not be doing its job. The title of this book in no way suggests that government must not do its job. On the contrary, it suggests that government must stick to its job and do it well too instead of doing other jobs which it is not obliged or expected to do.

In doing its expected job, government must produce solid and tangible results and not excuses. It must be results oriented, funding outputs and outcomes and not just activities or inputs. Government efforts must be measured in terms of efficiency (end product quantity per unit cost) and effectiveness (end product quality or purpose fitness) and not in terms of the amount of money, time or multiplicity of activities expended on trying to solve public challenges. In short, government must deliver. It has the duty and obligation to do just that. Anything less than service delivery would be unacceptable.

Government has the duty and obligation to empower

As the title of this book suggests, government must not do anything for anybody. That is not its duty, purpose, mission or function. As it governs, the mission or function of government is to empower individual people, corporate bodies, communities and the whole country to be able do things for themselves. This means that the activities of government must be geared towards empowerment or empowering. Such being the case, individual people, their communities and the whole country have the right to be empowered by government. And they also have the right to expect to be empowered by their government.

Government empowers individual people by ensuring that they access those public services which would make them to be born, live, grow and be able to look after themselves through their own means. Thus, as far as empowering individual people is concerned, government must first and foremost ensure that they have access to effective and efficient public health services which would enable them to be conceived, born and grow healthily throughout their whole lives. This means ensuring access to the right to life. Government must then go ahead to ensure that people have access to all their basic human rights as well, especially the ones which support the right to life such as food, shelter, education, training, transport, communication, safety, security and peace. After that, government must then ensure that an appropriate environment is created which would enable individuals to help themselves in terms of their physical, mental, psychological, social, economic, financial and environmental health and wellbeing. It is this enabling environment which the government must create or ensure that it is created which is its sole responsibility, duty, mandate and obligation as government as far as empowering individual people is concerned. Once it has created the enabling environment, government does not need to do anything else for anyone. It would then be up to individuals to get up and go out there to do things for themselves. This is the reason why this book still insists that government must not directly do anything for anybody. Government must just take the horse to the river in terms of creating the required and necessary enabling or empowering environment. Whether to drinking the water or not is the business of and up to the horse itself. For example, in the presence of affordable and accessible good basic education schools, universities and other training institutions, it is up to individuals whether or not they end up with good and useful academic and professional qualifications which would enable them to find decent jobs, start their own companies or even to work for themselves.

Government must empower corporate businesses too almost in the same or similar way it empowers individual people. As far as corporate businesses are concerned, government must create or ensure the creation of an enabling environment in which business corporations can freely and profitably conduct their own businesses. If that environment is the whole country, then the whole country must be practically open for all kinds businesses. This means that government must put in place conducive investment, financial, monetary and other business incentives, rules, laws and regulations for both local and foreign investors, and in all sectors of the economy too. It must also put in place any other stimuli or incentives for accelerated socioeconomic productivity, growth and development in a direction and towards a destination which is desired by the people. Any other things which may hinder or slow down socioeconomic growth and development such as conflict, corruption, fraud, theft and general lawlessness must be prevented or eliminated from all sectors of the economy. And that is the obligation of government too.

And as far as empowering whole communities is concerned, government must enable and allow communities to govern themselves. This is a very important point as far as the issue of community governance is concerned. National or central governments are usually far removed in terms of time and distance from the communities which they govern. For these reasons, national or central governments usually do not know or are not aware of what goes on daily in the local communities which they govern from afar. It is the local communities themselves which know better about these issues because they are their own issues. Such being the case, it is only logical for communities themselves to be able to govern themselves in terms of making and implementing those public government policy and other decisions which directly affect them, especially the ones which affect only them in the whole country. This is the main reason why there are state governments in large federal countries. This is also the reason why we have local governments such as district, town and city councils all over the world. The saying that the speed of decision making is the essence of good governance by Piyush Goyal rings true in this case.

As naturally existing and almost completely separate entities, individual communities have the right to some form of freedom, political independence and self-determination anywhere in this world. For that reason, they must be empowered, enabled and allowed to govern and serve themselves within themselves instead of being governed or served from outside or from afar. Thus local government must generally be community based and also community owned. Community or people ownership of government is very desirable if actually not mandatory even of central or national government itself. It is foregone that national government must be collectively owned by all the people it governs. That is the only way by which it can be government of the people in the first place. Such being the case, local community governments must also be owned by local people. Local communities must be allowed some leeway to freely make their own choices in terms of how they want to be governed locally and by whom. No one must begrudge or deny local communities their nature given right to freedom of choice and self-determination in this regard because it is their basic human right. In addition to decentralisation as alluded to in the preceding paragraphs, government has the mandate, duty and obligation to empower, enable and allow everyone to participate in government issues, one way or the other.

Individual people have the right to be heard, to vote and to lead. No one must be unduly prevented from participating in government. The right to participate in government is a basic human right which every person has and must be allowed to exercise and enjoy. Such being the case, disenfranchisement for whatever reason is not only a travesty of justice, but also a human rights infringement.

Government has the duty and obligation to compete

Government has the mandate, duty and obligation to enable and allow competition. It must empower, enable and allow individual people, corporate businesses and communities to strive to be the best that they can ever be. And it must also try to be the best government that there can ever be on earth for and on behalf of the people. Individual people, corporate bodies, communities and even governments all have the right to social esteem, self-esteem and self-actualisation. That is the reason why they all have the right to compete and must actually go out there and compete. Competition is an age old natural phenomenon. When the great naturalist Charles Darwin propounded his theory of evolutionary about how species emerged in a survival of the fittest kind of natural completion, he was not stating anything knew. He was simply putting across to scientists to perhaps realise for the first time how all living things including human beings have come to be who or what they are today through spontaneous and natural competition. Competition is not only a fact of life but it is also the mother of excellence. Competition breeds excellent leadership, businesses, goods, services and services delivery systems in all sectors of the economy. There must be transparent, free and fair competition in life in general and also in politics and in business in particular. Competition is the only way by which comprehensive, holistic, viable and sustainable socioeconomic growth and development of the highest calibre can be ensured or guaranteed. Without competition, there is nothing to live for. There would be no growth and there would be no development? What for really? The survival of the fittest theory illustrates this point very well. Such being the case, government must enable, encourage and allow open, transparent, and free and fair competition in every sector of the economy rather than institutionalise monopolies. Not even government operated monopolies must be allowed. Monopolies, public or private, are not good at all for business or for service delivery. Institutionalised monopolies breed sloppiness, poor service quality, inefficiency, conflict, corruption, fraud, theft and all sorts of chicanery throughout the whole country. Thus, government has the duty and obligation to compete and to enable and allow competition everywhere and in every sector of the economy. People do not only have the right to compete, but they also have the right to the best competitive services and service delivery systems there are.

Government has the duty and obligation to protect

Finally, there is no argument about the fact that government has the mandate, duty and obligation to protect all of its people from all and any risks which might confront them. Starting from the risk to life, liberty and happiness down to the risk to social protection itself, government must protect all of its people. In fact, the obligation to protect covers almost everything which government is there for. As far as the obligation to protect is concerned, there is not much difference between godly, governmental and parental functions, duties, obligations and responsibilities. And the best form of protection ever is to enable or empower someone to be able to protect himself or herself. At creation, the creator enabled all living things including people to protect themselves one way or the other and so do our parents as well when they teach us to grow up and fend for ourselves from an early age. That is exactly what government must also do to all of its people both as individuals and as communities. It must teach and empower them to protect and fend for themselves.

One very important thing which the duty to protect behoves on government is the obligation to be anticipatory, proactive and preventive in approach. Prevention is always better than cure. Such being the case, government must always do horizon scanning and anticipate challenges before they arise or become problems. It must proactively focus on prevention rather than remediation. Common wisdom tells us that remediation is not always possible with everything, and that even where remediation might be possible, the results would never be as good as prevention. Prevention usually preserves the situation as it currently is, while remediation tries to salvage the situation back to as near normal as is practically possible. That is not exactly the same thing as the situation being normal again. For that reason, the obligation of government to protect cannot be overemphasised.

Chapter 3: Government must not do anything for anybody

As you might have realised from the first two chapters of this book, government has the duty, obligation and responsibility to do a lot of things for its people but just not directly. The title of this book is about government not having to directly do anything for anybody as an individual, organisation or community. Individual people, organisations and communities must just be empowered by government and then left to directly do things for themselves and by themselves. That is the whole point of this book. I wonder if there is anybody who can argue with this rather reasonable, rational, logical and desirable proposition. The problem we have with our rather skewed view of government is that we expect government to directly do almost everything for us. For example, when we adjudge ourselves to be poor and also during very hard social and economic times, we as individuals, organisations or communities, often expect government to directly provide us with everything from free food, free shelter, free housing, free health services, free education, free transport and communication services, free safety and security services and sometimes even free entertainment. This is what this book is saying is expecting rather too much of government.

Government must just meet people half way

Those people who may be in need have the right to expect government to assist them one way or the other, but they have no right to expect government to assist them all the way through. Rather, they must seek government assistance with the view of being enabled to eventually be able to help themselves out of their own bad situations.

Usually, this means that they must and will have to meet government half way as it tries to help them out. For example, crime ridden communities must indeed get safety and security services from their government. But the communities themselves are the ones which must play a major or leading role within their own neighbourhoods if they really want to effectively and permanently get rid of crime. With government police services assistance and approval, affected communities themselves must set up neighbourhood crime-watch and crime-stop committees and go to work together with the police to indentify, prevent and stop crime and criminals. After all, it is the communities themselves which know better about who the criminals are in their midst, where they stay, live or hide, and how, when and where they operate. With national police services backing, individual communities can and have thus indeed managed to permanently get rid of rampant crime from their midst. In fact, everyday in our countries, cities, towns and villages, national police and other safety and security services have managed to prevent crime or catch notorious criminals only by roping in the general public in one way or the other and then doing nothing else much after that.

Sometimes the police use paid secret informers or the so called snitches. But snitching is a very risky and dangerous business which even national police and security services themselves are discouraged from routinely using. Most of the time though, police just put up once off anonymous rewards, awards or bounties on the heads of criminals who they want to catch. This is not very different from using snitches but apparently it is more effective and much safer for the involved informants. However, the best way to do it still remains to openly involve the whole community to hunt down and catch their own criminals and then to also protect those community organisations and their members who help to stop community crime in this way in much the same way as the national police services and their members are themselves also protected from revenge attacks by criminals. Thus, community policing is one of the best examples of how government can help people to help themselves without directly spoon feeding or doing things for them. In fact, in every sector of the economy and for every human need or want, there are very many ways by which government can just leverage on the existing social or economic systems, markets and market forces in order to enable self-help or self correction without itself having to directly go in there with guns blazing to put out the fires. As Abraham Lincoln said, "You cannot help men permanently by doing for them what they could and should do for themselves." This is the whole point of this book.

Government is not born to do things for people

First and foremost, the reason why government must not directly do anything for anybody is that government itself is not naturally primed to do things for or to give away things to people for free. On the contrary, government is naturally primed to take things away from its subjects through mandatory taxes of one kind or the other. This is what government actually does best. And this has also been the standard practice for all governments since the emergence of nation states almost 4300 years ago in Sumeria [1] (BC 2100). The old adage that when a man is born, the only two calamities he is sure to suffer in life are government taxes and death was not born out of idle talk but real practice. In the greater scheme of things, the pretentiousness of government of trying to do things for people are its own basic predator and natural killer instincts. They are just political marketing gimmicks or tactics which are cleverly designed to capture public consensus or buy-in so that government can continue to govern and tax the governed people. Such shrewd conquering tactics make individuals and the general public at large, either consciously, sub-consciously or unconsciously, concede and submit to being governed and taxed by their own government. Anyone who has ever crossed government in terms of owing it anything, especially unpaid taxes, will leave to tell you the story. When it comes to collecting its tax dues or what it believes are its tax dues, government mercilessly collects everything that you own! So by nature, government is in fact an inborn control freak and merciless tax collector. That is hardly the face of a benevolent benefactor to me. It is thus not the natural or God given talent of government to directly do things for people in the first place, hence it just must not be expected to do that. This is the main reason why so called political conservatives have always advocated for less and not more government interference or participation in their private lives, especially their hallowed private business lives. Ronald Reagan succinctly summarised it well when he said that government's first duty is to protect the people, not run (read ruin) their lives.

People are born to do things for themselves

The secondly reason why government must not do anything for anybody is that people are born with a natural and basic instinct to survive and to directly do things for themselves. This is evidenced by the existence of primitive reflexes at birth such as the breathing, crying, startle, suckling, swallowing, grip, stepping (walking) and excretion reflexes among many other natural inborn reflexes. What this means is that government, just like God and parents, must not do things for people if, when and where people can do these thing for themselves. That seems to be the natural order of things. God seems to help those who help themselves. The only difference is that government and parents must also help even those people who do not want to help themselves. Government and parents must make such people want to help themselves and then go ahead to see to it that they in fact actually help themselves. This means that government and parents, unlike God, cannot just let people go kamikaze. This is to say that government, parents and other people cannot just let some psychiatric or psychologically disturbed people commit suicide while they watch. Such mentally ill people would always need external help because they cannot help themselves.

Government does not have adequate resources

The third reason why government must not do anything for anybody is that it simply has no capacity or resources in terms of money, knowledge, skills, time, motivation, experience and many other necessary requirements to do things for individual people, organisations and individual communities. The best government can do is to enable individual people and their communities to help themselves one way or the other as has already been stated above. For example, a look at the national financial statistics of any country in this world would show that average government income and expenditure per capita is always lower than average individual household income and expenditure per capita. People as one national group, always earn more money and tend to spend more money per head than their own government. So the truth of the matter is that government just does not have the kind of money which is needed for it to directly do things for individual people, organisations and individual communities, while individuals and individual communities themselves seem to have that kind of money, and with a little help from government, they can actually do greater things for themselves.

Government does not know what people want

As far as knowledge of what people, organisations and communities want or need, and how to do or deliver these things, government is not only out at sea, but it also does not have a compass or sailing chart on these issues. It is completely lost. Government would not know anything of that sort. The experts on these things are found amongst the people and within the communities themselves. This is a fact. For example, how can government know that as a matter of priority, one particular community needs a tarred road more than it needs a primary school while another community needs a primary school more than it needs a tarred road? When governments do things directly for people, they tend to do things which are not the priorities of those people. Unfortunately, this, among many other things, is the origin of many white elephant national projects which we see all over the world today. From small and simple things like bus stops and market stalls which no one wants to use to huge things like always empty and loss making five-star government built and operated hotels, there are plenty of white elephant projects everywhere in this world! What a waste of resources.

Government has no motivation

The issue of motivation is very important. Many a time we always say that whether or not you get something depends on how much you want it. This is very true. How much you want something speaks to how much motivated you are to go out there and get it. Would you do all it takes to get it or when the going gets tough, you would give up? There is no doubt that individual people, organisations and their communities would be much more motivated to fulfil their own immediate and local needs than any far placed and unaffected government could ever be. The truth is that it is the hungry man himself who is more motivated to provide for his own empty stomach than any benefactor who might want to help in that regard. After all, if there happens to be failure to get food, it is not the benefactor who goes to bed with sharp hunger pangs, but the one who carries the empty stomach – the hungry man himself. Motivation, that formidable driving force which makes us do the things which we do every day, is an intimately personal and heartfelt passion. Government does not have that kind of passion for the people and the communities it governs. The only motivation or passion which government definitely has is to stay in power forever. And that has nothing to do with fulfilling the needs of the governed people and their communities or doing anything for anybody. But it has got everything to do with doing everything, anything and whatever it takes to stay in power. Whether or not that has got anything to do with meeting the needs of the governed people is purely coincidental. That is the way government politicians are by nature regardless of what they would want the public to believe. How can someone feel hungry for another person?

Spoon feeding people is counterproductive

The fourth reason why government must not do anything for anybody is that doing things for people or spoon feeding them is a very counterproductive engagement. At the end of it all, spoon feeding actually destroys the intended beneficiary people and their communities by undermining individual and community endeavour, responsibility and accountability, personal and community accomplishment, fulfilment, pride and joy, and also community and societal cohesion. Spoon feeding eventually just about destroys everything instead of permanently helping out. If someone is hungry and they are given ready to eat food which they just eat and thereby quench their hunger, what motivation in terms of trying, effort, responsibility and accountability would that person have to go out there and grow food crops for himself or herself? Perhaps very little if anything at all! Would it not be better then, to give such a person a piece of arable land and teach them how to grow food crops, tend for them and how to harvest, store and prepared the food for themselves? Armed with a good piece of arable land, farming knowledge, skills and other required resources, and with the climate and weather permitting, such a man would never go hungry again, with or without government. This must be old wisdom really.

Good governments are unneeded governments

In fact, just like a good business manager whose presence or absence would eventually be immaterial to business productivity, profitability and success because he would have excellently taught, educated and trained all his employees on how to profitably manage and run, and also how to collectively and individually play their own appropriate roles in running the whole business at the highest level of productivity, efficiency and effectiveness, a good government must similarly also aim to make its presence or absence immaterial in the daily lives of the people it governs. Very good governments must make themselves eventually redundant or unneeded in the day to day lives of the people they govern. Where people continue to need the day to day presence and intervention of government in their normal lives, there would be complete and total failure of government to govern properly.

Good governments are unnoticeable governments

They say that the best indicator of an effective and efficient government is the extent to which people are aware or not aware of its presence in their midst. Where government is dysfunctional, ineffective and inefficient, almost everyone knows everything about government. They know about who the president or prime minister is by name, and also who are the ministers of each and every government ministry or department, their wives, children and relatives, where they leave, what they do on a daily basis and so forth and so on. People would know about all these things because they would have too many complaints about their government in terms of public service delivery. The government would not be working or delivering as it should. Such a well known government would be a dysfunctional government. On the other hand, where and when government is working well, is fully functional, effective and efficient, why would one want to know about who is in government or doing what in there? What for? Why would a child with a full stomach want to know where its mother is? What for?

Personal accomplishment synergises itself

Pride is something which comes naturally to all human beings and all other animals as well. It is an overt or covert joyful expression of personal satisfaction which comes from a deep sense of meritorious personal accomplishment. Pride is one of the most potent individual and community motivators there is. When one looks back at what a splendid thing one would have accomplished for oneself and through one's own effort, one can then afford to confidently and joyfully walk tall amongst other people. While others would wish to emulate him or her, the happy and proud achiever would want to do even much better next time or in another different field of competition. Thus, a joyful sense of achievement and pride can trigger a chain reaction of continuous achievement and pride at both individual and community levels. Doing things for people would take away all that, and take it away for good some times. That is definitely not good at all, and that is why government must not do anything for anybody.

Spoon feeding communities destroys social cohesion

In some religious circles they say that families which pray together stay together. In fact, the same applies to communities and societies as well. Communities which work together stay together. There is nothing as potent in bringing communities together and binding them together as working together for a common cause and achieving success together as a community in terms of solving community challenges or meeting community needs. One thing which government must know and understand is that communities are by nature actually self-contained, self-governing and cohesive entities which have existed, survived and maintained their unique individual identities over many years exactly because of their natural tendency to work together to solve their own problems or challenges. Doing things for communities would first of all take away the need, interest and willingness of individual community members to work together as one community before eventually taking away the same need, interest and willingness at community level and thereby finishing off the actual identity and existence of that community as a community. If government would provide, how and why then would individual members of the community see the need or feel obliged to cooperate or participate in community work at community level? And if government would provide, why and how would any community demand and enforce individual cooperation and participation at community level? There is no way all these things could happen or be enforced because the treason for their happening in the first place would have been directly taken away by government intervention. Spoon-feeding communities just about kills the spoon-fed communities by initially undermining and eventually destroying community cohesion.

Communities govern themselves better than government

My other previous book of which this one is a sequel to as indicated on the cover argues that government is a natural phenomenon and that government has always existed in human lives as well as in nature or in the wild. Naturally, individual communities have their own unwritten but very efficient and effective internal governments, governing systems, laws, rules and regulations in terms of their own traditions, cultures, practices, values, systems and norms. It is these unwritten laws which tame wayward individual members of society and help to preserve the peace in any given community. And it is also the very same laws which help to bind and keep communities cohesively together. Only communities themselves and not governments can monitor, evaluate, review and enforce such internal community laws and regulations. And, please believe me here, these natural community laws and regulations are far more effective and far more efficient at achieving what they were intended to achieve than any statutory laws can ever be. The impact of community behavioural standards is very high. Such being the case, communities enforce standards of practice and codes of acceptable behaviour far more effectively and efficiently than government bureaucracies or service professionals such as the police [2]. Police services would be the first to testify to this fact. Such being the case, government must, by and large enable, empower and assist communities to effectively govern themselves instead of wanting to dominate or directly govern them.

Communities are more committed than government

Government is better advised to keep communities intact and together because communities are better committed to governing themselves than government would ever dream of being committed to governing them. It is as simple as all that, and there are very many examples of how and why this is so. For instance, individual communities have far more commitment to themselves and to both their individual and collective membership than any government or public service delivery system would ever have towards the same communities, individuals or collectives. The reason for this much better commitment towards individual community members is that communities need each and every one of their members to be there and to play his or her part in order for the community to exist, manage or survive. As a small and closely knit family, communities cannot afford to lose even just a single community member, while with government one such loss is just but another statistic. For example, in a very small community, the loss of one member might just take away the only electrician which the community was one hundred percent reliant on! To government, there would always be another electrician in another village or community whom it can use, but to the affected community itself, that would be the end of local electrical services. This is the major difference and also the major reason for the difference between the commitment of communities to their individual members and that of government towards its individual subjects.

Communities know better than government

The other reason why communities can and actually govern themselves better than any national government is because communities know and understand their own challenges and problems better than anyone else, government included. This must be obvious because the challenges exist within the communities themselves and not outside. This question is much like the doctor patient question. Who knows better about how much in pain they are and how desperately they want the pain to go away between the doctor and the patient? Obviously the patient! To the doctor, pain is just another presenting complaint. Of course, this is not to suggest that doctors do not empathise with their patients, but empathy is not exactly like feeling it.

Besides knowing what their problems are, communities understand these problems much better than national government and even better than specialised government service professionals. Communities know what the problem is, where it came from, when it started, how it started, who started it or with it, what they want to be done about the problem, how that must be done, by whom and so forth and so on. This might sound like fiction but it is actually true. Any epidemiologist who has ever cracked the source of an infectious disease outbreak and helped to bring it down would be the first to acknowledge that they would never have done it without community involvement and participations all the way through from start to finish. Any other doctor would also acknowledge the fact that they would never be able to diagnose and treat any disease in any patient without involving the patient and also without getting the full and active cooperation and assistance of that patient. It is just not possible to treat a patient without involving the very same patient all the way through. Apparently, the very same community involvement and participation must be applied to all government systems and structures. Individual communities cannot be properly or even successfully governed without their involvement or participation just because they know better.

Community governments solve community problems [2]

The other reason why communities must be kept intact and be helped and allowed to govern themselves is that while national government and its service professionals and bureaucrats say that they are there to deliver public services to communities, communities themselves are there to solve both individual and community challenges and not just to deliver public services. Communities offer much needed care and support to their members while governments offer services. The best illustration here would once again be a medical one. A chronically ill patient who is admitted in hospital would benefit from splendid hospital health care services. But when that very same patient goes back home to continue treatment, he or she would get stupendously splendid home based care. Watch out for the fact that when at home, the words health and services are naturally taken out of the patient care vocabulary. This is because in hospitals and other health institutions, patients receive health care services with emphasis on the words health and services. This means that while in hospital, patients only receive the kind of care and services which are directly related to their specific health problem, challenge or diagnosis and perhaps nothing else much. In stark contrast, while at home, the patient just receives home based care. There is no health or services about that home based care because it is total, complete and holistic care. It is the kind of care which looks at the patient as a total person, a complete human being who comes in with all his human endowments, wants and needs. Such being the case, home based care does not only look at caring for the specific and immediate physical health and wellbeing needs of the patient, but it also looks at caring for his or her psychological, mental, emotional, family, social, economic, financial and environmental health and wellbeing as well. Home based care is total patient care. And this is the kind of care, and not just service provision, which communities can and want to provide when dealing with their own problems and challenges at community level. Hubert H. Humphrey got it right when he said that the impersonal hand of government can never replace the helping hand of a neighbour (read community). What else could be better than that? Such being the case, would it not be far better for government to just let communities govern themselves in terms of their own needs rather than to want to govern them from afar? The best thing which government would be advised to do under such circumstances would be to just empower, enable and allow communities to do what they do best, i.e. govern themselves, and nothing more.

Communities are more enterprising than government

Communities must be maintained as cohesive entities and be empowered, enabled and allowed to govern themselves and solve their own problems for many other good reasons as well other than the ones already stated above. One of them is that communities can and usually do it in a more enterprising, more flexible, more creative and cheaper way than government or any government service delivery professionals. The problem with government in terms of service delivery is too much bureaucracy. Bureaucracy makes service delivery inefficient and ineffective. There is also no creativity at all in government because of too much bureaucracy. Bureaucracy dictates that things are done or solved in particular given, written down and mandatory standard operating procedures (SOPs). Unauthorised deviation from given SOPs can invite disciplinary procedures which may culminate in dismissal from work. Now, no one wants that to happen to anybody, especially to oneself. Such being the case, even when prescribed standard solutions to public service delivery challenges would obviously not work straight from the beginning, the experienced, disciplined and cautious public service delivery professional bureaucrat would follow SOPs to the letter and spirit of those SOPs and not necessarily straight away do what the challenge obviously invites him or her to do according to his or her vast knowledge and experience. He would only do what actually and obviously needed to be done right from the beginning in that specific situation only after first of all doing the SOPs dictated routine which he knew would obviously not work this time around, then he would report the failure to work of the routine SOPs to his superiors and then ask for permission to move on to the next line of therapy, the one which he knew he would need to use right at the beginning. He would do all this expensive, time wasting and unnecessary rigmarole just to cover his or her backside just in case something unexpected may go wrong in the process. This is because if and when that happens, bureaucratic investigative SOPs would unearth that there was indeed an overlooking or unauthorised breach of the relevant SOPs and therefore the operator would automatically be guilty of not following procedures whether or not it was the overlooking of the SOPs which caused things to go wrong in the first place. This kind of approach is much like saying that someone caused a road traffic accident just because they drove without a valid drivers' license without actually looking at the facts as to what exactly happened and how and why exactly it happen so as to determine the real cause of the accident. Government bureaucracies are so stiff, so dull, so unimaginative, so uncreative and so very wasteful like this.

Communities see the good in everyone [2]

Finally, as far as the need to foster and maintain community cohesion is concerned, government must keep individual communities together and intact and also enable and allow them to govern themselves because when governing themselves communities employ some of the best governance skills ever. Many governments would be better advised to learn a thing or two from their own individual communities in this regard. For example, communities usually focus on what they can do or are capable of doing to help out both as communities and also as individual members of the community. This way, they focus on the capacities and capabilities which they possess instead of focusing on their inherent deficiencies like what most government public service delivery systems would do. Communities prefer to focus on the question of what positives they could collectively as communities or as individual members contribute to community health, social wellbeing and development instead of focusing on what they cannot do or what is wrong with them. Focussing on deficiencies would not bring out any good from anything or anybody. It would just bring out the worst. Professor Ha-Joon Chang says just as much in Chapter 5 (Thing 5: Assume the worst about people and you get the worst) of his book entitled "23 Things they don't tell you about capitalism." [3] In practice, there is no one who is so completely and absolutely lacking or deficient to the extent that he or she does not possess any capacity for anything good at all no matter how trivial that good may be! Every one of us, no matter how bad or lacking we may be, are capable of at least one good thing. And that must be the starting point of getting something good out of each and every one of us. Focusing on our bad side all the time will not get us to change or get anything good out of us. This realisation is the reason why many governments have stopped from referring to places where offenders are confined to as prisons or detention centres but now respectfully and dignifiedly call them correctional or rehabilitation centres or facilities. And rather than continue to punish detainees at these correctional facilities by subjecting them to inhuman and degrading treatment as used to happen in the past, governments are now obliged by international law to focus on what each and every one of these offenders is capable of doing in terms of positively productive talent and then cultivate, grow and nurture that talent to the maximum while the person is still inside so that when they come outside, they could have the chance, capacity and capability to positively contribute to society instead of going back to their bad old negative ways of life.

There is indeed always something positive which every community can do for itself as much as there is indeed always something positive which every individual person can do for himself and for his family or community. Unfortunately, while individual families and communities usually maintain that positive attitude, government usually just sees what is wrong with us as individuals, families or communities. To prove this point, just walk into any police station anywhere in the world today and look at their city statistics board or map. Only crime statistics are displayed there. Different colour coded pins are used to mark places on city maps where particular kinds of crime are rampant such as burglaries, muggings, murders, rapes, hijackings and so forth and so on. There would be absolutely not even one pin which would be indicating where something good usually happens as if nothing good but only bad things ever happen in the city or town in question. And yet in reality, the opposite is actually very true. A lot more good things actually happen in every given community, town or city than the bad things which happen there. But the police, maybe because of their job, so maybe we must forgive them for that, only chose to focus on the bad happenings and where they happen most as they mark their crime statistics boards or maps. This is very unfortunate indeed.

The worst example of focusing on the bad side of things is unfortunately provided by the medical profession, my own profession, once again. In the medically profession, there is absolutely nothing which is harmless. Anything and everything can kill you. Medical doctors would tell you that everything is a toxin and that only the dose makes the difference! Yes, this is very true indeed, but why emphasise on toxicity alone? What about the other beneficial aspects as well? I wonder how many doctors know that the drug safety data sheets which they give to their patients together with their medicines frighten a lot of those patients into defaulting on the treatment because of the myriad of terrible and nasty side effects which are enumerated therein. Usually, there is many times more information about the side effects of a drug than about its beneficial effects in those drug information data sheets! Just check it out and see if it is not true. Then as doctors we wonder why our clients do not finish their courses of treatment? To conclude this chapter, it is pretty obvious from all what has been discussed in detail above that doing things for people when they can do those things for themselves and also when it is better to just empower, enable, assist, allow and then let them do those things for themselves is actually a very big mistake and a monumental waste of time, human, financial, economic, natural and many other scare resources. Even God just gives people the capacity to do things, but does not do anything for anybody.

Chapter 4: Government can deliver without doing

Government can deliver by just being strategic

If government has such solid mandates, duties and responsibilities which cannot be denied as we have seen in the preceding chapters, the question now is that how can government deliver on all those mandates without actually doing anything directly for anybody or for any of the communities which it governs? Is it even possible to do something and yet not do it at the same time, I can hear the reader asking. But yes, it is very possible.

In this chapter, and many other chapters to come, we are going to explore some of the innovative ways by which government can set itself up to deliver on all its fundamental mandates without necessarily having to be there on the ground to do it all by itself. In fact, as you shall see now in this chapter and later on in this book, the beauty of being government is not in directly controlling and ordering people around and then joyfully watching them jumping up and down to your beck and call. The beauty of it all lies in revelling in the amazing simplicity, efficiency, effectiveness and efficacy of your easy but intelligently, meticulously and wisely crafted service delivery strategies as they unravel themselves with such splendid and excellent automaticity right in front of your own and other people's unbelieving eyes. It would seem like government has the Midas or magic touch. That is the beauty of it all, and this is the beauty which this book seeks to impart in all our governments. By just adopting very simple day to day business principles, ideologies and strategies, government can deliver in very, very big ways.

Government can deliver through democracy

Government can actually deliver on all of its given mandates by simply just being a true democracy. For an in-depth discussion of what a true democracy looks like, the reader is once again referred back to my book of which this one is a sequel entitled "There is No Democracy At All in Government by Political Party Representatives." In this chapter, we are just going to browse through some of the basic tenets of true democracy and how they impact on public service delivery principles, systems and strategies.

In any given country, there are very many different government entities or structures which perform government functions. Starting with national government structures, there are state, provincial, city, town and district public government entities. And then there are specific public service delivery administration and governing entities such as environmental, transport, communication, water, energy, roads, health, food, drugs, minerals, agriculture and education administration bodies or authorities. The list of governmental institutions in individual countries goes on and on and on. The United States of America (USA) alone has a total of about 83 000 individual governmental units or institutions and more than half a million elected officials governing and administering them and about 12 million public servants employed full-time in these units [1]. The reason for this multiplicity of governing institution is simple. Central government alone cannot effectively and efficiently run the whole country, no matter how small that country may be. Governing decisions are better made on the ground where they are needed and implemented in order for there to be functional instead of dysfunctional government.

Commonsense therefore dictates that local government decisions must be decentralised to local levels. Centralised decision making would not work for localised government challenges. A lot of things can go wrong in between if decisions are made or implemented from afar. This is the reason why Piyush Goyal said that the speed of decision making is the essence of good governance.

The other reason why government must be decentralised is that it is what true democracy dictates. Democracy is government of the people by the people for the people, so said Abraham Lincoln. What this means is that all national governmental institutions from central government itself to the smallest hamlet administration, must conform to this dictum. This definition of democracy means that any governmental institution, entity or body must be composed of direct representatives of the people it governs, must be put in place directly by the governed people themselves and finally, must govern in the best interests of the people it governs and no one else. That is true democracy. One really needs to understand what true democracy is all about. For a start, a direct representative of the governed people is not the same thing as a political party based representative. A political party based representative of the governed people is not a direct representative of the people because the former takes orders first and foremost from his or her political party while the latter takes orders directly from the governed people themselves without any intermediary in between. Hence the latter scenario is the one which is truly democratic and not the former. The question is how many governmental bodies, entities or institutions in this world are made up entirely of only direct representatives of the governed people themselves? Some people would argue and claim that even political parties also take their orders directly from the governed people themselves, but the question is to what extent is that assertion true? And why have political party intermediation in the first place if representation can be done directly? If it ain't broken, why fix it? The truth of the matter is that there is no democracy at all in government by political party representatives. Anyway, the point here is that government can deliver by just being a true democracy at each and every level of government from central government down to local and institutional government. Democratic government is decentralised government. It is direct people representative and not indirect intermediary or political party based representative government.

Government can deliver through democratic governance

The story of true democracy does not end by a governing body just being a democracy or a truly democratically constituted body as argued above. There are also other very important considerations as well, the most prominent of which is the question of governance. "Governance is the process by which we collectively solve our problems and meet our society's needs. Government is the instrument we use." (David Osborne, Ted Gaebler; 1992: "Reinventing Government" pp 24. Addison-Wesley Publishing Company, Inc. USA). It is one thing to have true representatives of the people in a governing body and it is quite another different thing altogether to have the very same people governing democratically. Democratic governance is people centred and people oriented governance. It puts people first. It is the kind of governance which would always and without exception, make and manage public service delivery structures, policies, systems and operations in consultation and with the consent of the governed people themselves. Many governments just claim to consult the governed people first before they make or implement any public policy decisions. What they do not say is that they only do just that and nothing more. They just consult the people and then afterwards they would go ahead and do as they wish as government regardless of what the people would have said during the consultative process. Now, that would not be doing things in consultation with the governed people or with their consent.

Democratic governance implements people's wishes

Democratic governance is not just about consulting the people just for the sake of consultation itself and nothing more. Public consultation is not the be all and end all of democratic governance but just the beginning of it. Public consultation is not an end in itself but the beginning of a process. After public consultation, the actual views of the consulted people must be respected and implemented. Even those views which might at first seem contrary to logic or to what the government wants must also be respected. The thing here is that when dealing with social and behavioural issues, the science behind these issues is not very exact like the core sciences of physics, biology and chemistry. There are too many variables which influence human and social behaviour, a lot of which we usually do not know or take into consideration in our quest to understand how and why people and their societies function the way they do. Such being the case, what may seem to be quite a sensible priority to government may not at all be a priority to the governed community. Where there is true, effective and meaningful public consultation, it must be community views which carry the day instead of government views. Under such circumstances, the best thing which government could do would be to persuade the community to willingly see things the way the government sees them instead of forcing government views down the collective throats of the whole community. The use of force, coercion, corruption, fraud, cheating and any form of chicanery would not be part of democratic governance at all. Democratic governance is not just about consulting and listening to the views of the people. It is more about practically implementing the views and wishes of the people instead of just listening to them. That is what democratic governance is all about. What good is listening to a beautiful piece of music at a dance party and not dance to it if the goal was to dance? Would there be a dance party under such circumstances?

Government can deliver by just observing all human rights

Here is the big one, if not the biggest one of them all. Democracy is also inevitably intertwined with human rights issues to the extent that there cannot be true democracy without the correct and full observation of all basic human rights. If people are being wantonly killed, have absolutely no freedom of anything, are not happy, have no access to basic human needs and are being oppressed and exploited, then that is not democratic governance at all. By simply observing all basic human rights to their core, letter and spirit, any government anywhere in this world can deliver on all of its core mandates without doing anything much else. In fact, if you looked closely, you would see that this whole book is just about that and pretty much nothing else.

Democratic governances behoves that government does not have the right to dictate anything to the people it governs without their consent. It can only do so with their consent and that becomes not dictatorship at all because the people themselves would have empowered their government to do so for and on their behalf. Thus, the old adage that democracy is dictatorship of the majority is actually true here, even though such is not exactly a true dictatorship. The reason for the acceptability of majority dictatorship as true democracy is that there can never come a time when people would all agree on one thing in any given society. Never! A society in which everyone agrees with everyone else even on just one issue alone is a dead society. The normal thing is that no matter how obviously logical any issue may be, there would always be dissenting voices for one reason or the other, even for absolutely no reason at all other than just wanting to disagree. As far as human rights are concerned, the majority has the right to call the shots in terms of decisions on public service delivery issues while the minority has the obligation to go along with the views of the majority on these issues. This is where the acceptability of majority dictatorship comes from. However, not all questions about human rights need to be decided by majority votes because some of the issues are pretty straight forward. For example, no referendums will be held to decide if people have the right to all their natural freedoms or not and the same goes for the right to all basic human needs and human rights. The only question with human rights is about how best they can be delivered by government without government actually doing anything for anybody but just empowering, enabling and allowing things to happen almost on their own accord. Chapter 7 of this book deals in detail with all these issues.

Government can deliver by just sticking to governing

Principally, government is there to just govern, everything else is just incidental, and this is very true. The problem with many governments and politicians is that they also want to grab the limelight by interfering in issues which have absolutely nothing to do with them, so they end up messing up everything for everybody else. For example, government departments and ministries have been routinely disrupted and rendered dysfunctional by intense politically motivated interference from their own ministers and other politicians. A government minister is supposed to just stick to his or her duties of policy decision making and leave the rest to the experts (Chapter 6 of this book). But, no, these politicians do not want to do that. They want to, and actually also get involved with management decision making, management itself or even operational issues.

Most governments have separate and legally provided for Public or Civil Service Commissions which are tasked with engaging, disengaging, promoting or transferring public or civil servants. But government ministers end up interfering and getting themselves involved in such functions which are not at all their prerogatives. Interfering government ministers illegally and without following procedures, fire their ministerial director generals, heads of departments, operatives or even their own messengers, cleaners and general hands! At the end of the day, everything in the ministry would just become political and eventually complicate into a huge and dysfunctional mess. If only government ministers could stick to their job of policy decision making, then a lot of things would be helped. But no, these people do not do that but interfere.

Without pinpointing any particular group of politicians such as government ministers as being full of unwarranted political interference, even government as government itself in general, is also full of unwarranted government interference in the daily affairs of the country and its people. Former USA President Ronald Reagan was right when he said that government's first duty is to protect the people, not run their lives. Instead of just sticking to governing issues in terms of running the country and all sectors of the country's economy, sometimes government wants to and actually becomes an economic player or operative on the ground. For example, government has no business running business enterprises such as retail stores, supermarkets, banks, farms, mines, building construction companies, transport companies or even schools and hospitals, but many governments actually do that as a matter of routine. The obligation or duty of government in all sectors of the national economy is to just govern and nothing else. The role of governing means that government must just engineer into place the enabling legal, political, social and business environment, install the needed, necessary and relevant legal policy and regulatory frameworks, and then just allow the relevant natural and traditional economic players to take their positions and deliver public services. After that, then government would just legally monitor, evaluate, review and continuously improve whatever may need to be improved in the whole national economic delivery system as and when necessary. Such would be sticking to its actual mandate of governing and not interfering with economic processes on the ground.

There are many reasons why government must not get involved in operational issues of running the economy. As has already been said elsewhere in this book, besides the fact that it is not government business to do so, and also that government has no capacity to do that. Doing so would be overstretching itself because there would be too much for it to do or attend to in that regard. Depending on how one classifies the different types of economic sectors there are, one would only come up with five or less. For example, in terms of ownership, there are only two different types of economic sectors; the private sector and the public sector. In terms of the means of production, there are only four different sectors of the economy. These are the primary production economic sector (mining and agriculture), the secondary production economic sector (processing and manufacturing), the tertiary production economic sector (trade and commerce), and the service production economic sector or service industry (knowledge, skills, information and other services). In terms of classification by the nature of product which is produced, there are only five different sectors of the economy. These are the agricultural sector (agricultural products), mining sector (mineral products), processing and manufacturing sector (processed and manufactured goods), trade and commerce sector (buying and selling of goods) and the service sector (knowledge, skills and information services).

The point here is that if government just confines itself only to its governing duties, then it has got only five sectors of the economy tops to legislate for, regulate, monitor, evaluate, review and try to continuously improve at the very top or holistic level of doing its business. That sounds very much like an easier job to do than trying to stoop down to the lower level of getting involved in actual service delivery or operations where there are numerous and unimaginable numbers in terms of different business entities. Government would never afford to have adequate human skills, technical, financial and many other resources which are needed to run operations, and yet some governments still try their hand in operations. Government must just stick to the business of governing and nothing else. Operations are for trained and skilled operatives. Indeed, government can deliver on its given mandate by just concentrating on the bigger picture of governing in a sustainable, democratic, comprehensive and holistic way instead of splitting hairs down below in operations.

Government can deliver by just correctly strategising

A strategy is a cleverly, wisely and meticulously crafted plan of action which is designed and used to achieve a long term objective. Strategising is the process of coming up with such a plan. By merely just correctly strategising, government can deliver on all its obligations or mandates. And yet many national governments come into office without any tangible and practically implementable strategy or plan of action. They just breeze in together with all their electoral rhetoric and nothing else. Voters would have been promised free food, free housing, free health services, free education, and sometimes even free beer, transport and everything else imaginable. As to how such expensive things could possibly be provided for free to the public, no one would have asked any such questions during election campaigns, and no one would also have volunteered any answers either. And yet those would be the promises which would have won the day for the new government. Sometimes such is the sorry state of public administration politics.

Anyway, in real life, nothing can ever be accomplished in the absence of a proper strategy. Not even just munching and swallowing food! Absent mindedness while eating can result in choking! First of all, government must put all its cards on the table in terms of comprehensively, holistically and critically looking at all its mandates, obligations, duties and responsibilities. It must then strategically prioritise, position and focus these obligations towards the desired outcomes, results, goals or objectives. After doing that, government must then develop a feasible plan of action as to how it can cause its objectives to be achieved without itself necessarily getting involved in the actual action on the ground. This would obviously involve taking into account and planning for such things as resource mobilisation, business incentivisation, and subtle market manipulation and sometimes even the carrot and stick approach. If the adopted strategy is the correct one, government can actually score very many easy goals in terms of success in its given job of governing. It is as easy as all that. The only critical and crucial thing is that the strategy must be a winning strategy and not a losing one.

Correct and functional governance structures are winners

There are just two things which are crucially important in any product delivery system or production process. It is the structure and function of that system. Structure has to be conducive for or in line with function for there to be efficient and effective production or product delivery. This is the reason why people from all walks of life, from school to the factory shop floor, always talk about the structure and function of something. Structure always goes hand in hand with function. The very same logic also applies to government service delivery or governance systems. Structure and function are very important there too. The structure is the one which has to function to deliver the required good or services, and it can only function correctly and properly if it is the correct and proper structure for the given job or function. In other words, a structure can only function correctly if it is a functional structure and not a dysfunctional one in terms of what it is intended to do. Unfortunately, many public government structures or institutions are dysfunctional or not fit for purpose right from the way they were designed and built, and down to the way they were installed or put in place, let alone the way they operate or function. They cannot and actually do not deliver as intended because they are not fit for purpose. Chapter 6 of this book (also see book cover) details the five different, correct and proper government and governance structures which government much put in place and then just sit back and watch them delivering everything which is needed to serve the country and its people. These five basic structures which every government needs to put in place in order to optimise its chances of success in governing are as follows starting from the top: The government oversight structure as headed by the head of state; the government policy decision making structure as headed by the head of the legislature or parliament; the government policy implementation management structure as headed by the head of executive government; the government policy implementation structure as headed by the head of the public or civil service administration; and finally, the government policy implementation audit structure as headed by the head of the parliament of the people. These are the five original basic structures which any and every government must have in order for it to be functional.

The different functions, duties and responsibilities of all these intrinsic and basic structures of government are already given in their nomenclature. In terms of how these basic structures of government work, the doctrine of the separation of powers must be strictly adhered to. There must be complete and practical separation of both powers and people between each and everyone one of these structures of government. Not even one person must ever be allowed to operate or have influence in more than just one structure of government. The best example of what must not happen in terms of separation of powers is that the head of state must not also be the head of executive government. And yet many governments are guilty of combining these two distinct and separate offices into just one office and also into just one person. Such must not be the case if government must work or function properly. There are more detailed discussions on this very important issue of the doctrine of complete and practical separation of both powers and people in Chapter 6 of this book.

Government can deliver by just decentralising

National or central government can actually efficiently and effectively govern the whole country by just letting people govern themselves in their own various states, provinces, districts, cities, towns, villages and hamlets. This means that government can actually deliver by simply decentralising its authority, structures and functions. We have already seen that all these different local communities need to and must have their own local government structures in order for them to exist and functioning properly. What national government needs to do through legislation is to simply turn over local day to day governance issues to these local authorities and then just sit back to monitor, evaluate, review and continuously improve whatever may need to be improved as usual right from the top. Central government does not actually need to come down to interfere with local government on a daily basis. That would be disruptive and it would also render local government dysfunctional. Of course, for there to be law and order in any community, there must be some form of government and some form of governance going on in there, but that does not mean that it must necessarily always be done by national government.

Government can deliver by just being the enforcer

When one hears about enforcers one might immediately conjure up pictures of nasty and mean looking heavily tattooed shady characters in back street lanes who enforce "the law" in the underworld of illicit drugs, prostitution and other trades. But that is not the kind of enforcer which we are talking about here. No one wants government to be some kind of Pablo Escobar, Al Capone or something like that, but government must just stick to one of its natural mandates. This is the mandate to ensure that there is the all round accountability which goes hand in hand with certain privileges, duties and responsibilities of being a player in the service of the national economy. Local governments, private and public businesses and individual people as well cannot just be allowed to have their cake and eat it. They must also account for it. Everyone must comply with all national and local government laws, especially the laws concerned with how to conduct their own businesses and the observance of all basic human rights as they conduct these businesses. Those who do not comply with or breach the laws in any way whatsoever must be made to dance to the remedial music of the law itself and without any fears or favours too. This is the enforcement which we are talking about here. And the best way to be such an enforcer is for government itself to start by being responsible and accountable as far as religiously observing its own governing mandates and obligations is concerned, and then go out there to demand and enforce the very same responsibility and accountability equally and equitably and all round.

Come to think about it, one of the very good reasons why government must not be an active player or operative in terms of actually getting involved in running commercial businesses and some such enterprises in the national economy is that as the enforcer-in-chief of all national laws, how would government enforce the very same laws against itself if it should be caught on the wrong side of the law as one of the players in the service of the national economy? Under such circumstances, leading by example would be very tricky and the best way out would be to just not do it.

Government can deliver by just sticking to governing

Steering or controlling the economy is hard enough a job on its own without further complicating it with the actual rowing of the economy forward as was argued in previous chapters. Thus, government must just stick to governing issues alone and nothing else. The doctrine of complete and practical separation of powers and people must also apply here. The economy as a system can be split into four distinct and separate parts or components. The first and perhaps most important part of any economic system is the legislative component and it consists of the visible and invisible governing rules and regulations which govern how the system must work or how business is conducted in that economic system. The visible rules which govern any economic system are usually the ones which would have been enacted by government, and the invisible rules would be the unwritten but known business codes of ethics and morals and other business codes of conduct, practice and behaviour. Government as the enforcer-in-chief is there to enforce all these economic system governing laws, rules and regulations without any fear or favour. According to the doctrine of complete and practical separation of powers and people, this therefore means that government cannot be involved in any other component of the economy except in this legislative component alone. The remaining three components of any economy are the production, trade and consumption components. Goods and services are first of all produced, then traded and finally consumed. There must be strict rules and regulations which govern how all the four components of the economy must work and relate to each other. The doctrine of complete and practical separation of powers and people must continue to strictly apply here too. Thus, government must stick to governing, producers to producing, traders to trading and consumers to consuming. After all has been said and done, it then becomes clear and obvious that government can actually deliver on all its given obligations and mandates without itself necessarily getting involved in the action or activities of actually doing things on the ground. Thus, government can deliver without doing.

Chapter 5: The correct governance strategy

Strategy is a winner

In any war situation, the correct strategy does not only win the war, but it also wins every battle. In any business, the correct strategy does not only generate profits, but it also clinches every business deal. In public government systems, the correct strategy would not only deliver good governance for the nation, but it would also win every public vote. A strategy is not just a long term plan of action, but it is also a complete, comprehensive, holistic, viable and sustainable plan of action. A good strategy is flexible, malleable and ductile. It takes into account and considers all factors and possibilities, but still remains resolutely focused on the main goal or objective. The problem with government is that it usually focuses on the smaller picture rather than on the bigger picture. Government usually focuses more on winning the public vote and staying in power than on delivering good governance. Sometimes we forget that it is the bigger picture which counts more than anything else. For what use would be wining battles if that would not win the war and what use would be clinching deals if the company would not turn a profit at the end of the year? One can still win more battles than they lose but still lose the war, while one can also clinch more deals than they miss, but still make a huge loss at the end of the day. Actually just like what a lot of the United States of American (USA) presidential candidates have come to realise over the years, one can also will the popular vote in a presidential race bust still lose the elections! It is a good strategy which wins the war at the end of the day and not necessarily each and every little battle which happens on the ground. A winning strategy would always bring home the prize no matter what. And it is a winning strategy which government must put in place not only to win the votes and the elections, but mainly to win the war for good and better governance for its people. For government to succeed in doing this there are a few rules of thumb or strategies which it must of necessity follow. These are enumerated and discussed below.

Government must not divide but unite

For a start, government must realise, know and understand that people are already organised by nature or God into structurally and functionally natural families, communities and societies, and also that these natural societies or communities are already self-governing anyway, with or without the help of central government. Such being the case, government must not politically divide or disrupt people and their natural communities in any way whatsoever, more especially not through the artificial, unwarranted and counterproductive political party based sub-divisions. Natural communities, and this sometimes includes whole countries too, must be politically preserved as intact as is practically possible for the best possible results in terms of good governance. For more on the inadvisability, futility and counter-productiveness of political party based systems government and governance processes, please read my book "There is No Democracy At All in Government by Political Party Representatives." What government must do is to just support, empower, enable and allow natural human families, groups and other human communities such as states, provinces, districts, cities, towns and villages to remain united by the natural community blood which runs through them and unites and binds them all together as one. When united, people, families, communities, countries and nations can stand stronger than ever, but when divided, they can fall apart like houses built on sand. United communities can then be empowered, enabled and allowed by central government to govern themselves in the best way they want or need to without any fears of things falling apart. At the same time it empowers communities to govern themselves, government must never stop playing its governing role of ensuring that these natural communities of people are actually governing themselves correctly and properly by continuously monitoring, evaluating, reviewing and improving their capacities and capabilities as necessary and also by calling them to account for their own actions should that need arise. For such decentralisation to succeed, government must strategise on the appropriate structure and function of each and every decentralised governing body within each and every community. It must do this in consultation with and also with the full consent, support and participation of the intended beneficiary communities themselves.

Government must be the servant and not the master

Secondly, government must realise, know and understand that individual people, their families, communities and societies are by nature their own masters and saviours. Such being the case, government must just allow and assist them as individuals, families, communities and societies to govern and fend for themselves as they actually must do. Government must not as government seek to be or impose itself as the master or saviour of the governed people but it must just remain as their true, faithful and trusted servant.

Government must not dictate but listen

Thirdly, government must realise, know and understand that people already know what they want or need, so it must just let them say or express what they want freely, fairly, clearly and loudly without any fear or favour. Government must not tell people what they want or need, but instead, it must let them tell it what they want or need while it listens, and listens very, very carefully all the time! At the end of the day, a true listener would do as he or she heard and not as he or she wants. After listening to the governed people, government must then go ahead to implement what the people want and not what it wants, more especially when these two things are different. It is always what the people want which must be implemented.

Government must not do but just enable

Fourth, government must realise, know and understand that people know how to get what they want or need, so it must let them go out there and get it for themselves if they can. Government must not do for people that which they can and must do for themselves. Here, the rule of thumb is that if anyone can do something for themselves, then they must do it for themselves and not have it done for them by another person. That is the way it must be.

Government must let people ask for help, not offer it

Fifth, government must realise, know and understand that people know what help they want or need if they need any help, so it must just let them ask for and get the help which they want or need instead of offering any unasked for help.

Government must also not tell people what help they want or need from it or from anybody else for that matter. It must just let the people themselves tell it so instead. People always know what kind of help they want and if they are left alone to ask for it rather that have it offered to them, the bond between them and the helper would be stronger. The other thing is that letting people ask for the kind of help which they want from it or from anybody for that matter rather than offering it would prevent the scourge of unnecessary and rather useless white elephant public projects which adorn a lot of our communities today.

Help when approached, do not dictate helpers

Sixth, government must realise, know and understand that people know who can help them, with what, when, where, how and why, so it must just let them get help, the help which they want or need, and from whoever they want or think is best placed to help them and for whatever reason. Government must not prevent people from getting help or assistance from those who they want to help or assist them. This point brings to the fore the sore issue of governments absolutely prohibiting the employment of foreign workers in certain sectors of the national economy. If business entrepreneurs, for whatever reason, believe that certain foreign workers are best placed to help them and their businesses to thrive and would want to employ such workers, government has no business absolutely prohibiting such from happening. The best it can do is to put in place reasonable as opposed to unreasonable or prohibitive foreign workers employment levies on the concerned employers for employing such foreign workers. Absolute prohibition would violet not only most of the basic human rights in accordance with the United Nation (UN) Universal Declaration of Human Rights (UDHR), but it would also violet the very specific UN 1990 International Convention on the Protection of the Rights of All Migrant Workers and Members of Their Families (ICRMW).

Government must not capture but free talent

Seventh, government must realise, know and understand that the best way to get anything out of any person is to give that person his or her natural and God given freedom. This freedom includes the freedom to govern and regulate himself, freedom to express himself, freedom to think and reason for himself, freedom to innovate, formulate, crystallise and experiment with his own ideas, freedom to help himself, freedom to chose what he wants to do, when, where and with whom, and freedom to do anything else but harm himself, other people and his environment. With such realisation, government can then afford to turn over the responsibility and accountability of man's destiny to the man himself while at the same time, and as government, still hold man personally responsible and accountable for where he ends up in life as it must always do. Government must realise that the best way to unleash any hidden human potential or talent is to free it. A bird can only fly when it is out of the cage. When freed, only the sky would be the limit in terms of the bird's growth, development and productivity! Lack of necessary freedom tends to encase or imprison natural talent, thereby preventing it from reaching its full potential in terms of benefiting both the individual and his community or even the whole country at large. A free man is a very productive man.

Make laws which free people and not enslave them

One of the biggest drawbacks of any national economy is too many and too strict governing laws and regulations. Individual people and their commercial businesses must be given some room, a lot of room in fact, to freely move and manoeuvre as they do business in order for them to succeed and also in order for the whole country to succeed together with them. My own poor and very unfortunate country of birth once so tightly, rigidly and strictly regulated the business, financial and money markets so much so that not even a single cent would escape from the economy and from the country as well. This was during one self-made, self-inflicted and prolonged national socio-economic crisis. However, what that very tight and by and large also very unreasonable control only managed to successfully do was to completely shut down any capital inflows into the country, to exponentially accelerate capital outflows from the country, to shut down banks and all other businesses, to get almost everyone unemployed there and then, and to destroy the whole economy and the whole country as well. It was the dumbest thing which any government anywhere in the world could have ever done. I will not apologise for saying so not only because I also suffered immensely and intolerably because of it, but also because it is the truth anyway. Everyone in my country, perhaps only with the exception of government politicians themselves, suffered a lot and intolerably because of that kind of stupidity. Highly educated professionals suddenly became street vendors and street beggars in their own country, and miserable economic refugees outside of it. Law abiding citizens were turned into black market dealers and criminals overnight. Theft, fraud and corruption became normal ways of doing business. The collective psyche, conscience and morality of the whole country were instantaneously corrupted beyond recognition overnight. A people who were once upon a time a very good and proud people were turned upside down and inside out into some kind of animals which they never wanted to be in the first place. And all this just because of selfish and self-centred control freak government dictators who would not brook at anything but suck their victims like ticks until they dropped down dead!

Just focus on governing and nothing else

Government must just focus and concentrate on its core mandate which is to govern and any other governance related issues. In every situation which may need its attention, government must first of all, and before it does anything else, ask itself this question: What are the governing and governance issues which need government attention here? It must then isolate these governing issues and deal only with those issues alone before living the rest up to the affected people and their communities or organisations to deal with. Thus, government must not do anything for anybody apart from just assisting them with solving governing and governance issues which they may need to be solved by it. And if government can focus and concentrate only on governing and governance issues, it would kill two birds with just one stone. Firstly, it would most probably have the easier of the jobs there is in public service delivery systems because just putting the required legal policy framework in place is much simpler than the complicated and often very expensive process of trying to practically comply with that legal policy framework. Secondly, in case something goes wrong in the actual process of public service delivery, no one would blame government because it would not be the one at the helm of public service delivery operations. The people at the helm would be the public itself and businessmen and their businesses. These would be the ones to take the fall. When people break the law, they cannot blame the lawmakers for that! But if the lawmakers would also be the same people who would be breaking the law, then the lawmakers would have to answer not only to the law which they would have broken, but also to their wisdom in putting that law in place in the first place. That would be a double whammy which no government on this planet may want to be involved in.

If government descends down to the level of doing things on the ground or the level of actual policy implementation, then who would ensure that the environment is good and conducive enough for government policy implementation to happen? And also who would ensure that everyone else is actually playing their own public policy implementation role legally and appropriately as they must? And how much credible would it be for government as government policy implementer to audit and condemn another government policy implementer, say, the private sector for example, when itself is also failing to do the very same things correctly or according to its own laws? How can a match referee also be a player for one of the teams in the same game? That just does not make any sense at all.

Besides the valid point of the myriad of inherent deficiencies which bedevil government in terms of the actual on the ground implementation of public policy as already discussed elsewhere in this book, the above described catch 22 situation must just be enough to show that government must not directly involve itself with the actual implementation of its own policies on the ground, especially its own commercial business policies. It must leave that to others, preferably the highly competent private sector experts and other such players, while it concentrates on just being the national socioeconomic growth and development match referee, with the public service administration (PSA) executive as its linesman. When the helmsman abandons his boat steering role to join in with the rowing crew, there would of course be a lot of powerful rowing and vigorous boat movements which would ensue. And yes the boat would furiously jump, jerk and move forward, but only in circles and actually going nowhere because there would be no controlling helmsman to steer it in the right direction! Such being the case, government must just stick to its steering or governing role. That is what the doctrine of separation of powers behoves on it and everyone else to do. What is good for the goose must also be good for the gender.

Government must strategically deliver through POBEs [1]

And even where it seems that government has no choice but to actually go in there and deliver public services all by itself, there is always a way out in terms of government not being directly involved on the ground as shall be seen later on in subsequent chapters of this book. There is always the practical possibility of creating completely independent but public owned as opposed to government owned private sector commercial business organisations. Such public owned but private sector commercial business companies or organisations would be able to do what government was supposed to do for and on its behalf.

Besides just being public owned, these private sector public owned commercial business enterprises would still be true and complete private sector organisations. They would also still be using private sector principles and practices of conducting business such as being self-sustaining and thus of necessity also being dedicatedly profit focused or profit driven. Anything less than complete conformity with the dictates of the private sector would be a recipe for failure for such public owned private sector commercial business organisations. Thus, contrary to what many people would want to believe, all and any public services can actually be successfully and profitably delivered through the use of public owned but private sector commercial business enterprises or organisations. It is just the adopted business strategy which makes the whole difference.

Many governments have tried to put into place various such public owned private sector commercial business entities, enterprises or organisations with varying levels of success. Some governments call public owned commercial business organisations parastatal companies (PSCs) or Parastatals. Others just call them state owned enterprises (SOEs), state owned companies (SOCs) or state owned businesses (SOBs). Perhaps the best designation for such public owned private sector commercial business enterprises, organisations or companies would be public owned business enterprises (POBEs), companies (POBCs) or Organisations (POBOs). But maybe the actual designation in terms of name matters very little here. What matters most is what these public owned private sector companies are used for. Most of the time POBEs are used to provide those essential public services which could possibly not be left entirely up to or in the hands of the private sector alone without further creating future crisis situations because of their vital nature to human and social life and to the national economy as a whole. Because of their vital nature, essential public services are politically very sensitive services. The key phrase here is "essential public services." Most of these essential public services have everything to do with basic human needs such as fire and medical emergency services, disaster mitigation services, food, shelter, health, education and transport and communication services among others. There is definitely no question about the absolute necessity of essential public services delivering POBEs considering the fact that government cannot and must not do much of its own practical policy implementation on the ground as reasonably advocated for in this book, and yet there are also these essential public services which could not just be left in the hands of or up to the private sector to deliver without potentially creating more disasters or crises in the future. Although the private sector is very good at what it does, obviously, it cannot be trusted or relied upon to deliver everything, more especially essential public services.

As much as some POBEs are absolutely necessary, their Achilles heel is always the same, this being legalised but illegal government interference, corruption and fraud! In fact, the Achilles heel of POBEs is more than just corruption. The problem is also found in the poor and self-serving strategy which is adopted by government in constructing, structuring and managing POBEs. Government ineptitude is what eventually takes POBEs down and not any intrinsic, inherent or congenital disease which afflicts POBEs. Most of the failing POBEs were set up with the noble idea or goal of accomplishing certain very important national objectives. As stated above, government could not just leave essential services delivery objectives entirely in the hands of the private sector. And yet government could also not, for very good reasons too, directly get bogged down with providing such basic services all by itself. Thus POBEs hand to be created to fill in that gap.

POBEs are supposed to be truly public owned business enterprises and not government owned and yet in most cases they are actually government owned and not public owned organisations! And that is one of the biggest causes of their continued or repeated failure. For a start, many governments call POBEs state owned business enterprises (SOBEs) so that they could control and abuse them. Strictly speaking and also by definition, state owned business enterprises (SOBEs) are not exactly the same thing as public owned business enterprises (POBEs). This is because the state is defined as a given geopolitically bounded country together with all of its people, their government and everything else in it. The state is something which is very impersonal so no one can claim to be the state. People and organisations can claim to represent or belong to the state with varying degrees of justification. Government itself, the whole country and everything else in it are all state owned entities. In other words, they all belong to the state. However, people or the public occupy a special position in the state in that as people they are the actual owners of the state. The state belongs to the people or the public while the people belong to the state as people members of state and not as being owned by the state. On the other hand government and the whole country belong to the state and eventually to the people of that state. The state and the government are both public or people owned entities as are SOBEs which must actually be called POBEs and not SOBEs.

Government wants to refer to otherwise public owned business enterprises (POBEs) as state owned business enterprises (SOBEs) as a clever way of by-passing the public so that it could directly control and abuse these public owned entities. Government realises that there is no one who can claim to be the state and yet anyone and everyone can easily claim to be the public or a bona fide member of the public and therefore entitled to have a say in the way POBEs are administered. In fact, the public is not only one hundred percent entitled to have a say in the way POBEs are set up, managed and administered, but it must actually be the one which is completely in charge of POBEs and everything concerning POBEs with government being nowhere near there! The public is the owner of the state, government, the country and everything else in it, and this includes POBEs. Governments must therefore never refer to people as their people like what most of them do because they do not own any people at all but it is people who own governments. Governments deliberately, routinely and erroneously always refer to people as their people only as a clever psychological ploy of making people insidiously submit to their governing power and control.

There is therefore a very big difference between being public owned and being state owned or government owned as far as private sector business entities are concerned. Most of the current POBEs, erroneously called SOBEs by governments for the conniving, clever and tactical reasons given above, are not POBEs or SOBEs at all but just government owned business enterprises (GOBEs). They are GOBEs not only because these so called SOBEs report directly to ministers of government, but also because ministers of government have an absolutely free hand with them. Government ministers have the legal duty, right and responsibility to appoint and dismiss chief executive officers of SOBEs, to appoint and dismiss their token Boards of Directors, to audit them, to dictate company policy to them, and to actually run them as if they were their own chicken coops. Now, that does not sound very much like being anywhere near public owned. It sounds very much like being one hundred percent government owned. Such SOBEs should not be called SOBEs at all but GOBEs for government owned business enterprises, which is what they are in practice.

If SOBEs were public owned entities, then ministers of government would have absolutely nothing to do with them. Nothing at all! SOBEs as public owned business enterprises (POBEs), as they must correctly be referred to, would be answerable only to parliament and not to ministers of government, and that only in terms of performance auditing and nothing else. They would be answerable only to parliament because that is where the public or the people who actually own them can be found in government through their direct representative members of parliament (MPs). Truly public owned SOBEs (POBEs) would have completely independent Boards of Directors or governing structures which would be installed by the relevant stakeholders of each and every one of them and not by government ministers. Where the stakeholders are the general public, then the general public must be given the legal duty, right and responsibility to put in place the governing bodies of all such POBEs. For example, the governing bodies of such public institutions as national energy, water, roads, road transport, communication, health, education and many other similar authorities must all be directly elected into office by the affected general public itself. That is the only way by which such crucially important institutions can become true public institutions and not remain government institutions like what most of them are today. Cleverly referring to a government owned institution as a state or public owned institution does not change the fact that it would still be just another government institution in real practice. Public institutions, by nature and also by design, must outlive governments. POBEs cannot and must not also go up and down and in and out with governments as is the case with the majority of the so called state owned business enterprises (SOBEs) today. In fact, to say that the current government owned business enterprises (GOBEs) are SOBEs is just a ploy by government politicians to disguise the fact that these organisations are just government owned business enterprises which they as government ministers use and abuse for their own corrupt and private benefits. If the doctrine of complete and practical separation of powers and people was adhered to properly by most governments, we would probably never have a situation like this. What a sad state of affairs this is, but it is the naked truth anyway. And yet public owned business enterprises (POBEs) are very crucial public owned private sector commercial business organisations which the state must strategically employ to deliver essential and other vital public services to the people.

Chapter 6: Democratic governing structures

Complete and practical separation of powers and people

As far as correct democratic governing and governance structures and their functions (i.e. duties, responsibilities and accountabilities) are concerned, there must not only be complete and practical separation of powers between all the governing and governance structures of government which are discussed in this chapter, but there must also be complete and practical separation of the people involved in all these governing and governance structures as well. Not even a single person, no matter what, must ever be allowed to simultaneously hold positions or have influence in more than just one governing or governance structure of government at any one given time. Never!

Community based government

All the governing and governance structures discussed herein, as far as is practically possible, must preferably always be based and function in the very same governed communities themselves and not elsewhere. This means that government must be totally decentralised as far as is practically possible. Government must thus be practically owned by the governed people and their communities. And government must be physically present as close to where it functions as is practically possible. This is because for government to be efficient and effective, governing and governance decisions must be made as close as possible to where they are needed or implemented. This is just pure commonsense. The other good reason for being community based is that government must not just be there but it must also be seen to be there in practice and actually working for the governed people to appreciate and concede to being governed by it. Such would auger very well for national peace, stability, safety and security which are some of the most important prerequisites for viable and sustainable national socioeconomic growth and development.

In every economic sector, in every service delivery system, in every industrial sector and in every business organisation, institution or entity whether public or private, government must legally and strategically ensure that there are the following five separate basic organisational governing and governance structures: The organisational policy oversight structure; organisational policy decision making structure; the organisational policy implementation management structure; organisational policy implementation structure and the organisational policy performance audit structure.

The exact designation in terms of name and the exact composition in terms of the people and also the exact internal structure and function of all these five basic organisational governing and governance structures depend on the type of business organisation, institution or entity and the economic or industrial sector concerned. What government must legally insist on is that these five basic organisational governing and governance structures must be there in every organisation, public or private, and they must be given very specific duties, responsibilities and accountabilities too. The reason for this is that when government comes calling as it must do in terms of its other governing responsibility, duty or obligation of monitoring and enforcing things so as to ensure that every person and every organisation are legally doing what they are supposed to be doing in accordance with how they are supposed to be doing it without prejudicing other people and the whole country at large, and also in terms of calling those who might deviate from legal obligations to account for their deviant actions, government must then not be sent from pillar to post as people run away from responsibility as they would naturally always do. When someone needs to be brought to book for any kind of transgressing, public or private, they must be quickly found and easily brought to book rather than for government to get involved in a cat and mouse game of "who was it?" and "it wasn't me!" Right now, we are going to discuss what these five basic organisational governing and governance structures must look like and how they must function by using government itself as an example.

The five basic governing structures of government

Government policy oversight structure

In any and very organisation, public or private, there must always be a legally designated organisational policy oversight structure whose duty, responsibility, obligation and function is not only to take the final fall or accountability for and on behalf of the whole organisation, but also to ensure that the whole organisation, its policies and operations are fit for purpose and are thus delivering or achieving the intended or desired results or impact. At national or central government level this oversight structure would most probably be the office of the Head of State and not the office of the Head of Executive Government or Head of Cabinet as it is usually called. It is only logical for every country or state to have a government oversight structure.

As has already been suggested in the opening paragraph to this chapter and also in the previous chapter in relationship to complete and practical separation of both governing powers and governing people themselves, the Head of State must just be the Head of the Government Oversight Structure alone and nothing else. The Head of State must never be involved or have influence in any other structure of government besides the government oversight structure alone. Double, triple or even quadruple dipping by top government politicians and officials is one of the biggest causes of government failure. There would never be proper checks and balances if government politicians and officials are allowed to double dip. Such must be prevented and avoided at all costs.

The duties of the Head of State would include giving the final seal of approval to government policy decisions but not to debate or to make those decisions himself or herself. Decision making through thorough discussion and debates would be the sole prerogative of the policy decision making structure of government and not of the government policy oversight structure. Please note that government policy decisions include both legal policy and standard operating or governance policy decisions. In terms of its own governance policy, the Office of the Head of State must only give its final seal of approval to government policy decisions after it has satisfied itself that all laid down legal and other procedures were adequately followed in coming up with those government policy decisions. Trying to re-debate the substance of any government policy decisions would be out of bounds for the office of the Head of State. Such would be the sole responsibility and prerogative of the policy decision making structure of government alone and no one else.

Typical Central or National Government Level Hierarchy of Policy Governing and Governance Structures

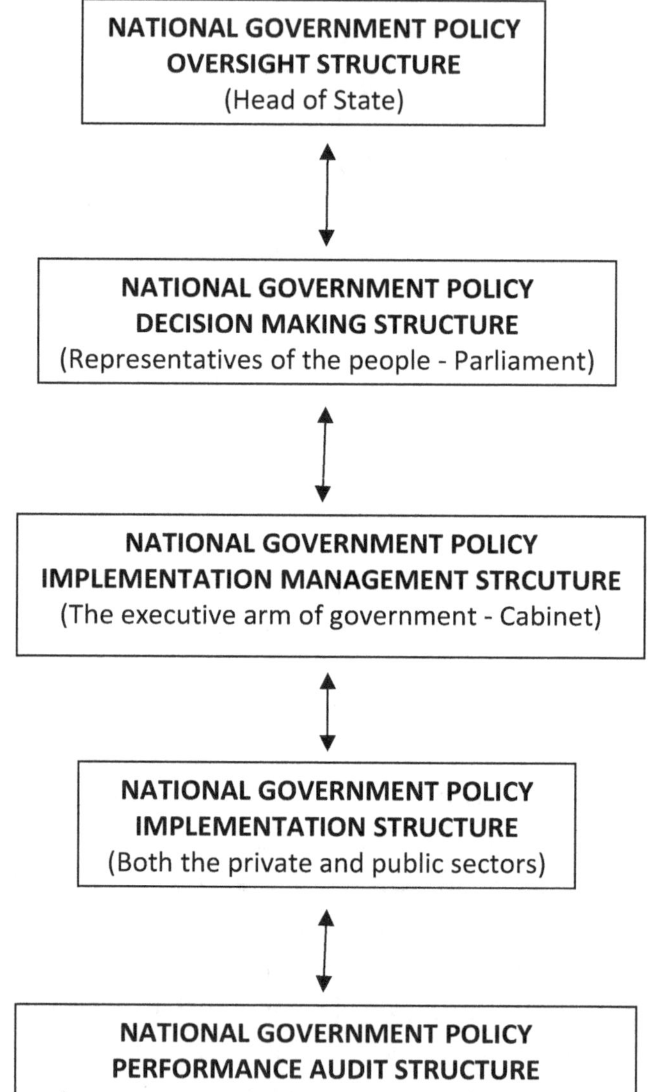

The other duty of the office of the Head of State as the legitimate government oversight structure is to represent the country at and in international forums where and when heads of state are required to do so. However, the office of the Head Of State can only do that with the full consent of the government policy decision making structure because even government foreign policy decisions would still need to be made by that responsible body alone and no one else.

The challenge there is in many countries of this world is that there is no stand alone (i.e. separate and independent) government policy oversight structure as there must be. The offices of Head of State and that of Head of Executive Government are routinely fused together into just one office and also into just one person. According to the principles of good governance of which the doctrine of complete and practical separation of both powers and people actually is part of, this is not at all acceptable and must be rectified. Remember we said that there must be true, complete and practical separation of both powers and people between each and every governing and governance structure in any organisation, public or private. The reasons for the common fusion of the offices of Head of State and Head of Executive Government lies in the republicanisation of many countries as they naturally moved away from being monarchical democracies to being republican democracies. In those countries which are still monarchical democracies, there is usually no problem of separation of powers and people between these two offices because the Monarch automatically becomes the head of state in charge of the government oversight structure, while the prime minister also automatically becomes the head of the executive arm of government in charge of the policy implementation management structure of government. The challenge arises in republican democracies where there is no obvious natural person who can assume the role of the Head of State. However, this is not actually a problem at all because such countries can still choose to have an elected Head of State instead of a monarchical one. In fact it is hereby recommended that they actually do so. The office of the Head of State is crucially important and also absolutely necessary in any country today because of its strategically inalienable and crucial role as the government overseer. Someone somewhere must make sure and see to it that government is not shot-changing the governed people.

Government policy decision making structure

The policy decision making structure of any national government must be the parliament of the people. Ideally, it would have been all the people in the country, but that is obviously not practicable. So the best that can be done in practice is to settle for parliamentary representatives of the governed people. The Head of Parliament would usually be the Speaker of Parliament. Where parliament is bicameral or tri-cameral, that would not change the fact that parliament as a whole still remains the policy decision making structure of government. It also would not change the fact that parliament as a whole must still have one natural person as its head. As to who exactly that natural person must be, that is the decision which parliament itself must make and no one else.

In true democracy, parliament would be composed of majority decision elected or however chosen direct representatives of the people and not political party based indirect representatives of the people. The difference here is that while direct representatives of the people are elected independent of political parties (but not necessarily independent of other political considerations such as representative constituencies) and directly into parliament, political party based indirect representatives of the people must be elected into political party candidatures first and foremost before they are then "re-elected" into parliament. Such indirect parliamentary representatives of the people would obviously be primed to take their voting orders from the political parties which they represent and which they are also directly answerable to as a matter of priority instead of being answerable directly and independently to the people or the constituencies which would have elected them into parliament. If one looks at it very closely one would have to admit to the fact that indirect parliamentary representation of the voters through political party based representatives is not exactly as democratic as it is touted to be. In political party based representative systems, the linkage between the people and their parliamentary representatives is definitely an indirect one, and perhaps even a false linkage!

Anyway, it does not really matter for the purposes of our discussion here as to how parliamentarians end up in parliament although it would help a lot if they were truly democratically elected. What is important here is to know, understand and appreciate the fact that parliament is the sole policy decision making structure of government. But that is not where parliament's functions start and end. Parliament must also be the government performance audit structure providing checks and balances not only to all the other structures of government, but to itself as well. This is because it is in parliament and through representative members of parliament that the people and their voices, eyes and ears all reside. My book "There is No Democracy At All in Government by Political Party Representatives" which has been repeatedly referred to in this book has more details on how parliament must work or deliver on its various people given mandates in Chapters 10, 11 and 12. It would be advisable to re-visit these chapters in that book.

The policy implementation management structure

The Executive Arm of Government or Cabinet would be the government policy implementation management structure. Because of it being in the forefront of government, this is the government structure which is commonly referred to as "government" by most people and yet it is just merely another component of the whole government and not the totality of government by itself as most people seem to assume or think that it is. However, in the present state of world governance practices or how most governments work or govern their people, those who assume or think that Cabinet is the government and that the government is Cabinet may not be far removed from the actual or practical truth which is happening on the ground. Many if not most Cabinets all over the world seem to have hijacked or completely taken over government!

The Head of Cabinet would naturally be the Prime Minister. If the doctrine of true, complete and practical separation of powers and people is followed, in countries where there is no Monarch, the Head of State must be the national President. This automatically disqualifies him or her from also being the Head of Executive Government. And yet in many republican countries, the national President is the designated Head of State and also the Head of Executive Government. This is contrary to the desirable dictates of the doctrine of complete and practical separation of both powers and people. This scenario is obviously inappropriate and must be corrected. It does not auger very well for good and accountable governance.

In many if not most countries, Cabinet Ministers are also elected Members of Parliament (MPs) who are appointed into Cabinet usually also by another elected Member of Parliament (MP) such as a national President or Prime Minister. Cabinet Ministers also sit, debate and vote on any and all issues in parliament just like ordinary MPs. At the end of the day, there is no clear cut demarcation as to who exactly is who and what exactly is whose prerogative in the bigger scheme of things because some people are found in each and every structure of government. This sad fact shows that contrary to common wisdom, there is no true, complete and practical separation of powers in most of our current government systems.

According to the revered doctrine of complete and practical separation of powers and people, Cabinet Ministers must only be Cabinet Ministers and nothing else. They must not even be Members of Parliament (MPs). And as Cabinet Ministers, they must concern themselves with government policy implementation management issues and nothing else. Cabinet Ministers must not be law makers but only managers of the processes of implementing that law. As government policy implementation managers, Cabinet Ministers actually have got a lot on their plates. The process of management involves strategic planning, mobilisation of needed resources and strategic manoeuvring or placement of those resources in readiness for service delivery in terms of putting them in the hands of the actual government policy implementers or operatives. And then once the needed resources have been delivered, management involves letting the actual government policy implementers or operatives on the ground do their job through the use of those resources while Cabinet just continuously monitors, evaluates, reviews and improves the situation as and when necessary from a management point of view. That is a hell of a lot of management work to do for Cabinet and its ministers without it having to involve itself in other things.

One would think that our government cabinet ministers already have too much work to do, but apparently they do not think so themselves if what they actually do is anything to go by. Most of our current crops of cabinet ministers are always interfering with the work of government policy implementers or operatives on the ground soon after they have delivered the necessary resources to these people for them to do what they know best and deliver public services in the true sense and spirit of public policy or of the law. Cabinet ministers interfere with government operatives or those who actually use public resources to implement government policy because they want to also get their hands onto those public resources. They want to illegally, clandestinely and corruptly stick their hands into the public pie and come out with some dough for themselves. And unfortunately, they actually do just that most of the time! This is the reason why our governments are dysfunctional. If cabinet ministers stuck to their duties of government policy implementation management and nothing else, nothing of the sort would ever happen.

Government policy implementation structures

In any country, there are basically just two sectors which practically implement government policy on the ground. These are the public sector and the private sector. The public sector government policy implementation structure may be called the Public Service Administration (PSA) or simply the public service. The PSA governing body must be politically independent or neutral and it must be put in place directly by the public itself as the name PSA suggests. The PSA governing body could be called the PSA Board. Its main job would be to appoint and oversee the executive management of the PSA. All members of the PSA executive management, just like all public servants, must not be actively involved in politics but be politically neutral. And they must also not belong to or be found in any other government structure besides the PSA.

It is very important to note that there is a big difference between government policy implementation management, which is the function of the executive arm of government or Cabinet, and government policy implementation proper, which would be the function of a public service delivery structure such as the PSA. It is very difficult to pinpoint as to who the head of the government policy implementation structure or the PSA could be in most current government systems. The obvious choice would have been the Secretary to Cabinet, but that would not do because already he or she is a member of Cabinet. According to the doctrine of true, complete and practical separation of both powers and people, there is definitely need for an independent head of the public service delivery team, the PSA, by whatever name in terms of designation that he or she might be called.

The designation Chief Executive Officer (CEO) of the PSA might just be suitable for the executive head of this public institution. The job of the PSA would be to actually get dirty and get involved in the practical processes of implementing government policies on the ground. Remember we said that government must not do anything for anybody, but must just create an empowering and enabling socioeconomic environment and then let people actually do things for themselves while it just continuously monitors, evaluates, reviews and improves the situation as and when necessary? The job of the Public Service Administration (PSA) would be to do exactly just that for and on behalf of government in each and every sector of the economy, and right down to the flow or ground level of the business end of things. Using the enacted national legal policy frameworks, rules, regulations, codes of practice and codes of conduct, the Public Service Administration (PSA) would comb through each and every sector of the economy ensuring that all government policies are properly implemented. The PSA would also implement government policy in terms of creating the required conducive or enabling operating environment for government policy implementation to happen in addition to actually empowering and enabling the actual economic players on the ground to play their part in driving the economy. Of course, the PSA would do all this through its own internal service delivery structures and employees, the so called public or civil servants.

The private sector as government policy implementer

As already alluded to above, the other very important arm of the government policy implementation structure is the private sector. The private sector is one of the most important, if not actually the most important, drivers or propellers of the national economy as a whole. And every person as a private individual is actually also a member of the private sector whether employed by government of not. It is the private sector which actually rows or powers the country forward towards the desired socioeconomic goal, objective or destination and not the public sector. Although the public sector actually does a lot of practical things on the ground on its own as a government policy implementer just like the private sector, it only does those things which are concerned with the government duties, obligations and responsibilities of providing an enabling environment and ensuring that things are happening as they are supposed to happen according to government policy and nothing much else. One can safely say that the public sector (PSA) is just the police force of government in terms of prevention of any legal deviations and enforcement of compliance with government policy on the ground. It is also the police force in terms of its role in the monitoring, evaluation, review and improvement of government policy implementation or oparationalisation on the ground. The public sector through the Public Service Administration (PSA) must not try to usurp the role of the private sector in terms of actual policy implementation or actually doing things on the ground in accordance with government policy. That is the preserve of the private sector and the private sector alone. This point and the reasons thereof have been clearly elaborate in some of the preceding chapters.

The private sector, although actually highly organised, cannot be pinpointed to a single organisation or entity with one head sitting at the top of it like the public service sector or at least like the Public Service Administration (PSA).

There are very many different and seemingly unrelated organisations and organisational leaders who constitute the private sector. But at the end of the day, they are all united as one in their quest to make things work, to provide public services and also to generate profits for themselves.

There are two different types of private sectors

There are actually two different types of private sectors. There is the privately owned private sector or the so called private private sector, and then there is also the publicly owned private sector or the so called private public sector. When people talk about the private sector, they would usually just be referring to the private private sector and not to the private public sector. The main reason for this, as was revealed previously under the discussion on POBEs, is that many governments and government politicians, for very self-centred, self-serving and sometimes outright corrupt reasons too, have not allowed for there to be true, complete and practical separations of both powers and people between the public sector and the private public sector as they must actually allow to happen.

The private private sector

The primary driving force or motive of the privately owned private sector or the so called private private sector is not public or any other service delivery at all but purely the commercial business profits thereof with service delivery being just the means to that end. And that profit motive is usually so strong that the private private sector actually outdoes itself most of the time in pursuit of profits. And yet that apparent weakness or aberration of being almost one hundred percent profit focused is also the biggest strength and contribution of the private private sector to both the national economy in general, and also to public service delivery in particular.

In its insatiable quest for profits, the private private sector has grown and developed to such high levels of skills, productivity, efficiency and effectiveness that have not been matched in other sectors of the economy, and it still continues to grow and develop even further in that regard! Consequently, those countries which have empowered, assisted and allowed their private private sectors to freely grow, develop and prosper without much hindrance are now reaping immense benefits as they become some of the most highly developed countries and also as their people enjoy some of the highest standards of living in this world. For every government, the trick is to know, realise, appreciate and understand the fact that in spite of its being squarely and strongly driven by the commercial business profit motive as nature would have it, the private private sector's other superlative abilities, qualities and attributes of superior skills, productivity, efficiency and effectiveness can and must in fact be harnessed for the greater national good. And there is no better way of doing so than to just free and allow the private private sector to just be the private private sector at its original and maximum best as much as is practically possible but, of course, always within the limits of national legally policy frameworks, and also in the best interests of the public and the country as a whole. Any government which successfully and strategically manages to do that would be a winner all the time! There is no question about that.

The private public sector

The private public sector is made up of publicly owned private commercial business companies, enterprises or organisations. These are the so called public owned business enterprises (POBEs), state owned business enterprises (SOBEs), companies (SOBCs), corporation (SOBCs), organisation (SOBOs) or parastatal companies, or by any other name which may be applicable from place to place and from country to country. In this book and for reasons already elucidated at the end of Chapter 5, we prefer calling these organisations POBEs. The difference between POBEs and the rest of the other public sector structures and organisations is that POBEs would actually be legally registered and incorporated as private business companies or corporations in accordance with local company registration laws. On the other hand, most of the other public sector management and administration structures or organisations, although sometimes legally constituted as well, do not have to be mandatorily legally registered or incorporated as private business companies, corporations or organisations.

Apparently, the similarity between private public sector organisations (POBEs) and their private private sector counterparts begins and ends at legal registration. Whilst private private sector companies would have governing bodies or boards of directors which are made up almost entirely and exclusively of shareholders and their representatives, private public sector companies would have theirs being made up of stakeholders and stakeholder representatives instead of shareholders. The reason for this is that private public sector companies belong to the general public and not to anyone in particular. As stated in Chapter 5, POBEs do not even belong to government as many people erroneously believe because government is not the people or the public.

The other major difference between private public sector commercial business companies or enterprises (POBEs) and their private private sector counterparts is that while the latter are purely profit motive driven, the former would be service delivery motive driven more than they would be profit motive driven. In other words, private public sector companies are in the business of serving the people or delivering public services and not in the business of making money although they must of necessity also make some money in order for them to be able to survive or to stay in business just like their private private sector counterparts. Otherwise if POBEs fail to turn profits, even them too would go bankrupt, collapse and completely disappear from the scene just like what would happen to any other unviable business entity because in that respect the business world and the business environment are very unforgiving, and justifiably so too. The only thing which might prevent non-viable POBEs from total bankruptcy, collapse and completely disappearing from the business scene altogether would be continuous capital injection from the public itself. And the need for continuous capital injection has actually been the Achilles heel of many POBEs, especially in third world countries. Instead of being the public assets which they were supposed and intended to be in the first place, many POBEs have turned out to be very undesirable public liabilities and huge financial drains on the fiscus. They have also been found to be swivelling and gigantic cesspools of politically engendered fraud and corruption. In fact, the scourges of illegal but legalised government interference, cheating, fraud, corruption and general mismanagement and maladministration are the main reasons why most POBEs are usually not viable organisations and not because of anything which is inherently wrong with them or with the business model on which they are founded or based. Under different circumstances and with true, complete and practical separation of both powers and people in place, POBEs can just be as dynamic and also as viable as any other private sector companies. And what is more, POBEs are in fact the best if not the only option in terms of essential public services delivery as was previously explained in Chapter 5 of this book. Anyway, the most important thing to note here is that there are in fact two very different types of private sectors, i.e. the private private sector and the private public sector which are both involved in government policy implementation proper on the ground.

Government policy performance audit structure

The best government policy performance audit structure is composed of all the governed people themselves. These are the people who own government and also these are the people who actually know whether or not the government and its policies are actually performing, delivering or achieving the desired impact on the ground. This is because they are the ones who are directly and practically affected by government and government policies every single day of their lives. However, because of many obvious practical limitations such as logistics alone, all the governed people cannot examine and tell government how it is performing or failing to do so at any given public forum or platform. But they can always do so through their elected parliamentary representatives, the MPs, in parliament. This is the reason why, by default, parliament is and must be the government policy performance audit structure. Parliament is where the people are, and the people are in parliament. In fact, parliament does not only audit all government service delivery structures right from the government policy oversight structure at the top and down to itself, but it also audits every other public service delivery institution as a matter of routine. And parliament also audits every private individual and private sector institution which may be called to account for or explain its actions as and when necessary. No one in any country must be above parliament, including parliament itself. In a truly democratic dispensation, the government of the people by the people for the people must start with and end in parliament. And in the eyes of parliament, there must not be any sacred cow or cows!

As the government policy performance audit structure, Parliament cannot just audit, find anomalies, condemn them and then do nothing else after that. Parliament must have teeth, and it must actually bite all those who transgress against the people and the nation at large, regardless of whom they are or which economic sector they operate in. Such being the case, parliament must have the right to sanction any person in any arm of government and all other public institutions as it sees fit, but always in accordance with government legal policies and procedures. Parliament must also have the legal right to refer any person and any institution to the courts of justice for prosecution if it adjudges there to have been some criminal breach of the law.

The principle of separation of powers revisited

The principle of separation of powers is the best principle which anyone could ever have conjured up for any governance system, public or private. This is because the principle of separation of powers ensures that there are clear-cut demarcation lines not just of power, but also of duties, obligations, responsibilities and accountabilities between related institutions, departments or operating units in the same organisation and also between the people who run these institutions. That is what the principle of separation of powers and people actually entails in practice. Unfortunately today the principle of separation of powers has been corrupted and defiled by governments and government politicians. Corrupt, wicked and avaricious government politicians have actually ruined a very good principle. They have done so by just yapping about the principle of separation of powers, pretending to be abiding by it while at the same time they would in fact be actually trashing it. Most politicians just talk of the principle of separation of powers when it suits them and not exactly as a matter of principle, priority, belief or practice. For how can there be any true, complete, practical and meaningful separation of both powers and people at all if one politician simultaneously sits in two different offices as both the Head of State and also as the Head of Executive Government as is currently the case in many if not most countries of this world today? How can there be true, complete, practical and meaningful separation of both powers and people when a member of the legislature or parliament (MP) is simultaneously also a member of cabinet or the executive arm of government as Cabinet minister and therefore simultaneously sits in two separate and different offices of government at the same time? Under such circumstances and in the presence of the patronising political party based system of government, how would parliament be able to effectively perform its government performance audit functions, for example, against executive government (Cabinet) or any other government ministry? We have all seen blundering executive governments and their Cabinet Ministers being spared the rod in parliament just because of the partisan support which they command amongst their other parliament based political party colleagues (MPs). Such is not good for democracy at all because where executive government must and needs to be called to order then executive government must indeed be called to order without any fear or favour. The truth of the matter is that for there to be complete, true, practical and meaningful separation of powers, there must of necessity also be simultaneous complete, true, practical and meaningful separation of both the people and the institutions or organisations which are involved as well. Without that, then the doctrine of the separation of powers would continue to be full of sound and fury but signifying nothing. This very valid and realistic point has been emphasised repeatedly in this book, and it is just as simple as all that.

Separation of powers must start in government

Although they are inherently connected in the sense that they are just multiple functional organs of the same body called government, each institution of government must be a visibly stand alone organ, complete with its own different cells and tissues, responsibilities, duties and functions, but united with all the other government organs only through the blood of government which must floor through and nourish them all as different organs of one organism called government, and also for the common good of that organism and the people it serves. Such being the case, in order for government machinery to function well, efficiently and effectively, there must be true, complete and practical separation of both powers and people between all of its structures and also between its structures and the structures of the public service administration (PSA).

Head of State and Cabinet must be two separate people

Thus, in conformity with the doctrine of the principle of separation of powers in its true, correct and meaningful sense as advocated above, if the national President is the Head of State, then he or she cannot also be the Head of Cabinet (the executive arm of government), and neither can he or she also be the Head of Parliament as is the case in many of our countries today. This is because the Head of State as the head of the government oversight structure must and needs to be truly, completely and meaningfully separated from any other structure of government in order to be able to serve government well without any prejudices, fears, favours or biases. Otherwise without true, complete, practical and meaningful separation of institutions, powers and people, such would not happen.

Separate Heads of Cabinet and Parliament

If the prime minister is the head of executive government or Cabinet, then he or she cannot also be the Head of Parliament or the Head of the Public or Civil Service Administration (PSA) or anything else for that matter. Parliament must have its own individual and separate head, be it the speaker or any other person but not a Cabinet Minister. This is because Cabinet and Parliament are two very distinct arms of government, each with its own distinct obligations, duties and responsibilities. Parliament is the policy decision making structure of government, while Cabinet is its policy implementation management structure. These are two very distinct duties and responsibilities. In accordance with the correct doctrine and principle of true, complete and meaningful separation of both powers and people, it therefore means that these two distinct institutions of government together with their distinct responsibilities must be manned by completely different people without any double dipping of any kind whatsoever.

Separate Heads of Cabinet and the Public Service

The head of executive government or Cabinet (the Prime Minister) cannot also be the head of the Public Service Administration (PSA). This is because in accordance with the doctrine of true, complete and meaningful separation of both powers and people, these are obviously two different institutions with two distinct duties or functions. The Public Service Administration (PSA) is the proper government policy implementation organ, while Cabinet is undeniably the government policy implementation management organ. In other words, Cabinet are the managers while the PSA are the workers. The two are just different and thus they must be as practically separated from each other as they are already separate institutions. And yet in most of our countries today, no one knows who exactly the head of the PSA is or even what the public service is in the first place? Is it any wonder therefore that most of our national public sectors have not been performing well or not even performing at all? How can a sector perform when no one knows about it, what it is, let alone what it is there for?

The non-existent Public Service Administration (PSA)

The author of this book has a confession to make with regards to the public service. I have been a well educated adult person for the better part of thirty-two years now, but I have absolutely no knowledge of the existence of the public service as an institution, or of any head of the public service, past or present, in my own country or in some of the countries which I have lived in for many years. What I am aware of is a government employment agency called the public or civil service commission whose sole duty and responsibility is to hire, fire, promote or transfer public servants. This single responsibility institution of government is definitely not the government policy implementation structure or institution which we are talking about here. Surely, there is much more to implementing government policy than just hiring, promoting and firing civil servants!

Government minister interfere with the public service

Apparently, with many governments, there is no clear-cut distinction between Cabinet and the public service. This means that there is no clear-cut distinction between politicians and public servants. It also means that contrary to the doctrine of separation of powers espoused above, there is absolutely no clear-cut distinction between two different and very important organs, institutions or structures of government, these being the government policy implementation management structure of which Cabinet is, and the government policy implementation structure proper of which the public service, or in full, the Public Service Administration (PSA) is. Government ministers are government policy implementation executive mangers and not line managers, and as executive mangers they must be practically separated from government policy implementers or workers of which public servants are. Government workers must have their own line managers who sit and work with them every day and not executive managers in the form of Cabinet Ministers on their backs all the time. And yet many government ministers usually sit at ministry headquarters and daily interfere with government workers (public servants) sometimes right from the top administrative heads of government ministries such as Director Generals, and down to general hands on the ground. Such public service delivery interference by Cabinet Ministers cannot be good at all not only in terms of the doctrine of separation of powers but also in terms of hampering the proper efficiency and effectiveness of public service delivery as a whole. Government ministers tend to prioritise politics in service deliver whereby they are apt to want to satisfy the political whims of their own electoral constituencies just in order to ensure re-election instead of prioritising the needs of the general public as a whole.

Public service delivery must be devoid of politics

Public service delivery must be devoid of any political considerations such as who voted for whom in the last elections or who supports who or which political party now. Members of ruling and opposition political parties must both be served impartially, equally and equitably by the public service. Such being the case, having already heavily politicised, vote seeking and therefore thoroughly politically compromised government ministers sitting right there at public service delivery counters would definitely jeopardise that impartiality regardless of the expected perpetrators' protestations to the contrary. This is a fact. The truth of the matter is that the presence of the inevitably and thoroughly politically compromised cabinet ministers at public service deliver counters such as ministry headquarters would never be good for the business of public service delivery. This would be especially so in political party based systems of government. And as far as the awarding of government contracts and tenders is concerned, such government ministerial presence at that level is by far one of the biggest contributory factors to the rampant cheating, corruption and fraud which bedevil many government ministries today, especially in third world countries.

The befuddled role of the Secretary to Cabinet

In some countries, the Secretary to Cabinet is also designated as the Head of the Civil or Public Service, but in a titular kind of way. Titular because in most cases what that just means is that the Secretary to Cabinet, in addition to taking and keeping Cabinet meeting minutes, would also act as the boss of Principal Secretaries or Director Generals of all government ministries but only just in terms of human resources functions such as approving their leave days and government personal loan applications and some such mundane things. In other countries the Secretary to Cabinet would also be given the duty of approving official international trips for all civil servants. Such a Secretary to Cabinet, although designated as the Head of the Public or Civil Service, would usually not be involved in anything else to do with proper public service delivery or proper government policy implementation on the ground or the proper government to people service delivery process itself of which the real public service must be concerned with. And that is definitely not the head of the public service by many miles away. Anyway, the massive confusion which is generated by the lack of true, complete, practical and meaningful separation of both powers and people between government institutions as exemplified above would testify to the vital nature of this doctrine in public service delivery. Perhaps one of the major causes of service delivery failures in many public service delivery systems could actually be just the lack of true, complete and practical separation of powers and people between government and public service institutions and also between the various public service institutions themselves. It could simply be just a matter of strategy as already explained in Chapter 5 of this book.

Separation of powers vital in the private sector too

The doctrine of true, meaningful, complete and practical separation of both powers and people applies to the private sector as well. In fact, most of the highly successful private sector organisations religiously adhere to this doctrine. One of the reasons why the private sector adheres to this doctrine is because this sector is very particular about accountability. When something goes wrong in any private sector organisation or corporate business, someone must account for it and that someone would be made to account for it for sure. That is the way things are done in the private sector because any other way would negatively impact on productivity and profits. Allowing employees to just do as they please, not to follow the rules and get away with it is definitely not good for business. For accountability to be enforceable or for it to be actually enforced, the responsible person must be precisely pin-pointed to the last decimal point. That cannot happen in the absence of true, complete and practical separation of both powers and people. So the private sector always exercises and implements the doctrine of the separations of powers down to its true and ultimate limits. The beauty of what happens in the private sector is not only about the obvious separation of powers and people between two or more institutions within the same group of companies, but also within one and the same institution. There is true, complete and practical separation of both powers and people between different management hierarchies of the same company from the shareholders down to the last man in operations. There is also complete and practical separation of powers and people between the different departments of the same company, and also between different operating units of the same department, and then also between the different management levels of each one of the different operating units. In the private sector, the doctrine of separation of powers and people is exercised down to the individual level. In the private sector, unlike in the public sector where there are a lot of laissez faire attitudes, everyone knows where he or she stands in terms of individual and personal duties, responsibilities, obligations and accountabilities. Failure to be responsible in terms of one's given duties and responsibilities can easily lead to permanent loss of the job and loss of income in the private sector, while in government or in the public sector, it could just mean a prolonged suspension on full pay or a transfer to another department, but rarely a job loss. Perhaps this is one of the major reasons why the private sector is much, much more successful than the public sector. And yet there is absolutely no reason at all as to why the public sector cannot adopt the same serious attitude in conducting its business as the private sector. A serious paradigm shift is therefore needed in the public sector not only in terms of personal or individual job commitment, but also in terms of rigorously enforcing responsibility and the accountability which comes along with that responsibility.

Private sector governing and governance structures

In the private sector and at company level for example, the organisational oversight structure would be made up of all company shareholders at an annual general meeting of the shareholders of the company. Thus, company shareholders would act as both the company policy oversight and policy performance audit structure. Reporting to the shareholders would be the Board of Directors as the company policy decision making body. And reporting to the Board of Directors would be the company executive management committee as the company policy implementation management structure. And reporting to executive management would be line management and the rest of the company employees who are the actual company policy implementation team on the ground, the ones who actually produce and deliver whatever goods the company produces or deals in. And running through them all would be the blood and lifeline of the whole company. This would be as it must be in terms of the doctrine of separation of powers. A few pertinent examples of how the doctrine of separation of powers can be implemented in all present day private and public sector service delivery institutions are given below. These examples can be replicated in almost any institution or organisation, public or private.

Typical private sector institution or company level hierarchy of policy governing and governance structures

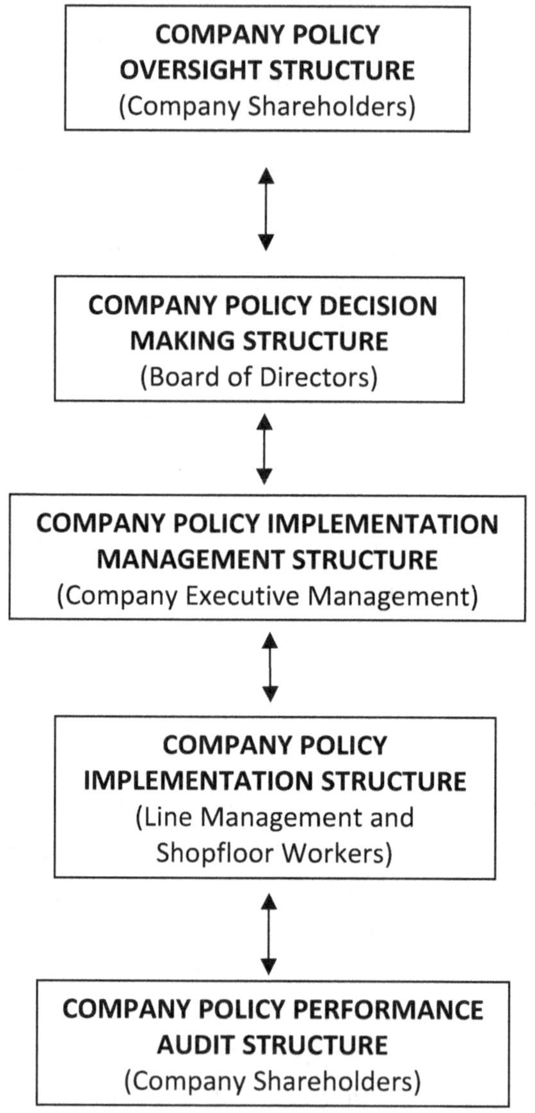

Typical local government institution level hierarchy of policy governing and governance structures

LOCAL GOVERNMENT POLICY OVERSIGHT STRUCTURE (Local Government Administration Authority)

LOCAL GOVERNMENT INSTITUTIONAL POLICY DECISION MAKING STRUCTURE (City, town or district council)

LOCAL GOVERNMENT INSTITIUTIONAL POLICY IMPLEMENTATION MANAGEMENT STRUCTURE (City, town or district council executive management)

LOCAL GOVERNMENT INSTITUTIONAL POLICY IMPLEMENTATION STRUCTURE (The private and public sectors)

LOCAL GOVERNMENT INSTITUTIONAL PERFORMANCE AUDIT STRUCTURE (Local Government Administration Authority)

Notes: Both the Local Government Administration Authority (LGAA) and individual local government institutions must be installed by the affected national and local public stakeholders through the ballot box. The LGAA ensures that each and every local government institution implements its own local government policies through the aegis of national local government policies, and that its own local government policies augment rather than contravene national policies. As at national level, actual local government policy implementation must be left to both the public and private sectors. The local public sector must confine itself to its governing role of just providing an enabling and empowering social, economic and business environment and then sitting back to monitor, evaluate, review and improve the situation as and when necessary. The local public sector must leave the actual doing part of things to the private sector. Where the local public sector feels obliged to do anything, it must do so through the aegis of public owned business enterprises (POBEs) and not directly for reasons discussed previously under POBEs. Government must try as much as possible to keep away from doing things on the ground.

Typical National Schools Administration Authority level hierarchy of policy governing and governance structures

NATIONAL SCHOOLS GOVERNING POLICY OVERSIGHT STRUCTURE (National Schools Administration Authority)

INDIVIDUAL SCHOOL GOVERNING POLICY DECISION MAKING STRUCTURE (Individual School Governing Body - SGB)

INDIVIDUAL SCHOOL GOVERNING POLICY IMPLEMENTATION MANAGEMENT STRUCTURE (Individual School Management)

INDIVIDUAL SCHOOL GOVERNING POLICY IMPLEMENTATION STRUCTURE (Individual school teachers, parents and learners)

INDIVUDUAL SCHOOL GOVERNING POLICY PERFORMANCE AUDIT STRUCTURE (National Schools Administration Authority)

Notes: The National Schools Administration Authority (NSAA) together with individual school governing bodies (SGBs) must all be installed by the affected national, local and individual schools public stakeholders through the ballot box. Owners of individual schools, local communities which schools serve, parents of students, school management and school teachers, must all be equally represented in individual school governing bodies. Where students are all or generally above the age of majority, even them too must also be equally represented in individual school governing bodies. The NSAA and SGBs must ensure that each and every individual school implements its own policies through the aegis of national and local schools governing policies, and that individual school governing policies augment rather than contravene national and local schools governing and other policies. The ownership of schools must be left to both the public and private sectors. Where the public sector owns schools, this must be done through public owned business enterprises (POBEs) and not directly for reasons discussed previously under POBEs. Government must try as much as possible to keep away from doing things on the ground.

Typical National Health Services Governing Authority level hierarchy of policy governing and governance structures

NATIONAL HEALTH SERVICES GOVERNING POLICY OVERSIGHT STRUCTURE (National Health Services Administration - NHSA)

HEALTH INSTITUTION GOVERNING POLICY DECISION MAKING STRUCTURE (Health Institution Governing Body - HIGB)

HEALTH INSTITUTION GOVERNING POLICY IMPLEMENTATION MANAGEMENT STRUCTURE (Health Institution Management)

HEALTH INSTITUTION GOVERNING POLICY IMPLEMENTATION STRUCTURE (Institutional healthcare workers and patients)

HEALTH INSTITUTION GOVERNING POLICY PERFORMANCE AUDIT STRUCTURE (National Health Services Administration)

Notes: The National Health Services Administration (NHSA) as well as individual health institution governing bodies must all be installed by the affected national and individual health institutions stakeholder public through the ballot box. Owners of individual health institutions, local communities which they serve, institutional management and key institutional healthcare workers must all be equally represented in individual health institution governing bodies. Note that unlike other private sector companies, public service delivery institutions cannot have 100% shareholder appointed Boards of Directors. They can only have Stakeholders Governing Bodies (SGBs) because in the case of essential public services delivery, government needs to ensure the involvement of all affected stakeholders and not just shareholders. The National Health Services Administration (NHAS) ensures that each and every health institution implements its own policies through the aegis of national health and other policies, and that individual health institution governing policies augment rather than contravene national policies. The ownership of health institutions must be left to both the public and private sectors as usual. Where the public sector owns health institutions, this must be done through public owned business enterprises (POBEs) and not directly for reasons discussed previously under POBEs. As usual, government must try as much as possible to keep away from doing things on the ground.

Typical National Water Governing Authority level hierarchy of policy governing and governance structures

NATIONAL WATER GOVERNING OVERSIGHT STRUCTURE
(National Water Authority - NWA)

INDIVUDUAL WATER INSTITUTION GOVERNING POLICY DECISION MAKING STRUCTURE (Individual water institution governing body)

INDIVIDUAL WATER INSTITUTION GOVERNING POLICY IMPLEMENTATION MANAGEMENT STRUCTURE (Individual water institution management)

INDIVIDUAL WATER INSTITUTION GOVERNING POLICY IMPLEMENTATION STRUCTURE (Individual water institution workers and customers)

INDIVIDUAL WATER INSTITUTION GOVERNING POLICY PERFORMANCE AUDIT STRUCTURE
(National Water Authority - NWA)

Notes: The National Water Authority (NWA) as well as individual water institution governing bodies must all be installed by the affected national and individual water institution stakeholder public through the ballot box. The owners of water institutions, serviced local communities, institutional management and other key individual water institution workers must all be equally represented in individual water institution governing bodies. As usual, individual water institutions, as essential public services delivery institutions, cannot have 100% shareholder appointed boards of directors but just stakeholder governing bodies. In the case of essential public services delivery institutions, whether privately or publicly owned, government needs to ensure the involvement of all stakeholders and not just shareholders alone. The National Water Authority (NWA) ensures that each and every water institution implements its own water policies through the aegis of national water and other policies, and that its policies augment rather than contravene national policies. The ownership of water institutions must be left to both the public and private sectors. Where the public sector owns water institutions, this must be done through the aegis of public owned business enterprises (POBEs) and not directly for reasons discussed previously under POBEs. Government must as usual try as much as possible to keep away from directly doing things on the ground.

Typical National Electricity Governing Authority level hierarchy of policy governing and governance structures

NATIONAL ELECTRICITY SUPPLY OVERSIGHT STRUCTURE
(National Electricity Supply Authority - NESA)

INDIVIDUAL ELECTRICITY INSTITUTION GOVERNING POLICY DECISION MAKING STRUCTURE
(Individual institution governing body)

INDIVIDUAL ELECTRICITY INSTITUTION GOVERNING POLICY IMPLEMENTATION MANAGEMENT STRUCTURE
(Individual electricity supply institution management)

INDIVIDUAL ELECTRICITY INSTITUTION GOVERNING POLICY IMPLEMENTATION STRUCTURE
(Institutional workers and customers)

INDIVIDUAL ELECTRICITY INSTITUTION GOVERNING POLICY PERFORMANCE AUDIT STRUCTURE
(National Electricity Supply Authority - NESA)

Notes: The National Electricity Supply Authority (NESA) as well as individual electricity institution governing bodies must all be installed by the affected national and individual electricity supply institution stakeholder public through the ballot box. Owners of electricity supply institutions, serviced local communities, institutional management and workers must all be equally represented in individual electricity institution governing bodies. As usual, individual electricity institutions, as essential public services delivery institutions, cannot have 100% shareholder appointed boards of directors but just stakeholder governing bodies (SGBs). With essential public services delivery institutions, government needs to ensure the involvement of all stakeholders and not just shareholders. NESA must ensure that each and every electricity supply institution implements its own electricity supply policies through the aegis of national electricity supply and other policies, and that its policies augment rather than contravene national policies. The ownership of electricity supply institutions must be left to both the public and private sectors. Where the public sector owns electricity supply institutions, this must be done through the aegis of public owned business enterprises (POBEs) as usual and not directly for reasons already discussed previously under POBEs. And as usual, government must try as much as possible to keep away from directly doing things on the ground.

No matter how far gone down the wrong road, turn back

To conclude this chapter, the reader must now sit back and take a very good and critical look at his and her own country and try to answer some of the following pertinent governance questions as truthfully as possible. First of all, does your country have in place all of the above five basic democratic governing and governance structures which were discussed in this chapter at both national and local government levels, and also at institutional level, in both the public and private sectors? To recap, these five basic governing structures are as follows: the organisational oversight structure, the policy decision making structure, the policy implementation management structure, the policy implementation structure, and finally the policy performance audit structure.

Secondly, are all these five basic organisational governance structures correctly positioned in the governing hierarchy as emphasised on in this book, and are they also correctly and appropriately staffed in terms of expertise? Thirdly, and perhaps most importantly, is there complete, true, practical and meaningful separation of both powers and people between these governing and governance structures all round as emphasised in this book, i.e. in government and also in the public and private sectors as well? And last but not least, does your country enjoy good governance in general all round, i.e. in politics and also in both the public and private sectors of the national productive economy? Truthful answers to these questions would automatically show the reader where and how his or her country needs to improve its own governing and governance strategies and techniques so as to position itself for optimum public service delivery and the resultant socioeconomic growth and development which come along with that.

However, it is not enough for you the reader alone to know that your country could do much better than it is doing right now, or where and how it is not doing things right and where and how it can make improvements in that regard. This information must be shared with others for it to work for you. It must be shared especially with those in positions of power so that they can influence governing authorities to change the direction which the country is moving in for the better. Old wisdom says that continuing on the wrong path no matter how far down the road you might be would never take you to the correct destination or to where you want to go. Thus, no matter how far gone you are down the wrong road, you can always turn back.

Many of our countries actually need to turn back and reposition themselves correctly before attempting to move forward again. Otherwise, many of our countries seem to be in a great hurry and moving fast to nowhere in particular in terms of the way they are governed. We really need a complete paradigm shift in the way we govern ourselves and our countries, otherwise we may never get it right. What is amazing about all this apparent failure to strike the right code as far as governance issues are concerned is the fact that over the years our technological advancements have been so rapid and so spectacular that had they been matched by similar advancements in our public governance systems, then we would not be talking about such very basic and rather elementary governance issues which we seem to be really struggling with right now!

Chapter 7: Democratic governance of the right to life

From this chapter onwards, and starting with the right to life, we shall now discuss the democratic governance of each and every one of the major basic human rights and major basic human needs in detail. Our discussions will be centred on what governments are obliged to do for people side by side with what people are also obliged to do for themselves with regards to the same basic human rights and basic human needs.

The intricacies of the right to life

In Chapter 2 of this book, we touched a bit on the right to life and what government must do to ensure that the people it governs access their right to life. This is more or less a continuation of that discussion. It might be helpful to revisit Chapter 2 in this regard before continuing.

The right to life means that once there is human life, either born or unborn, government must legally, if nothing else, ensure that that life is individually and separately protected from being prematurely snuffed out or taken out, even by its own mother. Government must then also ensure that human life is protected throughout its entire existence thereafter. The concept of a human being and human life are very simple to understand if people want to. Like all other forms of life, it all starts at the cellular level. Gametocytes are primordial gonadal germ cells which give rise to cell gametes or sexual reproductive cells (or half cells actually). These are the sperm and the ovum or egg in human beings. Both gametocytes and cell gametes cannot be regarded as human beings or human life because they are just individual cells with no discernible characteristic human or human body features, tissues or organs yet. The only discernible organs gametocytes and cell gametes have are the normal intracellular micro-organs such as mitochondria and cell nuclei. When cell gametes sexually unite, they form the zygote or fertilised egg cell, just another individual cell as well, but this time, the original precursor of a human being or human life. The zygote goes through various stages of growth and development starting by becoming a multi-cellular bunch-of-berries-like structure called a morula through becoming a fluid filled multi-cell-layered cyst-like structure called a blastula to then become a single-cell-layered cyst called a blastocyst inside which an inner-cell-mass or clump of cells at one pole begin to differentiate into a human embryo. The human embryo then develops, grows and finally metamorphoses into a human foetus which then continues to grow and develop further into a ready to be born human being.

A human foetus is actually a fully developed or fully formed structurally and functionally alive miniature human being who is just waiting to grow further before being born. But a human embryo is not quite there yet. Thus, it is at the foetal stage of human life that we can safely and objectively say that a separate although not yet physically independent human being or human life begins. Such being the case, the human foetus, as a physically recognisable human being, has its own God given basic right to life as well, just like all the other already born human beings. Thus, first and foremost, human foetuses have and must also be allowed to enjoy their basic right to life just like everybody else who is already born. Apparently, this is a very controversial issue when pitted against the basic rights of women to choose if they want to keep a pregnancy or to terminate it. But that should not be the case at all if only brut logic, rationality and commonsense are employed without mixing things up with spiritual and religious myths, beliefs or many other such apparently extraneous considerations. The world of beliefs is a world where nothing is true or false, wrong or right, correct or incorrect. It is a world in which things are spiritually good or bad, moral or immoral, ethical or unethical and evil or not evil. It is a mystical world fully loaded with unchallengeable myths and beliefs which no one would be advised to go against. The world of beliefs is another totally different world altogether from the world of objective reality by which human life is born and by which it lives, even though human life also lives in and around but not by the spiritual world as well. The important difference to note here is the fact that human life does not live by the rules of the spiritual world even though it lives in or is lived within the rules of the spiritual world as well. Actually and in reality, human life just obeys or lives by the rules nature. These are the natural rules which govern the way all matter and live matter in particular, relate to and interact with itself in the fields of the pure and real sciences such as mathematics, biology, physics, chemistry, biochemistry, physiology, anatomy, medicine and so forth and so on. It would be better to just confine ourselves to this world of objective reality when we debate and consider the basic human rights of all human beings, including the right to life, rather than confound and confuse ourselves with myths, beliefs and other spiritual considerations even if these things also subjectively, if not objectively, actually exist in all our societies in this world today. The spiritual world is a world in which we do not know anything.

So as far as ensuring that people access their right to life is concerned, and rationally and logically speaking as has been argued above, government must start doing that at the foetal stage of human life. No one must have a carte blanche right to take away the life of a foetus. The rights of women to choose if they want to abort or not must be rationally, logically and delicately counter balanced with the right to life or to live which both the mother and the foetus are naturally entitled to as separate individuals.

To begin with, in order to ensure that everyone including unborn foetuses access their right to life, government must legally and otherwise ensure and insure that all people have such correct and appropriate kind of health, religious, social, moral and any other kind of specific and relevant education throughout all levels of basic schooling which would enable them to know what choices, decisions or actions the enjoyment of their basic sexual rights would require or obligate them to make and take. In fact, education itself is also another basic and fundamental human right as shall be seen later on in this book. However, for now we are talking about the right to have sex vis-a-vis the right to life of the resultant foetus thereof.

From an early age, people must be taught that the right to have sex and actually going ahead to have it has got consequences which they as voluntary sexual participants must know and also take responsibility for. They must also understand and fully appreciate these consequences before they just blindly plunge into it. For a start, there are sexually transmitted diseases, and then, there is pregnancy, among other things. As we have already seen, it can be rationally and logically argued that termination of pregnancy before the foetal stage is reached is not exactly tantamount to taking human life. But one would realise that it would be far better not to allow things to get to that hazy and controversial red line in the first place. The predicament of whether to legally allow abortion or not is compounded by the fact that there is no easy, readily available and cheap way or method of ascertaining if a particular pregnancy has as yet graduated into a foetus or not. This is very true even in the developed countries of this world. And the situation is obviously worse in poor and developing countries. In countries where pre-foetal stage abortion is allowed, which would be somewhere between eight and twelve weeks of gestation, the risk of foetal abortion is ever present and actually materialises as a matter of routine. This is very unfortunate indeed. Rather than get to the stage of the need for abortion, women must be better educated and better advised about their right to contraception. Prevention is always better than cure in this case, more especially in the presence of a legal catch such as such an absolute or developmental stage related prohibition of abortion. All the other traditional, cultural, spiritual, moral and religious beliefs, do's and don'ts, and consequences thereof too must also be taken into account as well, especially at individual level. Under such circumstances, maybe it would be much, much better for someone to just not fall pregnant at all in the first place rather than to have to deal with the question of abortion.

On the other hand, a blanket ban on abortion does not appear to be very rational or logical at all considering the already known biological and obstetric facts and timelines about gametogenesis, sex, fertilisation, implantation, gestation and the whole process of embryonic and foetal growth and development. The fact is that, biologically, a human embryo is not exactly the same thing as a human foetus, but spiritually, who knows? That is where the challenge lies. And that is a lifelong challenge from one generation to another! At the end of the day, whether to legalise abortion or not, and at what gestational stage, must be a matter for the general public to decide for their government, perhaps in a national referendum. However, even a national referendum has got its own intractable challenges as well, like what kind of majority must be allowed to carry the day and why? Must it be a simple or two thirds or more kind of majority decision? These are not easy questions at all! And yet, surprise, surprise, some very enterprising politicians have often used their being pro or anti abortion as a rallying point to win elections. Never mind the logic which they apply to their arguments for or against, as long as it wins them votes, politicians do not care much about such mundane things as logic or rationality!

Further implications of the right to life

Observation of the right to life further implies that anything which is a basic human need or necessity for life also becomes a basic human right too, and actually such is the case. Thus, Abraham Maslow's hierarchy of basic human needs and social protection as a whole actually become basic human rights as well because all of these things are actually basic human needs or needs which people must access in order to sustain their lives, survive or continue to live. Social protection encompasses such basic human needs as food, housing, shelter, clothing, health, hygiene, water, breathing air, sanitation, education, training, transport, communication, safety, security, peace and many others. All of these things too are actually basic human rights. What this means is that as it ensures the right to life, government must also ensure that people under its jurisdiction have access to all these basic and life giving human needs. As for actually providing for all these basic human needs by itself, that, as you have already realised by now, and also as you shall continue to see further on in this book, is actually not the obligation, mandate or preserve of government alone. Government must only do that as a last resort when there is no other alternative way of ensuring that these basic human needs are provided and accessible to all the people. And when government does that, it must always do so indirectly through the aegis of public owned business enterprises (POBEs) for reasons already stated in previous chapters of this book. And when it does that, government would have ensured and insured access to these basic human needs as it must always eventually do with all basic human needs and human rights.

Basic human rights are not absolute

The trick about democratic governance of human rights is that even basic human rights are not absolute and neither are they unilateral. For example, the right to life does not mean that someone may not get killed come what may. It just means that no one, even government itself, has the right to intentionally kill another person. But killing in self defence can be and is in fact permissible. The act of killing in self-defence premises a situation whereby the primary driving motive or intention would be to defend oneself and not to kill. But then the only available option in terms of the modality of that self defence would be nothing else but to kill the attacker. Killing under such circumstances, although also very intentional just like in any other intentional killing case, would in fact not be the primary or forefront driving motive. Defending oneself from a life threatening situation would be the primary objective while killing becomes just an acceptable way of doing that. On the contrary, in pure murder cases, the primary driving motive or intention is to kill for reasons other than self-defence.

Now, compare and contrast the above scenario with the carrying out of a death sentence. The primary motive or intention of carrying out a death sentence right from the start would be to actually kill the convict and ensure that he or she is very dead for reasons other than self-defence. That is unacceptable in terms of the dictates of the right to life. And that is one of the reasons why many governments have outlawed the death penalty.

Of course, the other very good reason against the death penalty is the question of certainty. What if conviction was erroneous? How would one remedy the situation once someone has already been wrongly executed? Under such circumstances, it would be much better to err on the side of caution and not execute anybody rather than to regret it later after wrongly executing someone. Regret would never resurrect a dead person.

But what if the death penalty is what the affected community wants? What must government do in terms of democratic governance under such circumstances? The above questions sound like very tricky questions indeed, but they actually have got very easy answers to them. Before trying to persuade the public to change its mind about capital punishment, government needs to and must first of all try to understand why the majority of the general public would want capital punishment to be implemented before making any rash decisions. That would be the rational and logical thing to do under such circumstances. In any country ravaged by rampant violent crimes such as murder, rape, aggravated robbery, hijackings and many such social maladies, who would blame the angry general public for wanting revenge? Would it not be better for government to fist of all and working together with the affected communities as has already been pointed out in Chapter 3 of this book, try to get rid of violent crime first and foremost before persuading the affected communities to accept to repeal capital punishment from the statute books? The danger of repealing capital punishment first when the operating environment is not yet ready or not yet conducive for such is that it can actually be very counterproductive. Resultant public anger may just increase the rate of murder cases as the public would take the law into its own hands in revenge. Such is the real danger, and such has actually happened in many countries of the third world which prematurely abolished capital punishment just to please their western donors by masquerading as true democracies. And yet these western donors themselves only repealed their own capital punishment laws after their own violent crime rates had noticeably and appreciably gone down, and when their own people were psychologically ready and prepared for that.

People sometimes forget that capital punishment was there at the very beginning of times. It is not a new invention. Such being the case, there must be good and valid reasons why capital punishment was there in the first place. And those reasons cannot just be because there was no true democracy way back then, or that people way back then did not know or understand anything about the doctrines and the gospels of basic human rights. Of course, capital punishment can be corruptly used for political purposes, but that may not be the major reason why society may want to see it maintained or repealed. The bottom line is that society always has its own very good and valid reasons why it wants something to be done one way or the other and those reasons must always be respected, especially by government, because they really and actually do matter. Even when those reasons verge on so close to just being mere beliefs, they still hold water and do matter! The beliefs of people are true in their consequences, always said my social science Professor Gordon Chavhunduka way back in 1989 at the University of Zimbabwe School of Medicine. If government took some time to find out why the general public may prefer to retain capital punishment for the time being, it would definitely find out why and then act accordingly to address those valid reasons rather than to bulldoze its way through with what it wants, for its own reasons, and not what the people want. Unfortunately, in the case of whether or not to have capital punishment, many developing world governments prioritise pleasing their developed world western donors and their western countries or just appearing to be truly democratic. And yet their own communities and people prioritise the reduction of savage and violent crimes which pervade them, and not just pretending to be civilised gentlemen. That is where the problem arises in terms of good governance. In a true democracy, government priorities must not diverge from public priorities! In true democracy, government priorities and public priorities or the priorities of the people must converge. Human rights are there to serve the basic needs of people and not for people to serve the needs of human rights. Sometimes the right to life of savagely murderous criminals cannot be absolute if and when the majority in the affected communities do not believe or think, for whatever reason, that such a right must be absolute for such kind of people. Government must realise and accept this simple fact and then also act accordingly. Now, that is want I would call democratic governance par excellence!

The right to life is the right to basic human needs

The right to life is not only a very complex issue when one interrogates it in terms of the obvious cases of life and death of which abortion and capital punishment are all about as has already been discussed above in this and other chapters, but it is also a very complex issue when one extrapolates what it actually means in relationship to all the basic necessities of life itself, the so called basic human needs. For the fact that there would not be life if and when basic human needs are not met, then basic human needs themselves also become basic human rights in their own right. For a fact, no one can survive for long without food, water, breathing air, shelter, health, education, transport, communication, safety, security, peace and so forth and so on. All of these things constitute basic human needs as propounded by Abraham Maslow. Thus, the right to life is also the right to all basic human needs.

Chapter 8: Democratic governance of the right to freedom

Governments always restrict freedom

Many governments have the attitude that if you want freedom of anything in any of their public service delivery systems then you must just move out of the system and look out for yourself. It's like if you want your freedom, then be independent. Governments seem to believe that as far as public service delivery is concerned, having freedom is the same thing as being independent and as such you cannot have your cake and eat it too. If you want to be free to make a choice, either you have no choice but to abide by the rules of government sponsored public service delivery systems which sometimes severely limit your various God given freedoms, or you do not depend on those public service delivery systems at all (i.e. you are completely independent). Unfortunately, this either you are in or out attitude, and the resultant one size fits all approach or way of doing business pervades most public service delivery systems today.

For example, public health, education, housing and many other public programmes provide you with set menus which you either eat or go out to buy your own. This is really not fair, more especially because government can actually do much better than this if it wants. The question is not about whether or not it is possible for someone to be dependent on another person but still enjoy freedom of choice, for example, in the very same thing which one is dependent on the other person for because that is actually very possible. The question is whether or not government is naturally inclined to let its clients have freedom? Governments are control freaks by nature, and free people are usually not easy to control. This is the main reason why government is averse to any sort of freedom in its public service delivery systems. And yet freedom is what people want and what people are also naturally entitled to.

For example, people want to be free to choose where and from whom they get medical help, where their children go to school, in what sort of house and in what kind of locality they live. But many public service delivery systems routinely take away such freedoms. Most government sponsored public services are zoned for use by certain people within given surrounding localities. If you want such services in a different locality from the one which is zoned for your use, access is normally denied or you then have to pay in full by yourself instead of being served partly for free as usual. Such is very unfair and actually uncalled for as you shall see further on in this chapter. People can still enjoy freedom of choice and various other freedoms too in any and all government sponsored public service delivery systems.

Freedom and independence are not mutually exclusive

People sometimes joke that everyone is free except from gravity and yet life itself is actually a constant struggle for freedom and independence. Even though sometimes the two are confused for each other, there is a difference, no matter how small, between freedom and independence. Freedom is defined as lack of control, restrictions or influence by something. On the other hand, independence is defined as being separate from or not being connected to something. What these two definitions mean is that being free from something does not necessarily entail being independent from it and vice versa. The fact that someone may be dependent on another person does not necessarily mean that they are also not free or cannot be free from the influence of the person they are dependent on. And the fact that someone may be free from the influence of another person does not necessarily mean that they are not or cannot be dependent on that person. These two different situations are not mutually exclusive.

For example, all human beings, from foetuses to adults, must be free and are actually free to access and enjoy all their basic human rights from the right to life to the right to happiness. And yet during the early stages of human life, growth and development, children and youths are heavily dependent on adults for survival. However, this dependency or lack of independence does not preclude them from independently enjoying their God given rights and freedoms just like everyone else. This is the reason why the right to life of the unborn foetus must be taken into consideration and granted independently from the right to life or any other rights of its biological mother. It is not like if the biological mother is dead, then there cannot be any live foetus as would be explained in a moment. Yes, children are naturally dependent on their biological parents from gestation through birth and childhood until they become independent adults. But nowadays we know that at any stage in their lives, children can be freed from their biological parents for one reason or another and still successfully grow up to adulthood. For instance, nowadays there is ovum and sperm harvesting, in vitro fertilisation, and even surrogate motherhood whereby some women volunteer or are financially induced to carry pregnancies which biologically belong to other women who would, for whatever reason, not be in a position to carry their own pregnancies by themselves. Thus even pregnancy can now be liberated or freed from its biological mother. Abusive parents have their children routinely freed or liberated from their abusive hands and put up for adoption or into foster care. And of course, adult children and their parents are naturally both free and independent from each other. In the same vein, public service clients can and must enjoy their various freedoms while they still continue to depend on those public services, if only they can be allowed to do so by government. And there is absolutely no reason why they must not be allowed to do so because that is the right thing to do. It is only a matter of willingness on the part of government as you shall see later on in this chapter.

Freedom is a basic human right

Anyway, as far as freedom is concerned, people are born with the right not to be unnecessarily restricted, controlled or influenced in many aspects of their lives. Those aspects of people's lives in which the people ought to have the right to freedom constitute the various freedoms which people are born with. Thus people are born with the freedom to be who they are and who they want to be. They are also born with the freedom of thought, ideology, speech, expression, association and choice among many other freedoms. They also have the right or freedom to self-determination and independence both of which actually denote the right to be free to do whatever one wants. Thus, in short, people are born with the right to be free!

However, freedom is not limitless of unlimited. As Cullen Hightower said "Freedom without discipline is chaos, while discipline without freedom is tyranny." Discipline talks to the innate behavioural preparedness to obey or follow rules. In life, there are rules everywhere, some written but many of them unwritten. Ethics, morals and other social behavioural codes of conduct and codes of practice are not written but are usually informally taught both at home and within communities and societies in general. Disciplined people or characters are apt to behave well or follow the rules more than undisciplined characters. Usually, normal societal rules do not necessarily limit freedom but they allow freedom to be exercised within the confines of those rules. And there in fact is plenty of freedom within the confines of many normal societal rules. However, tyranny totally removes or restricts any freedom even within the confines of normal societal rules and then goes further to insist that it would be indiscipline to want to be free even if it would be just within the confines of normal societal rules. On the other hand, chaos is the kind of freedom which does not want to recognise the existence of or obey normal societal rules. So as far as freedom is concerned, it must always be exercised within the delicate balance between discipline and tyranny.

In real life though, most people are not free at all even though they were born with the right to be free. Some people always seem to want to take away other people's freedoms for their own usually selfish benefit. The people who diminish the freedoms of others are usually those in power or with the power to do so. At home, parents and other adults would be the first ones to diminish the freedom of the small people, the children, then schools and universities would be next, followed by employers and finally the ever present control freak government.

Freedom of choice

Freedom of choice is a basic human right. Everyone must therefore be free to choose. Where someone, for whatever reason, cannot make their own choice, usually government has the ultimate right to choose for such a person. Not even parents can be trusted with choosing what is best for their own children. If that was the case, then there would be no need for all those child protection laws which we have today. Apparently, even pregnancies have to be protected by governments from their own rather "murderous" carrier mothers as evidenced by anti-abortion laws. Governments must be the ultimate insurers of all our basic human rights, and yet sometimes they are the ones at the forefront of trashing some of these rights, especially the right to freedom. This is really unfortunate and must change.

Just like every other basic human right, freedom is not absolute. For example, one cannot enjoy one's own freedom at the expense of the freedom of other people. One can also have one's own freedom reduced by choice. If one freely, fairly and voluntarily goes into a contractual arrangement or agreement, then one is agreeing to abide by the terms and conditions of such an agreement. Some of these terms and conditions would obviously limit certain freedoms which one naturally enjoys. But the bottom line here is that such limitations would have been freely, voluntarily and fairly exercised through one's own freedom of choice. Such would be okay because everyone is free to choose to do what they want to do. The problem only arises if the act of going into that contractual agreement was not exercised by free, fair and voluntary choice but as a forced matter. Either directly or indirectly, it does not matter which, a forced matter is always a forced matter. And forced matters are violations of the right to freedom of choice. Thus, many international human rights standards outlaw such things as forced labour, indirect slavery, forced marriages, forced genital mutilations and other rituals, forced confessions and in fact forced everything else. The duty and obligation of government is to ensure that no one under its jurisdiction is forced to do anything which they do not want to do and which, by nature, they have the right to chose to want to do or not to want to do.

An yet governments routinely and indirectly force matters upon public service beneficiary clients in terms of exercising their various freedoms, especially the freedom of choice. For what freedom of choice can a poor and sick person have if he or she wants to live but to seek the services of the "free at the point of use" government funded public health sector in accordance with the sector's laid down, strict and non-negotiable rules, regulations and standard operating procedures, all of which usually limit the freedom of the beneficiary to chose where they can be treated, by whom and with what? Under such circumstances, there is absolutely no freedom of choice at all and it is just not right. The fact that someone desperately needs something and the other person is the only source of such a thing does not give the source person the right to restrict someone's freedom to choice whatever thing they may want if there are many such things to choose from, whether someone is paying for it or not. For example, if you are offered one mango for free from a large bowel full of mangoes, surely you have as much freedom of choice to pick whatever mango you want in much the same manner as another person who is actually buying one of the mangoes. In terms of the freedom of choice of its clients, government must approach public service delivery with the same benevolent spirit and in the same robust manner. Most of the time there would be absolutely no need to restrict the freedom of choice of public service clients, but our control freak governments still go ahead to do that, directly or indirectly.

There are certain things which logically and rationally speaking, one may not have the natural individual choice to want or not to want to do. For example, in a majority rule kind of democracy, one has no choice but to go along with the voluntarily, freely and fairly expressed and obtained decisions of the majority even if one may not agree with those decisions. That is the hallmark of majority rule. Another thing, even though one may be free to kill oneself, one may not be allowed, encouraged or left alone to do so based on moral, ethical and other considerations.

Freedom of choice is restricted in public healthcare

As far as freedom of choice is concerned, what government must look out for is the frequent and inadvertent limitation of the right to this freedom which usually pops up in many government laws, regulations, codes of practice and codes of conduct. For example, all medical patients, and that includes public healthcare patients as well, have the inherent moral and ethical right to choose where they may want to seek medical treatment in terms of healthcare institution and from whom in terms of the consulting or treating medical practitioner. The reason for this inherent patient freedom of choice is pretty obvious. In medicine, a lot of things can seriously go wrong, especially things to do with human error or ineptitude. The consequences of something going seriously wrong in the course of medical treatment could include loss of life. And where there is the possibility of loss of life, it is only right, fair and morally and ethically correct to let someone freely chose the healthcare institution and also the treating medical or healthcare practitioner who might end up being responsible for his or her own death. This perhaps is the main reason why even the internationally recognised patients' charter puts the freedom of choice of any and every patient, no matter who is paying for the medical bills, high up there.

But what do most governments do with regards to the right to chose or freedom of choice of their sick and poor fellow countrymen and women who have no other alternative but to use the public healthcare delivery system which is normally funded from the fiscal budget and administered by government? In real practice, and perhaps inadvertently so, many governments absolutely restrict or even eliminate the inherent rights of patients to freely choose where they are treated and who treats them, much against the dictates of the patients' charter and even the dictates of their own national laws and constitutions which usually just make blanket provisions for freedom of choice. For what freedom of choice is there for patients if there is rigid zoning? This is true of most of our public funded so called "free at the point of use" healthcare delivery systems. Zoning is a practice whereby patients from one given community are only allowed to seek and obtain healthcare from just one designated and one given chain of local healthcare institutions, and only from one institution after another in a rigid hierarchical order which cannot be broken. Any attempted deviation would usually be met with being sent back to the "correct" institution.

Thus, in many public healthcare systems, seeking healthcare services from public healthcare institutions other than from the ones designated for you according to where you live would normally be strictly prohibited. This is a very clear violation of the inherent rights of public healthcare patients to seek treatment from any healthcare institution of their choice within the same public healthcare delivery system. It does not matter how good the reasons which government may proffer for doing so may be, limitation of freedom of choice is wrong. The limitation of freedom of choice of public healthcare patients is ethically, morally and legally inexcusable, more especially considering the fact that lives may be lost just because of that kind of rather absurd, unreasonable and self-serving limitation. What is worse is the fact that at most if not all of these forcibly designated public healthcare institutions, public healthcare patients also have absolutely no choice as to which doctor treats or serves them! They are always served by the doctor who happens to be on duty on that particular day and also at that particular time of the day. The concept of having one's own doctor only applies to the private healthcare sector and not to the public healthcare sector according to the attitudes of many governments and their public healthcare delivery systems. The unfortunate consequence of the lack of choice of treating medical doctor is that our poor public healthcare patients end up passing through the hands of so many same level medical doctors, each one with his or her own different opinion, code of ethics and code of practice as far as individual practitioner attitudes are concerned, so much so that the possibility of the patient dying from iatrogenic and nosocomial causes is much higher than the risk of dying from the original ailment! This is really tragic.

The above depicted practical scenario is really unfortunate, but it actually happens every day in the public healthcare delivery systems of a lot of our third world countries or the so called developing nations. And such happens only because governments inadvertently restrict the freedom of choice of public healthcare delivery system patients through completely unnecessary and very rigid zoning systems and other standard operating procedures. This unfortunate practice unnecessarily, immorally, unethically and unsympathetically removes the inherent rights of public healthcare patients to choose where they can get treatment and from whom. What is worse is that top government officials themselves would be fully exercising this right to choose because they usually do not use public healthcare institutions but private ones. And even in cases where they have to use public healthcare institutions for whatever reasons, top government politicians and officials would usually be accorded the exact same rights and privileges which they would get in the private sector. Such behaviour, such unconscionable double standards, amount to cruelty of the highest order on the part of governments and all the involved government politicians and top ranking officials.

Freedom of choice in public healthcare is very possible

Regardless of protestations by politicians that there is no way out of such restrictions as would take away the patient's right to chose in so called "free at the point of use" public healthcare delivery systems, the opposite is actually very true as you shall see below just now. The problem with government politicians is that they think they know a lot of things which they actually do not have any clue about. If they would only ask and listen to the experts as has been repeatedly emphasised in this book, then everything would be okay because then the politicians would be educated and know for sure, and perhaps behave differently. The main reason why government thinks that rigid zoning is the only way to go in public healthcare delivery systems is that it is the same government which both funds and runs the system, contrary to what this book advocates for throughout. When a funder also runs what he or she funds, getting obsessed with saving and becoming a control freak as a result is the next obvious thing which would inevitably happen. This actually happens in almost every public services delivery system where government does both of these things simultaneously. Education, housing, transport and communication are some examples which quickly come to the fore in this regard.

Every beneficiary client of the so called "free at the point of use" public healthcare delivery system can be given a token public health medical aid (Medicaid) card. Such a medical aid card would be issued out for free as services are already for free anyway. The beauty of this is that the Medicaid card, as it may be called, would be issued in the name and specific personal identity number (PIN) of the prospective public healthcare beneficiary. There are many side bargains or benefits which would accrue to government just because of the issuance of these proposed public health Medicaid cards. This very simple but novel suggestion would afford government prior identification of all prospective public healthcare clients before they even seek medical treatment. It would also afford government prior quantification of these prospective clients and a whole lot of other useful metadata such as their ages, sex, where they live or stay, where they come from, what they do in life and more other useful information. Such vital advance information would enable government to do what it cannot do right now because it does not have this kind of prior knowledge. For a start, public healthcare Medicaid beneficiary cards would enable government to know in advance as to who exactly it is responsible for on the "free at the point of use" public healthcare roll of beneficiaries, and also how and why it must be responsible for paying for each and every particular beneficiary. Government would know all this kind of very important information down to specific pinpoint individual beneficiary clients' identities and all, even before spending a single cent on those clients. At present, many third world governments do not have this kind of advance information even though they actually need it for budgeting or planning purposes. They might not even know that they actually need to have this kind of information in the first place!

Anyway, at present, what many third world governments have is only historical information about public healthcare delivery, which information they cannot even validate. We all know that national health budgets are some of the biggest budgets in any country all over the world. But how many countries know by name as to who exactly are the prospective beneficiaries of all that money? Would such information not be handy, necessary or even mandatory to have considering the huge amounts of money involved? The answer must be pretty obvious. Anyway, what most third world governments currently end up with in terms of their public healthcare system beneficiaries is just historical data denoting who was treated where, when, by whom, what for and for how much. As to whether or not these historical beneficiaries of their public healthcare systems were actually bona fide people or deserving beneficiaries in the first place, most of our governments have absolutely no clue! They also have absolutely no capacity whatsoever to retrospectively answer the very same important audit questions because they usually cannot even trace or find these beneficiaries anywhere in the country. And yet they would already have spent millions or even billions of monies on clients who they do not know whether or not they deserved that kind money in the first place, let alone, whether or not these clients actually exist at all. Some crooked, innovative, techno savvy and enterprising public healthcare workers have been known to have managed to siphon millions of monies from such lax systems by routinely submitting phantom annual healthcare delivery statistics as justification for bigger budget allocations and expenditure while in fact there would be no one to treat.

Besides providing the much needed advance knowledge in terms of specific or exact individual or personal identities, and the total number of all prospective public healthcare system beneficiaries, Medicaid cards would also allow government to ensure that only those who really deserve to benefit from the system actually benefit. And the beauty of it is that with the use of current cutting edge information technological innovations such as internet based electronic healthcare information management systems, governments could actually make this verification in real time as and when benefits are being accessed instead of retrospectively as is the case right now in most of our developing countries.

If there was ever a smart and innovative method by which financially strapped third world governments could save money while at the same time ensuring efficient and effective utilisation of scarce public healthcare resources, the use of these proposed public healthcare Medicaid cards must definitely be one of them! The biggest beneficiaries of this proposed public health Medicaid card system would not be the government but the individual public healthcare prospective clients themselves. This is as it must be because in any public service delivery system, it is the public or the people themselves who must always come first and also benefit the most. This proposed public health Medicaid card system would enable individual public healthcare system beneficiaries to seek and obtain medical treatment from anywhere they like in terms of healthcare facility or institution, and also from any medical practitioner of their choice, as long as it would be within the same government sponsored public healthcare delivery system as it is right now. This means that in an instant, this proposed public healthcare Medicaid card alone can revamp, revitalise and revolutionise most of our insensitive, archaic and ailing public healthcare delivery systems in unimaginable ways.

First of all, our poverty stricken and long neglected public healthcare patients would, perhaps for the very first time ever in their lives, enjoy their God given freedom of choice! And for the very first time ever too, they would also taste what it would feel like to have someone whom they could confidently call their own private doctor even if that doctor would be just another employee of the public healthcare delivery system. What would be different and important would be the fact that public healthcare patients would be able to book appointments with any doctor of their own choice as and when necessary regardless of the public health institution in which that doctor may be found at any one time. As long as they could fix an appointment, then they would be able to see him or her, just like what currently happens in the private healthcare sector. In fact, the Medicaid card can privatise the public healthcare delivery system overnight in terms of fitness for purpose and standards of care. And improved standards of care are some of the things which our third world public healthcare delivery systems have been in real need of for all these years. Who could be against such improvements?

What is also very fascinating about this simple proposal is that it can actually be done. It is actually feasible right now as things stand in most of our developing countries, and it has always been feasible! The reason for it being feasible right now is that there are no extra funds which are required or needed to implement it. No one needs to contribute anything in terms of proper medical aid premiums because public healthcare is already free at the point of delivery anyway. And this proposed Medicaid card changes nothing in that regard. The only new thing it does is to bring in the new, important and immensely beneficial factor of prior identification and verification of public healthcare system beneficiaries together with all the other resultant benefits thereof as already discussed above. The normal public health budget would still be employed more or less in the same normal way as before.

What this proposed "Medicaid" card system would also do is to ensure that government public healthcare expenditure resources follow the individual choices of public healthcare beneficiary clients. This is as it should have been all along. Because of the inherent individual claims based service delivery payment system which Medicaid cards would bring about, the budgeted for government public healthcare resources would only be expended where and when they are needed. This would be significantly different from the present scenario whereby government spends stupendous amounts of public funds sustaining healthcare institutions and healthcare workers from whom no one wants to seek treatment even if they have no choice, for example, because of bad service delivery or professional misconduct reputations among other things. As things stand right now, there are many public healthcare institutions and their healthcare workers who are paid for doing pretty little or nothing at all in our needy third world countries because very few people or no one at all wants to go to these institutions for one reason or another. Many people may not be aware of this, but public healthcare patients would always devise ways and means of beating any system which aims to work against them and their various God given rights and freedoms. This is only natural. Even in the presence of strict zoning, public healthcare clients would and have always found ways and means to avoid those public healthcare institutions and healthcare workers whom they do not like for whatever reason, while government usually continues to blindly waste money on such and other underutilised healthcare institutions and workers.

This proposed "Medicaid" public healthcare delivery system can also be a source of greatly improved morale for those performing healthcare institutions and their healthcare workers because their budgets and salaries could be pegged against the volume of work which they dispatch over a given period of time. Because of the claims based system of funding public healthcare service delivery which Medicaid brings along with it, all public healthcare institutions would be funded according to the volume of work which they accomplish, say, every month, just like what currently happens between private medical aid schemes and their private healthcare institutions. This would mean that high performance public healthcare institutions together with their healthcare workers would also be rewarded highly, while low performance ones would also be rewarded lowly. The morale of hard workers would thus obviously and deservedly be boosted. And it would be just about time too! Such an innovative and robust approach would be very different from the performance blind and demoralising uniform budget and uniform reward systems which pervade most public service delivery systems today.

With "Medicaid," government can actually save mountains of money while at the same time affording all public healthcare clients their long awaited and deserved freedom of choice. Medicaid would also induce much needed competition between public healthcare services delivery institutions and their workers. Such competition would obviously improve the quality of public healthcare service delivery. Competition would also improve the morale and level of satisfaction of public healthcare clients with the services which they would get, perhaps also for the very first time ever considering what we all know about public service delivery standards in general. And what is more, the commensurate remuneration resulting from winning that competition would tremendously improve the morale and job satisfaction of the affected healthcare workers as well.

It may be difficult to imagine that all the above awesome benefits can be reaped almost overnight by just merely introducing the proposed token Medicaid card in the public healthcare delivery system, but it is actually very possible. What a mouthful of benefits in just one go, one might be tempted to excitedly exclaim! However, the reader would be cautioned not to rejoice like that as yet just because politicians usually do not listen, especially to things which do not bring them any immediate and personal benefits. And politicians have not been listening to this kind of logic for years now. The other thing which the reader may want to note is that this Medicaid card proposal is actually not the best thing which can happen to our public healthcare delivery systems. Medicaid is just the best thing which could happen under the present circumstances without injecting any extra money into the system. In other words, Medicaid is just the best we can do with what we have right now. The actual best thing which can ever happen to any public healthcare delivery system in this world and not only in poor third world countries but also in the rich and developed countries as well is a social security based public healthcare delivery system called national or public health insurance. And this kind of public health services delivery system is discussed in detail in Chapter 10 of this book.

What was discussed above in this Chapter in relationship to affording public health clients their freedom of choice can also be replicated in other public service delivery systems such as education, housing, transport, communication and many others in pretty much the same way as long as government would be willing to do so. Just imagine the amount of savings and the improvements in service quality which the public sector could enjoy all round!

Freedom of expression

Anyway, let us look at other freedoms now that we have tackled the mother of all freedoms, the freedom of choice.

Logically, next and right on the heels of freedom of choice would be freedom of expression, for how can one fully exercise their freedom of choice if one is not free to express that choice? Freedom of expression is sometimes loosely referred to as freedom of speech, but it is definitely more than just freedom to speak out. Freedom of speech is the freedom to say whatever one may want to say by word of mouth, but that is not the only way by with one can express oneself. People can also express themselves in writing and in action and also on various platforms, public or private. The public media, i.e. theatre, newspapers, radio, televisions and nowadays the internet, are some of the favourite platforms on which people can freely express themselves. When people take to the streets to demonstrate or march, they would also be expressing themselves, but this time in action. The same applies also when people engage in work related strikes and any other demonstrations. When people go out to vote in national elections, they would be simultaneously exercising both their freedom of choice and also their freedom of expression, and also both in writing and in action.

Governments must be very wary of public laws, actions and practices which may inadvertently take away people's freedom of expression. In order to safeguard the media from ever being muzzled by disaffected politicians, the constitution of the United States of America [1] simply provides that no one shall make any laws about the press or media. And it has been like that in the USA since the begging of times. However, not many countries have been as lucky as the USA in terms of freedom of expression. Most of our young democracies have draconian media laws which severely restrict or curtail freedom of expression while heavily protecting those in power and giving them carte blanche powers and rights to muzzle up anyone and everyone whenever they want. This is really unfortunate.

I have heard some USA National Presidents being publicly called unprintable choice names, and also being described in very unimaginable and horribly graphic uncomplimentary superlatives which have left me cowering for cover just in case sparks began to fly. But then I forgot that we were talking about the USA here, the land of fame and fortune, and also the land of the free and the brave, and not about my beloved Africa, the land of who or what by the way? I know of a media law in one African country which is called by the nice and innocent name of the Access to Information and Protection of Privacy Act (AIPPA). And yet in real practice this law was originally designed and actually used to completely muzzle the press and everyone else who would dare to speak out against government and its holly cow politicians. In this one unfortunate country, AIPPA criminalised and outlawed journalism in general and investigative journalism in particular. It did this under the guise of opening up access to information and also protecting privacy at the same time. How on earth could there be access to any information if and when that information would also simultaneously be legally protected from access? This is a classic case of political double speak, gobbledegook and crooked and fallacious thinking. And yet our African governments routinely do just that.

Freedom of expression is not meant to mean that one has the freedom to say whatever one may want to say as long as the authorities agree with the substance of what one would be saying. It is meant to mean that even if the authorities or anyone else for that matter may disagree with the substance of what one may be saying, they must still let one say what they want to say without any hindrance whatsoever. Better still they must actually even go as far as to facilitate one to freely say what one wants to say even if they may strongly disagree with it. They must not shout the person down while he or she would still be expressing himself or herself. However, they could then if they want also shout out their own disagreeing opinions in response as loud and also as long as they could but only afterwards. That would be the wholemark of freedom of expressing. Everyone is free and must be allowed to freely express themselves especially on public platforms.

Repression of freedom of expression is instinctive

Apparently, human beings have a natural tendency to want to minimise the freedom of expression of other people other than themselves. This is especially when those other people are expressing views which they themselves do not subscribe to or like. This tendency is almost automatic. And this is the reason why people always tend to shout each other down at public debating forums or meetings, thereby increasing the heat of the meeting or debate and making things even worse in terms of not listening to each other.

Once upon a time, I was invited to a public discussion in a certain African country by an alleged human rights focused voluntary institution which called itself the Institute of Democracy and Leadership (IDEAL). The public discussion was supposed to be about the opinions expressed in my previous book entitled "There is No Democracy At All in Government by Political Party Representatives" to which this book is a sequel as depicted on the cover. I was informed prior to the discussion that there would also be participants from local political party formations, more human rights groups, non-governmental organisations, and even religious groups as well. Naturally, I agreed to attend the discussion with the caveat that participants were supposed to be well behaved, stick to debating issues rather than personalities, and no name calling or violent behaviour of any kind. I got the assurance.

Maybe it is also worth noting that in this particular country, political parties had not been legally recognised in its electoral and government systems for decades by then, and this was one very sore point with all those who wanted political parties to be recognised, especially the political party formations themselves. What was even worse was the fact that my previous book mentioned above had been reported about in not so critical terms in what most political party supporters in that country considered to be the government press. In fact, although press reports never really reviewed the book but simply published whatever extracts they wanted to publish from the book almost verbatim and for their own reasons too which had absolutely nothing to do with the author or what the book was actually all about, most people misconstrued that as an indication that my book was supporting the status quo and that the status quo also supported my book. However, nothing could be further from the truth than that. And this fact would have been obvious to anyone who may have read the book, but most of the people who came to this public discussion meeting had not read the book at all, let alone even seen it besides reading about it in the press.

Anyway, off I happily went to the public discussion meeting on the day in question. I could never have been prepared for what I met at that forum. The guest of honour was none other than the person of USA Ambassador to that country. Apparently, it later dawned on me that it was the USA Embassy which had met the costs of hosting the debate in the respectable hotel in which it was held. When the USA Ambassador told the audience that a repeat Afro Barometer conducted survey had revealed that the majority of people in that country still did not want a political party based system of government, and then insisted that this was an accurate reflection of the truth on the ground, I was pleasantly excited and thought that I was going to have a really good day at the debate even though my book, which was the main topic of discussion, is not exactly about political systems of any given country in particular but just a general observation and opinion of mine with regards to the undemocratic nature of most political parties and public government systems based on them. But I was very wrong.

As soon as the USA Ambassador had said her piece and left, I was verbally abused, assaulted, ridiculed and mocked by almost everyone who spoke after I had spoken. My speech was just about summarizing and restating the opinions in my book. But instead of focusing on the opinions as they are expressed in the book and debating just those, speaker after speaker just focused on calling me all sorts of names for writing such a book when they were supposedly fighting for democracy in their country, more especially when they were vigorously fighting for the right to have political parties recognised in the electoral and governance system of that country, so they ranted. I was literally torn apart!

One religious priest, in the name of the Lord and also almost speaking in tongues, said that I was supposed to be deported from the country for writing the book. And yet I had stayed in that country for nearly ten years by that time working for government and paying my taxes without fail. A supposedly respected veteran human rights activist and long time aspirant political party based politician said that he had burnt a copy of my book in anger and would not want anyone to read it. He also advocated for the book to be banned. Another veteran trade unionist whom I thought was my friend said that I must not be allowed to benefit a single cent from my book, so no one was supposed to buy it, and he was going to make sure that no one bought it. A supposedly respected university professor and political activist said that the way my book was written was not the correct academic way to right a book. He, in his calculated, pompous and egocentric professorial demeanour, just heavily criticised and rubbished the way the book was styled and did not even touch on the actual substance or opinions therein as if that was not at all important.

Everyone was very angry with me and they all furiously said and showed it. They were all very angry because all of them were ardent political party members, supporters or aspiring political party based politicians. And yet, sitting there in front of them was a book which said that political parties were not good at all for true democracy! Obviously, this opinion was contrary to the strongly entrenched political beliefs which they held and also very contrary to what they wanted to happen in their own country. To say that these people were livid, seething or raging with anger would be understating things by very huge margins. They were hopping mad!

However, through all this, all the abuse and all the insults, I just sat there, not stone faced, angry or embarrassed, but laughing my lungs out and shaking my head in amazed wonderment. Here was a bunch of self-anointed human rights activists and self-enthroned doyens of all sorts of freedoms, completely losing their heads and becoming the exact opposite of what they claimed to be just because in my book I had expressed opinions which they did not like or agree with! That definitely was something worth raucously laughing about! Anyway, the organisers of the debate gave me the last word and my last word was; "Guys, just look at yourselves in the mirror and see who exactly you are and what exactly you stand for, and not who you think you are or what you want people to believe that you stand for!"

These pretentious human rights activist comrades displayed behaviour which was completely the polar opposite of what real human rights activists would do. I told them that freedom of expression was one human right tenet which any self-respecting human rights activist would uphold and yet they had failed to do just that on the day. Any self-respecting human rights activist would have said that "I totally disagree with your opinions, but I would one hundred percent fight for your right to hold and freely express those opinions." But these comrades said the exact opposite of that. Point blank, they told me that I had no right to say what I said in my book or even to think that way! What is worse, they said that they would actively support instead of just passively not opposing my being gagged, my book being banned or burnt, and me being deported forthwith as if I had committed a very heinous crime! And yet I had committed no crime at all but just expressed a different opinion from their preferred one.

Later on as I reflected of this discussion, I just wondered as to what kind of politicians these comrades would become should they one day ever came into power. And I realised that they would just become the very same bad old politicians whom we have everywhere today. These pretentious comrades proved to me that as politicians, they were all just the same usual wolves in sheep's clothing. Repression of freedom of expression is indeed instinctive.

Freedom of association

Freedom of association should naturally follow through right on the heels of freedom of expression. An association is a group of people organised for a joint purpose. And to associate is to be connected to such a group. By nature, people are free to associate with whoever they may want to associate with and for whatever reason they may choose. No one must tell anybody who they can or cannot associate with or what association they can or cannot form or join unless if it is for a natural illegality such as for the purposes of committing crimes. And no one must illegalise an association just because they do not like it or they want to believe it is a criminal association without the necessary proof thereof. And yet many governments do just that.

In terms of ensuring that people enjoy their freedom of association, government must again guard against and refrain from inadvertently enacting and enforcing laws, rules and regulations and other codes of practice and conduct which may diminish this kind freedom. Some governments legally proscribe certain social groups or associations for no good reasons at all other than that they just do not like what these associations stand for. Once an association is legally proscribed, membership to that association is automatically legally proscribed too. Many political formations with the potential to unseat incumbent governments have been dealt with in such a manner for very frivolous reasons as part of bigger and broader underhand schemes by affected governments to get rid of all potential opponents especially towards national general elections. This would be obvious gerrymandering and a blatantly deliberate limitation of freedom of association. And yet it happens all the time in this world today.

Most of the time governments fall into the cesspool of limiting freedom of association because they make the mistake of making themselves the self-appointed moral touch bearers of society. And yet we all know that no government on earth can lay any claims on morality of any kind. Government must just stick to its core mandate of governing through making and enforcing legislation. It must keep away from making any value judgements about morals which even itself does not have. The best way by which government can avoid unfairly limiting freedom of association is perhaps to ask the people it governs in a referendum if such freedom must or must not be limited with particular reference to very specific societal issues rather than for it to make its own value judgements by itself and then unilaterally going ahead to impose such on society. If governments ask their people as proposed, one pleasant surprise they may discover is that a very large majority of people do not really care much about a lot social miscreants, nincompoops, scallywags and other good for nothing "scallybeggers" and their internet based social groups or associations all of whom somehow seem to irritate governments a lot. But many governments seem to honestly think that the general public really cares or believes every kind of internet based trash which is thrown at it. Consequently, governments embarrassingly find good reasons to take action at national level, against a lot of the kind of internet trash which no one really cares about or pays any attention to. This kind of illogical paranoia has led governments to legally proscribe social media entities which they adjudge to be threats to national security and also to put into place laws which compel internet service providers to take down such websites or permanently block them. The paranoia has crystallised into governments confidently linking public shootings and bombings in their countries with people whom they say were radicalised by this kind of internet based social media. If one would listen to such government propaganda, one could easily be sold the dummy because it is done with so much charisma and passion, especially soon after every tragic public bombing with unwarranted loss of innocent lives. In fact, most of the public have been sold the dummy already and they believe the association or link between internet based so called radical social groups and the apparently senseless street bombings and shootings which have escalated in their own countries. Such being the case, many people have blindly supported the legal limitation of the freedom of association even on the internet social media and especially for the young and impressionable minds of the youth. But maybe things are not exactly as we have been made to believe. A closer look at most of the violent and fatal street shootings and bombings which society has experienced over the years seem to reveal that they usually are the result of almost uncontrollable outburst of lots of longstanding, cumulative and fervently held passionate anger, disappointment and frustration with local communities about purely local issues and not about or due to any misguided inspirations from the internet. This observation is much closer to home than most of the contrary assertions by many governments which they usually make in the heat of the moment and soon after such tragic incidences. As long as governments continue to externalise social problems like this, perhaps we shall never be able to get on top of them. But we must all know and be aware of the fact that it is usually very hard to accept that the problem is with me!

Our natural refusal to accept that the problem is with me reminds me of this real life story. My own late father always told me that everything which happened to me, good or bad, would always have been caused by me somehow. He said that I was supposed to refrain from being too quick to take credit for all good happenings and also refrain from adamantly refusing to accept any responsibility for all bad happenings. He implored me, with an open mind, to always ask myself what I could have personally done wrong to cause any and every bad thing which would have happened to me until I found the answer because that answer would always be there somewhere. Thinking that I was clever, I then asked the old man to tell me how I would have personally erred if I lent a friend in need some money, for example, and the friend then eventually failed to pay back the money? The old man then said to me that just as an example, if the money was for recurrent expenditure such as payment of rent, electricity or water bills, would it not have crossed my mind that any normal working person like my friend would ensure that they reserved money for such essential bills rather than borrow? If that was the case, what would I have thought was the capacity to pay back loans of someone who obviously was not capable of saving money for essential future needs? Obviously if someone could not save money for his own essential future needs, it obviously also meant that he would not be able to pay back any loans. I was supposed to know that before lending that friend the money. So whose fault would it be that I would have leant such a person any money? Obviously mine! This revelation shocked me into realising that indeed we are always responsible for everything which happens to us, good or bad. Such being the case, governments which are too quick to externalise the causes of their own internal problems must think twice before they do that.

Going back to the internet, there is something which I have observed about human beings or people in general. This is in connection with what seems to interest people to the point of either joining in a debate and making comments or taking practical action. What I have noticed, especially on the internet and other social media is that if you clowned, said a lot of stupid things and generally made a big fool of yourself, you would definitely have a tremendous amount of responses and followers in terms of numbers, even hundreds of times more than if you did not clown, say a lot of stupid things or did not generally make a fool of yourself.

Perhaps the best example of what I want to say here is provided by some of our sisters who think that they are very beautiful and sexy. These egocentric sisters usually post practically nude pictures of themselves posing in one sexually provocative way or another on the internet social media and then furtively invite comments from followers and other internet admirers. Within minutes, such pictures would accumulate thousands of hits, likes and followers, all drooling with admiration and praises for the sexual beauty on display. One would think that posing naked like that is the best thing which people want to see, and yet nothing is further from the truth than that. If our bimbo sisters ever make the grave mistake of thinking that the general public actually loves to see them in the nude and then they go ahead and actually pose in flesh in the same nude manner right in the centre of town, then they would get quite a very rude awakening. There would never be any or even just one admirer to ogle or drool at and cheer them on as on the internet. Instead, there would be lots of very angry and disgusted protestors, jeerers and ridiculers, with arresting police officers right behind them. If she is very lucky, the poor beautiful bimbo sister would not even last for a few minutes on display before she is spirited away by the law for public indecency and perhaps also for soliciting for the purposes of prostitution. Otherwise by the time the police arrive, they might find her in an unidentifiable heap of flesh, bones and blood after the public has finished administering their own mob variety of moral and social justice.

The big questions is that why is there such a very big difference between the reaction of people on the internet and their reaction on the street to the exact same thing? The reason for this big difference could that perhaps people react differently on different media platforms. If that is the case, then one of those reactions must be phoney and the other one must be genuine. If something is truly disgusting to you, it must certainly remain just as disgusting whether in a picture or live and direct. And as far as the internet is concerned, everyone knows that people are phoneys on that platform. Even our dear sister here would never dare to go out live and pose naked in the middle of the street as she easily does on the internet.

The other possible explanation for the different public reactions on different media platforms is that perhaps we would be dealing with two completely different crowds here, the internet crowd and the street crowd. And again this seems to be true. The internet crowd seems to be very different from the real life crowd. The real life crowd, which seems to be in the majority in all our societies, does not care a hoot about the internet or what goes on there. These are the people who are not on Facebook, Twitter, Instagram or any other such internet based social media platforms. And admittedly, these are the majority of the people in any given country. Such being the case, maybe governments must just stop going bananas about who is doing what on the internet and with whom, and then seeking to interdict, ban or restrict them in terms of their freedom of association and expression thereof. Governments need not waste their precious time and energy chasing down useless internet gangs instead of looking at solving real life issues which daily affect us on the ground and on our streets.

In another example, your country may be going through very challenging socioeconomic times such as economic depression, hyper-inflation, a financial crisis or famine. You may then decide to research about the reasons why things are that way and the possible solutions thereof and then post your findings and recommendations on the internet and other public and social media platforms so as to share with your countrymen and invite their comments in a public debate kind of way. If you are very new to social media you would be very much disappointed. Your disappointment would come from the social and public media responses which you would get both in terms of numbers and also in terms of quality or substance thereof. First, you would get complete apathy, and then you would get snide remarks or comments from people who would obviously not have read your article at all. They would probably say something like who the hell do you think you are to imagine that you know everything, what's in it for you, what do you want them to do about it, or something like that. And to add salt to your wounded ego, you might see that on the same internet page, there would be a very stupid story about an obscure couple which was caught red-handed cavorting and doing the nasty right in the middle of the local recreation park and in broad daylight. That stupid story would be having several times more hits, likes and excited comments than your well considered, well researched and rather relevant article considering the hard times which would be afflicting your country at that very point in time!

On social and other media platforms, people just do not care much about things which really matter in terms of responding to them. To most people, it seems like social media is there for trashy talk and not for any serious business at all. If you want to do or talk serious business, go somewhere else and not on social media. For example, exposure on social media alone would not get you very far in business. Anyone who has ever tried to market or sell anything on the internet would tell you that. Such being the case as the examples given above show, the current frenzied paranoia about the internet which is frequently exhibited by many world governments is very unwarranted. Government must just let people associate with the internet and other social media platforms any way which they may want to because, as Professor Ha-Joon Chang said, at the present moment, the social and economic impact of the internet is actually overrated [2]. Trying to restrain freedom of association on or with the internet would just give many national governments undeserved reputations as being anti-freedom of association and for absolutely no good reason at all. That would be my considered advice to any government in this world.

In conclusion, the fact of the matter is that people do not seem to do as they say or behave on social media. But maybe the kind of people who are active on social media are not the same kind of people who are active in real life. The latter seems to be true. There must be more to the apparently crazy street bombings and shootings which we have witnessed than just being radicalised on social media. Such being the case, restricting freedom of association on social media would not reduce street bombings and street shootings. It might just work to take away the freedom of association and other human rights of those who may want to share stupid stories, jokes, fallacies and fantasies on that public media platform and nothing else. But if a precedent like that is set, then one day government might want to take away the freedom of people to associate and share serious and helpful information on other media platforms as well using that precedent as a convenient pretext and yet it would be all for political reasons. That is where the danger lies. People must never allow government to diminish their freedom of association arbitrarily and for very frivolous reasons too. Freedom of association is a basic human right which must always be respected.

Chapter 9: The right to happiness

The USA constitution puts it across very well. Everyone has the right to life, liberty and the pursuit of happiness, it says. These are actually three different basic human rights all put together in just one swoop. And these three basic human rights are very closely related to each other for the reason that what is life worth if one is not free or happy? And conversely, how can one be alive and happy if one is not free? Every one of us has the right to be happy. There are obviously many forms, kinds or types of happiness and we are entitled to all of them. These different kinds, types or forms of happiness include physical, social, psychological, spiritual and emotional happiness among others. Although we all want to be happy or enjoy ourselves, very few people know and understand that joy and happiness are actually basic human rights too, just like the rest of the other more common basic human rights.

It is only in recent times that many governments have begun to recognise the value of happiness in the lives of people. This is only after so many behavioural scientists and other psycho-sociologists have repeatedly demonstrated the undeniable association of high levels of general public joy and happiness with peace, good health, longevity, high productivity and high living standards among other things. After this belated realisation, some upfront, innovative and enterprising governments have even gone as far as to officially appoint ministers of national joy and happiness! Whatever these minsters actually do is hard to imagine, but the thought of such a minister alone is definitely exciting. It automatically evokes feelings of joy and happiness! Sadly, there are many things which governments do which do not make people happy. A lot of times, such things make people angry, while a few times, they make them sad. Anyhow, both ways, the results are the same because an angry person is not a happy person and so is a sad one.

Most of the fairy tales there are emphasise a lot on the necessity of happiness in life because people always end up living happily ever after in those stories. In my traditional fairy tales, people do not just end up living happily ever after, but they end up living lives specifically full of eating, full stomachs and happiness! Thus my tradition does not leave it up to the imagination to picture what kind of happiness some fairy tale hero or heroine ends up enjoying as a reward for some exemplary heroism. It tells it like it is, and what that tells me is that eating and a full stomach are some of the basic ingredients of happiness. Who can argue with that? And these are just two of the rest of the Abraham Maslow hierarchy of basic human needs.

Happiness is a much more fundamental feeling

Happiness is an inner state of pleasure, delight, satisfaction, contentment or gratification, while joy is the outward cheery, jubilant, merry, jovial, jolly and elated expression of happiness. Happiness is therefore much more fundamental than joy. As has already been said in the first three chapters of this book, every government has a duty and obligation to satisfy the needs and aspirations of its people. In other words, every government has a duty and obligation to make its people happy. This just about summarises everything which government is there for! People will be happy if government delivers on all its responsibilities, duties and obligations. This mean that people will be happy if their government governs them well, if it legislates properly and appropriately, if it serves them well, listens to them all the time, actually works or functions for them, if it delivers on all its obligations, if it empowers, enables and allows them to do things for themselves, and if it allows competition and also competes to be the best government it can ever be. And finally, they would be very happy if their government is always protective of them. In short, people would be happy to be happy with their government. Conversely, what would make government happy? That must be food for thought.

When people are happy with their government, they can then express their happiness or show their joy in many different ways. They do not necessarily have to cheerily, jubilantly, merrily, jovially, jollily or elatedly invade the streets shouting, singing, and dancing about it, although they sometimes actually do just that on certain national occasions. But they can simply show their happiness with their government in the way they do the things which they do every day. For example, happy people would be inclined to be less violent or criminal minded, less prone to diseases, harder working and more productive than unhappy people. Such being the case, a nation which enjoys high levels of public happiness would show or express its deeply felt joy through reduced violence, less crime, low morbidity and mortality, and high levels of productivity. Singing and dancing on the streets would just be added bonuses. Lately there have been people who have gone around trying to measure what they call national happiness levels through some sort of happiness index. Since people would be happy to be happy with their government, perhaps the happiness index is actually the best measurement of the performance of any and very government!

People must be allowed to be happy

After having said all the above things about joy and happiness, people still need to be allowed to be outwardly happy and show it both as communities and also as individuals. They still need to be enabled, empowered and allowed to enjoy themselves both publicly and privately as well. Maybe this is the actual job of the Minister of Happiness. People cannot be completely happy if they are not allowed to joyously express or show it.

What the above means is that people must be empowered, enabled and allowed to meet and socialise, drink alcohol if they want, smoke, bet, gamble, sing and dance if that is what makes them happy or how they want or choose to enjoy themselves. Legally outlawing or banning activities and things which give people joy will not make them happy at all, and yet many governments in this world routinely do exactly just that. They usually do so based on some extraneous traditional, cultural, religious, moral or social grounds which normally would be completely out of touch with the actual reality on the ground. Such actions make people extremely unhappy at best, and at worst, they drive happiness underground into the dark and shady world of the black market, gangsterism and the mafia. And no government may want to have such on its hands. Why not just let people be happy and let them show it any way which and how they want to? As long as they do not commit crimes or bring any harm to anybody or anything, does it really matter how people choose to be happy or to enjoy themselves? After all, happiness is just as good a basic human right as any other, so why not just let them have it the way they want to have it?

Physical happiness

Governments are warned to always be cognisant of the fact that happiness is a basic human right every time they conduct their business in our communities. Such being the case, governments must enable and allow people and their communities to be physically happy by letting them do those things which give them physical happiness such as socialising, singing, dancing and drinking. Banning such things and closing places which provide them would definitely not make people happy at all. Doing such would only succeed in creating an underground happiness or entertainment industry as already pointed out above. And as with anything which happens underground, such would be accompanied by all sorts of illegalities, crimes and criminal activities which governments can well do without!

Social happiness

Government must also let and actually enable people to be socially happy as well. People derive social happiness from socialising with other people in many different social groups or organisations and on many different social platforms such as social clubs, churches, synagogues and mosques for the welfare and religiously inclined, bars, restaurants, discotheques and nightclubs for the free spirited ones, and the internet based social media for the dreamers. Besides just providing social welfare, governments must provide social happiness as well by just allowing people to be socially connected and socially happy. Government does not actually have to socialise people by itself even though a social welfare department must be part of any people oriented government. It must just leave people to socialise.

Psychological, mental and emotional happiness

As far as psychological, mental or emotional happiness is concerned, government must ensure that as it conducts any of its business, it does not deliberately or inadvertently psychologically, mentally or emotionally stress or depress people. And that is easier said than done. A lot of things which governments do to people are very depressing. For a start, as if having more than fifty percent of your individual earnings directly deducted from your salary every month in mandatory pay-as-you-earn tax is not depressing already, government then goes ahead to corruptly use and abuse that money in broad daylight and without a single care in the world! That is very depressing indeed. Basic public services such as food, housing, health, education, transport and communication are usually in very sorry and depressing states in many countries. Government treatment of political opponents is usually depressing too, just like the attitude of government towards all basic human rights. In fact, many governments are just depressing all by themselves as they are just sitting there! I hereby advise that before agreeing to any government proposal in parliament, perhaps every MP must ask himself or herself how that proposal makes him or her feel personally. If the answer is not happy at all or not exactly happy, then they must not agree to it. The heart may not be so smart, but it is always wiser as far as happiness or any other feelings are concerned. Government is also better advised to one day just go out there onto the streets and ask its people just two questions thus: Are you happy or not happy with your government, and why? Revelations which it would get from such a very simple but effective exercise would go a very long way towards helping government to work better for its people.

Spiritual happiness

Spirituality talks to religious, traditional, cultural and many other such myths and mysteries which people strongly believe in both as individuals and also as communities. These spiritual beliefs must also be respected, especially by government, regardless of whether or not they make any sense at all to outsiders or those who do not believe in such things. Beliefs always make sense to those on the inside or to those who believe in them, and that is what is important.

Also remember that the beliefs of people are true in their consequences (Prof Gordon Chavhunduka). For example, when a particular redline is crossed even by an outsider, a religious insider may feel religiously obligated to take very practical steps to rectify or atone for that breach in all manners possible and religiously permissible, and that may include violence or even death. Actually, such is the origin of religious fanatic suicide bombings and no one wants that to happen anywhere in society. Such being the case, government has the duty, obligation and responsibility to keep its entire population spiritually happy in the way they want to be spiritually happy and at all times. Those who want places to build churches, synagogues or mosques must be afforded such places and the time to worship even on the national calendar. And government must not dictate the spiritual inclination of anybody, any community or even the whole country. Doing so would be a recipe for religious persecutions and religious crusades or jihads. Governments must ensure that people are physically, psychologically, socially and spiritually happy. All round happiness is just as good a basic human right as any other human right.

Chapter 10: The right to social protection

Definition of social protection

By definition, social protection is any public owned scheme of arrangement which guarantees individual people, families or communities protection as and when necessary, either in cash or in kind, from risks which are occasioned by lack of basic human needs. And some of these basic human needs are food, shelter, health, education, transport, communication, peace, safety, security, self-esteem, self-actualisation, socialisation and social esteem among many others. Noteworthy in this definition of social protection and in line with the title of this book is the fact that the definition says public owned and not necessarily public operated. Social protection schemes must be public owned and not government owned, but they do not have to be also public, let alone government operated.

Social protection can be legally compulsory or non-compulsory and it can also be mandatorily contributory or non-contributory. Social security is social protection which is legally compulsory and mandatorily contributory. On the other hand, social welfare is social protection which is both non-compulsory and also not mandatorily contributory. Social security is interchangeably also referred to as social insurance, while social welfare can also be referred to as social assistance. However, some people use the phrase social protection in its narrowest sense to refer only to social assistance or social welfare and not to include social security. In my own opinion, the broader and all inclusive definition of social protection would be the preferred one. It covers everything which social protection is all about.

Government must ensure access to social protection

Government has the responsibility, duty and obligation to ensure that all people are provided with social protection, either individually or as groups or communities. Of course, government does not have to provide social protection directly and all by itself as we have already said elsewhere in this book. It must just ensure that such happens, and it can do that by just putting in place strategic legal policy frameworks and other operational standards which would make sure that such actually happens. In providing social protection, legal enforcement is the main function of government. All social protection schemes must be public owned and not government owned. Here, the reader would be referred back to Chapters 5 and 6 of this book for detailed discussions on the differences between public owned business enterprises (POBEs) and government owned business enterprises (GOBEs). The reason why social protection must be public and not government owned is that while governments come and go, the public stays there forever. Social protection is actually the public protecting other members of the public. And such important functions as ensuring that people always access their most basic human needs cannot be entrusted to temporary institutions such as governments but to permanent institutions such as the institution of the public itself. Of course, public means people, with or without government. In this chapter, we are going to examine how government can legally and practically ensure that people are indeed socially protected by exemplifying with how this can be done on the ground in relationship to a few selected basic human needs. These will be food, shelter, health, education, transport and communication, and safety and security.

The right to food

If there is one basic human need which is more basic than basic, it is food. Without food and water, there would quickly be no life. There must be no argument about this fact. But how many people sleep with empty stomachs, go hungry or do not have enough food to eat in all our various countries today? In 2015, the World Food Programme (WFP) [1] quoting the UN Food and Agricultural Organisation (FAO) [2], issued ten facts about hunger among which were that about "795 million people or about one person out of nine in the world do not have enough food to lead a healthy active life. About 12.5% of the third world population is undernourished. Asia is the continent with the hungriest people at two thirds of total population. Sub-Saharan Africa is the region with the highest prevalence of hunger with one in every four persons being undernourished. Poor nutrition causes 45% of deaths in under fives (3.1 million children every year). One in four of the world's children are stunted (up to one in three in the third world). One in six children (about 100 million children in all) in developing countries is underweight. And finally, sixty-six million primary school age children attend classes hungry across the developing world, with 23 million in Africa alone." Intermittently, huge chunks of local community populations in one country or another face famine or starvation, and yet in other parts of the world or even in the same country, the problem would be over-eating and obesity.

Food is a basic human right because it is one of the most basic human needs. Governments must ensure that people are food secure at all times. Food security means having enough food to eat not just for now but also going into the foreseeable future. And this foreseeable future must be measured in several years time and not just in a few months or seasons. Thus, a food secure country would have enough and guaranteed stocks of food for all its people for at least three to five or more years to come.

Food security

Many government politicians always talk about food security during election times. They promise the electorate that once in power, they would somehow magically make the country food secure. As something which does not only give people life but also gives them a lot of enjoyment, pleasure, satisfaction or happiness, especially when eating it, the talk of food usually automatically warms up the bellies of the hungry audiences and appropriately focuses them on the ballot paper as well. Thus our food security promising politicians usually carry the day at the polls, and yet food security continues to elude many countries today. The big question though would be how can government ensure in practice that the country is food secure at national, community, household and individual levels? Usually, politicians do not offer answers to this question during election campaigns, but perhaps we must forgive them because they are usually also not asked this question by their hungry election rally audiences. Most election rally audiences would usually be there just for the food and drinks which would be served and nothing else.

Anyway, at national government level, a very logical and systematic approach is needed to tackle food security issues. Government must and needs to go back to absolute basics here. It must go back to answering such basic questions as what are the country's staple foods, who produces what food in the country, where, when, how and why? Since the job of government is not to actually do things on the ground as we have repeatedly said in this book, if government features anywhere in the answers to these pertinent food security questions, then a red flag must be raised wherever and whenever that happens so that the situation can be remedied later on when the national food security strategy is being crafted. Let us now rationally, logically and systematically examine each and every one of these basic food security questions and also try to provide some food secure answers to them.

National staple foods

The national staple food is the main food item or food product which the majority of people in a country eat most of the time. Naturally, national staple food is also food which is usually grown or produced locally as opposed to imported food. Rarely would staple food be imported food, but sometimes it happens. Anyway, knowing the national staple food and other high ranking foods in terms of aggregate consumption would greatly assist in pointing government where and on which food stuffs it must concentrate in terms of food security. All food is important, but it is food which is consumed by almost everyone and also almost all the time, whose availability, affordability and accessibility must be secured by government. That is what food security means and is all about. And that is exactly what government must ensure at all times. Although there would be one food item which would top all other food items in terms of consumption in the whole country, it would be more appropriate, accurate and proper to talk about staple foods and not just one staple food. The reason for this is that even in a very small country, staple foods vary from local region to local region depending on the local soils, climate and weather conditions. Hence the correct or appropriate question to be answered as far as national food security is concerned would be about national staple foods and not just about one national staple food.

Who produces food?

Once the various national staple foods have been indentified, the next important question to be answered in terms of food security would be who actually produces food on the ground in the country? All food and not just staple foods! This question is very important because usually the national primary producers of food (i.e. famers) do not just produce staple foods only but also other food and even non-food agricultural products such as the so called cash crops. If it really wants to ensure national food security, government must holistically empower famers in all aspects of their faming businesses and not only where and when it concerns the production of staple foods. It is only natural that any business person would be concerned about all aspects of his or her business and not just some parts of it. As important as any part of machinery may be, that part acting alone would never enable the whole machinery to function efficiently and effectively, or even to function at all sometimes! Thus primary producers of staple foods must first be identified and then effectively, comprehensively and holistically supported and empowered by government to produce staple foods, each according to his or her own specific needs, first, as a food producer, and secondly, also just as a farmer in the business of farming in general.

Where is food produced in the country?

After indentifying what the national staple foods are and who produces them, government must then try to identify where that food is produced in the country. This is very important because barring augmented and assisted agriculture (i.e. irrigation, etc) most food which people eat and depend on is produced through natural and unassisted means. We can actually say that food is usually produced by the grace of nature in terms of the necessary soils, rainfall, temperature and other climatic and weather conditions. Most of the food we eat is normally produced in those areas, places or regions of the country where the natural soils, climate and weather conditions would allow that to happen. People have always depended on nature for their food and that is not about to change any time soon regardless of our highly improved current agricultural techniques and technologies. The reason for this is that natural ways of producing food are every easy and inexpensive, so almost everyone and anyone can do it. And that is actually the tradition and culture in most of our societies. Almost everyone and anyone can grow or farm something and they usually do so too, whether formally educated about it or not. As already pointed out above, natural ways of producing food are also very cheap in terms of inputs because besides labour, the costs involved are very small and bearable on the part of the individual producer since, as natural resources, the land, soils and hydrology thereof, the local climate, weather, rainfall, environmental temperature, the presence or absence of agricultural pests or diseases, and all other contributory factors are all God given and basically for free.

Thus, it is very important for government to know where all the national staple foods are produced in the country so that such places and regions can be protected from things which may disturb them or make them unsuitable for food production. And yet this is where many governments have actually lost it! Instead of identifying areas where staple foods are naturally produced and then zoning them off to be used for that purpose alone, many governments have neglected or even actively destroyed such areas thereby permanently damaging or diminishing the capacities of their countries to be food secure. They have done this by knowingly or unknowingly permitting other industrial activities to encroach onto those areas thereby displacing food production. Residential, industrial, trade and other commercial activities have all been allowed to displace farming or agricultural activities from the only natural places where they could be practiced productively with very dire consequences for the whole country and for everyone else. Many countries have thus become food insecure.

It is no exaggeration that one of the first and most important steps towards national food security in any given country would be the legal identification and securing of all prime agricultural land anywhere and everywhere it may be found in the whole country. This must mandatorily be done by government and also as a matter of national security and national priority. And such legally identified and secured agricultural land must be agricultural land by nature. This does not mean in terms of the prevailing climate and weather conditions alone, but also in terms of soil types, hydrology and fitness for purpose among many other relevant considerations. The consideration of land fitness for purpose is crucially important in attaining food security at national level. This is because sometimes if left alone to just do as they please, individual farmers, especially of the subsistence variety, would use prime agricultural land to grow crops for which the land itself and the prevailing climatic and weather conditions are absolutely not suited. There is no better way of ensuring perennial crop failure than that! Government must ensure that prime agricultural land is utilised for purposes for which it is naturally best suited. Anyway, all in all, no one must ever be allowed by government to use agricultural land for anything else other than agriculture unless if there would be plenty of it to go around or even to spare, which is rare.

When is food produced?

Staple foods are usually produced seasonally. This is because most food crops naturally grow best during one particular season or the other depending on the prevailing natural climate and weather conditions during that season. No artificial agricultural production method has yet beaten the natural method of doing things both in terms of efficiency (quantity of output per given input) and effectiveness (output quality or purpose fitness). This is the reason why as far as food security is concerned, food production must always be timed to coincide with the natural times during which the food crops would normally grow and ripen in nature. Augmented or artificial agriculture is very costly and it would never make any country food secure just because of that. Not many people can afford irrigation for example. What government must do is to make sure that our food producers are strategically empowered and enable to optimally produce food wherever and whenever they produce it. This means that needed agricultural inputs must always be strategically available, affordable and accessible to food producers (farmers) where and when they are needed without fail. Anything less than this would not make the country food secure. Please note that there is no suggestion herein to give farmers anything for free. As was discussed in Chapters 2, 3 and 4 of this book, empowering people is not the same thing as doing things for them or giving them any material benefits for free. Free handouts are in fact very much discouraged as they would create dependency syndromes. Dependency and food security are polar opposites.

How is food produced?

Of course food is produced through farming or agriculture, but this is not what this question is about here. Here, we are asking about the exact agricultural methods employed. How is the bulk of the food which feeds the nation practically produced on the ground? Is it through straight forward natural agriculture, or is it through augmented or even artificial agriculture? The majority of people who partake in the primary production of staple foods or farming in terms of numbers are actually the so called peasant or subsistence farmers. And they are also the very same people who, cumulatively in terms of aggregate quantities, produce most of the staple foods in most third world countries. The situation is different in the so called developed world because of the almost total urbanisation of the whole population which has happened there.

Subsistence farmers mostly use straight forward natural and unadulterated agricultural production methods. If one wants to eat really organic, then one must only eat food which is produced by subsistence farmers. However, whether subsistence farmers end up with a good harvest or not depends largely on natural conditions which they cannot control such as soil types and climate, and on seasonal weather conditions such as rainfall, environmental temperatures and the presence or otherwise of natural agricultural pests and diseases. Government must know not only who specifically produces what staple food and where they produce it but also how they produce it so that it may be able to strategically empower and support them to be highly productive. Peasant farmers usually require a lot of agricultural education, financial and other technical assistance from their government almost all year round. If government wants national food security to be a reality, then it must empower and support its subsistence farmers, at least as the situation stands right now in most of the developing countries. However, government must support not only peasant farmers but every other category of food producers as well, to each according to their own specific needs as and when necessary.

Why is food produced?

Subsistence farmers, as the name suggests, produce food mostly for their own consumption. But most of the time, they also end up with some excess food to sell, usually very small quantities per each farmer. However, due to their overwhelmingly large numbers compared to the numbers of pure commercial farmers at national level, the aggregate production from subsistence farmers is usually several times more than that from commercial farmers both in terms of what they produce in total and also in terms of the excess which they end up selling to national agricultural marketing boards and other buyers of agricultural produce. The correct answer to the question as to why primary producers like farmers would produce food is obviously for both consumption and selling. Anyone who grew up in the village knows that. However, it is the sold food which ends up in national granaries and thus feeds the whole nation. And it is these national food stores which would make any country food secure. Producer retained food for personal consumption usually only lasts for a season or two and nothing more. This is because most peasant farmers have no capacity in terms of knowledge, skills, facilities and finances to store harvested food for long periods of time. Commercial farmers do not store much excess food either because doing so is very expensive and would also defeat the whole purpose of commercial farming as a business venture. Thus, national food stores are very vital in terms of food security. National food storage is actually an essential public service which can only be assigned to public owned business enterprises (POBEs) such as national agricultural marketing authorities, boards of commissions. Government must realise that people do not produce food just to feed the nation but to eat and sell the excess. In order for there to be guaranteed food security at both local and national levels, government must emphasise on and appropriately incentivise the commercial business aspect of agriculture in general and of food production in particular at both the peasant and commercial production levels. Both peasant and commercial farmers must the empowered, assisted and supported to produce much more and as much as they can produce, each one of them according to their own needs and capacities to produce. That is the only way by which any country can become food secure in the long run.

Augmented food security

With or without government, people would still produce food for both their own consumption and to sell as well. No government must ever delude itself with the notion that it is the one which is primarily responsible for national food production. The role of government is to augment national food security and not to create it. In the bigger scheme of things, government is just a supporter and not a player here. Such being the case, government is better advised to stick to its supportive role in agricultural productivity and nothing else. But government still must support with both the passionate commitment and the frenzied verve with which any real and dedicated supporter would usually support a cause which they truly believe in. Government support for national food security must just be for the benefit of national food security alone and not for political reasons such as trying to secure more votes at the next general elections or any other self-centred reasons.

Wrong kind of support for food security

Supporters must know that they are just mere supporters and nothing else in order for them to be able to exercise that supportive role correctly. In this case, government is a supporter of national food security and not its creator or the supporter of personal food security. This is very important because some African governments have gotten so much carried away in their supportive role for agriculture in their countries that they ended up running away with the whole country and its agricultural productivity (actually lack of productivity) to places where no one ever wanted to go in the first place. They just ruined things for everybody!

One African country I know embarked, in an impromptu sort of way, on a politically motivated national agricultural land reform programme which government claimed was intended to simultaneously correct past land grab injustices and also make the country food secure. But the result was tremendous national food insecurity and much, much more than that! This was after most government politicians had personally grabbed all fertile and arable agricultural land from most of the then existing commercial farmers and then parcelled it out in very large chunks to themselves, their relatives and their friends all of whom knew nothing about farming in general, let alone commercial farming. A few politically connected peasant farmers were also allowed to grab some prime farm land for themselves in an apparently spontaneous and therefore unstoppable land reform revolution. But what ensured thereafter was a disastrous catastrophe of very great and unimaginable proportions. The whole country, its economy and its entire population went through hell and never came back!

Due to the haphazard and free-for-all manner in which the so called national land reform programme was conducted or rather left to unfold, meaningful national agricultural productivity vanished overnight. Most of the new farmers concentrated on striping assets from the farms which they had seized and selling them for a living instead of doing any farming. Thus, they cut down centuries old forests in order to sell them as firewood. And they hunted down all the wild animals on these farms too in order to sell them as game meat. They sold game meat down to mice! At the end of the day, the country was not only highly food insecure, but its land and vegetation were absolutely destroyed! All working people who had previously been employed lost their jobs, not only in the agriculturally industry, but also in every other industry as well because as a primary production industry, agriculture supported every other industry as well. At its peak, unemployment hit the 97% mark. Consumer goods price inflation inflated even the local currency out of existence and made monthly salaries completely irrelevant. People ended up being paid in essential foods and other products instead of money. Poverty ravaged, decimated and devastated locals daily trekked out of the country to become economic refugees in neighbouring and other states. There was so much unhappiness, so much hunger and so much pain and suffering in the whole country. What was surprising was that in all this self-induced hardship, government blamed everyone else except itself! But then government had not remained just a supporter of agriculture in this whole saga. Government took an active participant role and yet it refused to take responsibility, let alone to account for its own actions. Anyway, the point here is that the wrong kind of support such as the one exemplified above is the kind of support which no one and no country needs in terms of ensuring that there indeed is national food security.

Correct kind of support for food security

In summary, here is the correct kind of support for national food security. Government must know what the national staple foods are, who produces them, where, when, how and why. It must then strategically empower and support those who produce these staple foods as and when necessary. The strategy must be comprehensive and holistic in nature in that it must jealously preserve agricultural land as well as give the farmer the reason to want to produce even more year in and year out, or even throughout the whole year. Part of that strategy would include things like strict zoning of agricultural land and the prevention of it being misused, abused or underutilised. It would also include materially, technically and financially supporting and empowering the producer to produce even more in addition to providing a ready and assured market for the produce through public owned national food products buying, selling and storage facilities such as agricultural marketing boards. This is the correct way of doing it and not politically motivated and self-benefiting farm invasions as was describe above in the case of that poor and unfortunate country of mine.

The right to shelter

Naturally, everyone has the right to shelter. Many people think of shelter as referring only to housing. Although such kind of thinking makes it easier to see why shelter is a basic human need and therefore also a basic human right, it does not enable someone to see the whole picture. Shelter refers to everything which people live in, on or around and are sheltered in, on or around and not just a house. As such, the whole environment which people live in provides them with shelter, the shelter which enables them to survive in that environment. Thus, shelter encompasses such other things as the whole environment itself plus specific things which are found in that environment such as soil and other minerals, water, vegetation and other animals, air and even just the "empty" environmental space all by itself. Come to think of it, even the country as a whole provides shelter to all its inhabitants just as a country by itself. This is the reason why in later chapters of this book we shall discuss the management of natural resources and why natural resources belong to all people to whom they were given by the creator. However, in this chapter, we shall discuss shelter as it mostly relates to housing and other housing related matters such as land.

Government must empower people to access shelter

Again the function of government in terms of ensuring that people have access to adequate, habitable and hygienic shelter is to just empower and enable people to do it all by themselves and for themselves. There must never be any dolling out of free houses to anybody by government. Not even under the pretext of correcting past injustices! Government must empower people to build their own houses through legislation and also through leveraging on the free market and free market forces as has already been discussed elsewhere in this book. This does not mean that government must not put money into housing. It just means that it must not directly fund or build a house by itself and then hand it over to someone for free.

If left alone to provide shelter for themselves, people would usually build anything, anywhere and anyhow. Now, that would not be the best way to conserve scare resources such as land. Just like agricultural land, housing land must also be legally zoned off specifically for housing and it must also be land which is specifically fit for that purpose. Such national land management and administration must mostly be done at local government level. This is the level where it is most suited. National government must just come up with the governing laws, rules, regulations and any other operating standards which must govern and control national housing administration and development, and then leave it up to local government authorities to implement these laws (see Chapter 15 of this book). However, it is not enough for government to just zone off housing land, demarcate housing plots, allocate them to individuals and then tell them to go ahead and build houses for themselves. As has already been said above, such would lead to unsightly chaos because people would build anything and anyhow. There must be legal building standards in place and these standards must be enforced and followed. There are some countries which I know whose huge burden of TB (tuberculosis) and HIV (Immunodeficiency virus) infections can be attributed squarely to very poor national housing standards. Yes, national housing standards are that very, very important in the lives of people! They can affect a lot of other crucial outcomes in society.

The other down side of letting everybody to build their own house whichever way they want is that of environmental aesthetics in relationship to the value of real estate. Where people have been allocated (not to mean given for free) housing plots and left to their own means and devices in terms of building, there has been lamentably variable rates of progress and completion of that task at individual household level. While some houses would be completed in record time, others would just stand there half complete like ancient ruins for years and years on end. What such differential rates of completion would do is to bring down the market value of the completed houses much to the detriment of their owners. Thus one of the best ways of ensuring that houses within a given locality are all built up to the required legal standards and also completed almost simultaneously and on time too is to rope in private sector land and housing developers to do the job. Strategically leveraging on the market and market forces, government can generate housing development resources from both private and public enterprises, from government itself and also from building societies, banks and many other financial institutions. Such resources must then be managed and administered in a prudent and business-like manner by the concerned stakeholders to provide privately owned public housing to those in need of such housing.

As far as is practically possible, a house just like a car or any other private property, is better looked after if it is one hundred percent owned by the one in whose hands it is or by the one who is occupying it. Many public housing programmes have failed because of the huge maintenance costs which are generated by tenants who just rent the properties and not own them. Such being the case, every national housing development project or programme must aim to put houses completely and squarely in the hands of tenants in terms of both occupation and ownership.

It is not feasible for everyone who wants a house in any country to be able to afford to independently pay for one, either in cash, in kind or in instalments, all by himself or by herself alone. The majority of people need some kind of outside assistance (outside of themselves) in one way or another in this regard. However, what government must do in this regard is not to go in there headlong like a lone ranger and attempt some short sighted heroic Houdini stuff for political and other self-serving purposes. Instead, it must put into place long standing public housing, social, legal, economic and other strategies which would stimulate and channel the investment capital awash and innovative free market and other free market forces towards public housing development. Government must be able to strategically cultivate the public housing development industrial sector into becoming an important national socioeconomic growth and development sector on its own. For example, employers who assist their employees to buy or build houses of their own could get tax rebates or preferential treatment as far as supplying goods and services to government and the public sector is concerned. Private property developers could get certain incentives if they go into public housing development such as getting the required land at its intrinsic instead of its commercial value among many other trade-ins. Public housing development by private developers can also be used as quid pro quo for permission to develop certain private business properties which this sector may want to develop for purely commercial business purposes in areas which must be legally rezoned first in order for that to happen. Government itself may incentivise the public sector housing market by providing housing loan guarantees, tax rebates and subsidised land to all its permanent employees and all the other public service employees as it tries to also play its part as an employer in that regard.

Everyone must be sheltered

On the huge and dicey matter of helping the out-of-employment (unemployed) general public, government must always link any assistance it offers directly to anyone, be it housing assistance, food, education or anything else for that matter, to some sort of personal productivity. For example, unemployed households which would be benefiting from government sponsored public housing may be required to ensure that their underage children seriously attend school without bunking lessons, while the parents and over-age unemployed children join job skills training and other self-help programmes both of which would also be sponsored by the same government. This would ensure that eventually such people, together with their families, can be weaned from government assistance and be able to stand alone socioeconomically. Being unemployed does not mean being unable to work to help oneself. There are many different things which an unemployed person can do to help himself or herself, least of all being to synergistically or symbiotically help those who are helping them to be able to help themselves in one way or the other.

Whatever kind of housing assistance it gives to anybody, government must never give a house to anybody for free. It must never even temporarily house anybody completely for free. That would not only create unacceptable dependency, but it would also eventually undermine the capacity of the people in helps in that way to do things for themselves in more ways than one. For a start, it would take away that highly motivating sense of personal achievement, self-accomplishment, self-esteem and the pride which comes along with doing things for oneself. And yet these are the sort of inbuilt behavioural drivers which everyone needs to propel them forward and to keep on personally achieving even greater things in the future. First of all, those who get government housing assistance must merit that kind of assistance. Secondly, government housing assistance or any other government assistance for that matter must always be paid back. Whether it is paid back in full or in part, in cash or in kind, it really does not matter. What matters most is that it must always be paid back somehow.

To go back to the beginning, government does not have to only legally zone off housing land and then parcel it out. There are other important things which it must also do first or as a matter of priority before such housing land can be developed. Soon after zoning any piece of land for housing development, government must categorise it in terms of what sort of housing would be developed on that piece of land. This categorization would be in terms of whether it would be high, medium, low or luxurious density houses which would be developed on that piece of land. The next thing would be for government to ensure that individual housing plots are surveyed and demarcated on that piece of land and also that the plots are serviced in terms of providing the required access roads, street lighting, water and sewage reticulation systems. It would be only after all these things have been done that the land would then be said to be ready for purchasing and housing construction or development. At this juncture, private sector developers and building construction companies can come in and work.

The right to health

Right on the heels of the right to food and shelter is the right to health. This is not just the right to health but the right to good health, the kind of health which gives life or prolongs life. Government has the obligation to ensure that all people have access to such kind of health in their times of need. They say that health is the most valuable wealth there is. That is why it is better to be poor and healthy than to be rich and unhealthy. Ralph Waldo Emerson said that "the first wealth is health." But apparently poor people do not see things the same way which led Charles Caleb Colton to say that "The poorest men will part with health for money, but the richest men would gladly part with all their money for health." There is nothing which when it is really needed is needed with such urgency as medical or health services. One can go for days or even weeks without food and still be alive. One can go on for years and years living on the open streets (at least anywhere around and within the tropics) without any appreciable shelter and still live. But one cannot hope to survive even for just a few minutes in any real medical emergency situation without appropriate and needed medical help. The relationship between health and life is quite acute and this acuteness is acutely visible most of the time. The state of national health services alone can determine the viability or otherwise of any national government in terms of retaining power. Where matters of life and death are concerned, people do not think straight but just become emotional.

The best possible solution to health services delivery

In Chapter 9 of this book we talked a lot about how, under the circumstances whereby government is both the funder and provider of public health services, things can be improved therein in order to afford public health clients their deserved and rather mandatory freedom of choice. What that discussion just did was to suggest the best possible solution to the situation at hand and not the best possible solution there is to public health services delivery as a whole and in general. As was alluded to in that chapter, the best possible solution to public health services deliver in any country is called national health insurance (NHI) under which there would be a national health insurance medical aid scheme (NHIMAS) and a national health insurance fund (NHIF) to finance the whole scheme.

National Health Insurance

National health insurance (NHI) is a legalised, mandatory and contributory national social protection (social security) arrangement whereby every single individual person in the country would be covered from before birth to after death, by a compulsory public owned but not necessarily public operated or administered medical aid scheme and fund. By definition, national health insurance (NHI) is actually health focused social security, not social welfare. NHI is as simple as all that, and also just as complicated. But it is something that can be done and has been done successfully in many developed countries. The medical aid scheme under NHI would be called the national health insurance medical aid scheme (NHIMAS) and the medical aid fund thereof would be called the national health insurance fund (NHIF).

The inhibitive idea which most developing countries must disabuse themselves of is the notion that NHI or social protection in general is only implementable when a certain magical and higher level of national socioeconomic growth and development has been achieved and never prior to that. The opposite is actually very true. The widespread availability of social protection services at national level has been proved to be one of the strongest and most effective drivers of national socioeconomic growth and development instead of social protection being the result of that socioeconomic growth and development [3]. What this means is that every country can afford to and must actually put social protection services in place, one way or the other. After all, social protection is a basic human right as we have been saying all along and everywhere in this book. People of all nations must be enabled to enjoy their basic human rights. In fact, social protection is not new but an age old phenomenon. For a quick discussion on this aspect of social protection one is referred to my previous book entitled "There is No Democracy At All in Government by Political Party Representatives" pages 216 to 223.

National Health Insurance Medical Aid Scheme

National health insurance medical aid scheme (NHIMAS) is a public owned social security medical aid scheme whereby everyone in the country would have a medical aid card as we discussed in chapter 9 but this time the card would have to be paid for and not just issued out almost free of charge. And it would be paid for in a very systematic, logical and rational way in terms of determining who contributes what amount, for whom, when, how and why.

NHIMAS stakeholder identification

Individuals: The logic or rationale of it is all very simple. Individual health is naturally the business and responsibility of the concerned individual person. Such being the case, everyone is and must be responsible for his or her own health, including paying for it as and when necessary. Thus each and every individual person would be responsible for his or her own portion of monthly premium contributions to NHIMAS for and on his or her own behalf as a primary stakeholder of the scheme. Of course, the equity principle of from each according to his capacity to contribute and to each according to his needs would apply especially here as well. Such being the case, employed adults would directly fund their own portions of the bill and their own portions of those dependents that they are responsible for.

Parents: Obviously, parents are naturally responsible for the health of their own dependent minor children. Such being the case, all parents have an obligation to pay for the health of their own minor children under NHIMAS, whether such parents would be employed or not. Besides being mandatorily obliged to pay for their own children, affording parents and other affording relatives have the moral duty and obligation to also pay for their less fortunate closest dependent relatives who would not afford to pay for themselves, but such moral duties would be voluntary and not mandatory. Incentivised voluntarism would be the best approach for government to take in such cases.

Government: As was suggested in preceding chapters of this book, government acts as the Godparent if not the real parent of all people under its jurisdiction in terms of its obligations to ensure that they access their right to social protection and all their basic human needs and basic human rights as well in return for the power to govern. Such being the case, government is and must be responsible for the health of everyone under its jurisdiction. In fact that public responsibility is what gives any government legitimacy and the right to govern. Such being the case, government is automatically also liable to pay NHIMAS monthly premium contributions for everybody in the country whether they are employed, dependent or not. Under NHIMAS, everyone becomes a dependent of government.

Employers: Employers benefit a lot from the good health of their employees in terms of productivity and the profits thereof. As much as the employee must look out for his or her own health, the employer has a mandatory moral duty and obligation to also chip in. Such being the case, employers are also liable to pay for the health of their employees in terms of monthly premium contributions to NHIMAS in the same way they may already be doing so under private medical aid schemes. Just like what they may already be doing under private medical aid schemes, employers also have the moral duty and obligation to assist their employees in paying NHIMAS subscriptions for both their dependent children and some other dependent relatives as well such as parents, brothers and sisters.

Unemployed: Finally, the major challenge of unemployed adults rests squarely with government. It is government alone which must pay for the health of these people in terms of monthly premium contributions to NHIMAS. But of course government would always make the public pay for that through taxes as channelled through the public health fiscal budget. That is as it must be, but at least the monthly premium payments to NHIMAS in this case must all come directly from government.

In summary, what we have established above in terms of payment responsibilities under NHIMAS is that government must pay its own portion for everyone, while adults who can afford to pay (i.e. those with an enabling income) must pay their own personal portions for themselves and also pay their parental responsibility portions for their children and other dependents. And finally, employers must pay the employer portion for their own employees and even help those employees to pay their portions for their minor children and other dependents. In short, those who must mandatorily contribute equal monthly premium portions to NHIMAS as principal stakeholders and for each and every person under their care and responsibility would be individuals (for themselves), parents (for minor children), government (for everyone) and employers (for employees and their dependents). NHIMAS payment responsibilities having been thus established, the next step is to establish the rationale and logic of both the amount to be paid and the mechanisms of payment thereof, and finally followed by establishing the modalities of how exactly NHIMAS must operate, be managed and administered.

Monthly premium contributions to NHIMAS

There is definitely an optimum level of NHIMAS monthly premium contributions per capita which would make the scheme sustainably viable in terms of both maintenance and service delivery. Such an optimum level would take many things into consideration such as national morbidity and mortality rates, consultation and hospital admission rates, national per capita expenditure rate on health per annum, government per capita expenditure rate on health per annum, other population demographics, national wage bill, wage rate and distribution, consumer price inflation rates, employment and unemployment rates, consumer bread basket index, cost of living index, poverty datum line and many, many other relevant variables. As to the exact formula of how all these relevant and dynamic variables can be simultaneously integrated, computed and worked out to arrive at the very exact desired optimum level of NHIMAS monthly premium contributions per capita, no one knows that. Even seasoned actuarial scientists have absolutely no clue about that. The fact is that such an optimum level is very difficult if not well neigh impossible to calculate or establish. And yet it must be there somewhere and it must be calculated and established somehow and then be put to use in order to operationalise NHIMAS. Without that figure, there would be no monthly premium contributions to the NHIF and consequently there would be no NHIMAS as well.

After being hopelessly vexed by some convoluted actuarial logic and rationalisation expressed in terms of differential calculus when trying to arrive at a very simple everyday insurance solution, someone once quipped that actuarial science, like economics, was actually ninety-five percent commonsense just made complicated. To every common man out there on the street, it sounds like this observation may be very accurate and true. As individuals, we all make several decisions every day about what we want to do and actually go ahead to implement those decisions all the time. Usually, we do this on the go or on our feet without even consciously or visibly employing any complicated actuarial evaluations about the validity or otherwise of those decisions or their chances of success or failure in terms of implementation. Most of the decisions which we make every day and on the go like this are actually very complicated decisions to make if they were subjected to proper actuarial evaluation. But then somehow, we just make those decisions in an instant and then immediately implement them and, dada, most of the time we successfully achieve what we wanted to achieve, no actuarial science needed or used! If we waited for scientific actuarial evaluations before we made or implemented any decisions which we make every day in our lives, then we would most likely if not most definitely not be able to do or accomplish anything at all. This is a fact. The other fact is that actuarial science, just like economics and other social sciences, is not exactly a real or pure science regardless of what they call it because it is not an exact science like physics, chemistry, biology and mathematics. With actuarial science, you are never one hundred percent sure of anything. Perhaps this is the reason why Norman Vincent Peale said that if you put off something till you are sure of it, you will never get anything done, while Carrie Wilkerson said that your only limitation is how much action you are willing to take and Amelia Earthart said that the most effective way to do it is to do it!

The point here is that there is in fact a very easy and everyday method by which the optimum level of NHIMAS monthly premium contributions per capita which would make the scheme sustainably viable in terms of both maintenance and service delivery can be arrived at. And the starting point of this search is none other than national healthcare expenditure rates themselves. No complicated applied statistics, integrated mathematics or differential calculus is needed here. The rationale and logic of this is that whatever the country would have been spending on health, although it may not have been enough, would at least have been providing some sort of acceptable level of healthcare services which the country and its people could live with because they would actually have managed to live with that thus far as envisaged by their still being alive and healthy up to that point in time. Simple! Every country must know what its annual per capita expenditure on health is, at least retrospectively. It must similarly also know what that figure is in terms of government per capita expenditure on health as well. Most of the time government annual per capita expenditure on health is lower than the national figure. This is as it must be. And in order to come up with an optimum NHIMAS individual stakeholder monthly premium contributions level, the average national per capita expenditure on health per annum adjusted for inflation over a period of three to five years must be calculated. In order for the country not to overstretch itself in terms of its annual fiscal budget, the average annual government per capita expenditure on health over the same period of time as the average national per capita expenditure on health per annum figure must also be calculated and be used as an index or reference point. In a country where the average government per capita expenditure on health per annum multiplied by three is more than the average national per capita expenditure on health per annum, then the average government per capita expenditure on health per annum divided by twelve must be used as the individual stakeholder minimum monthly premium contribution to the National Health Insurance Fund (NHIF) of the National Health Insurance Medical Aid Scheme (NHIMAS). Where the average government per capita expenditure on health per annum multiplied by three is less than the average national per capita expenditure on health per annum, then the average national per capita expenditure on health per annum divided by twelve must be used as the optimum individual stakeholder minimum monthly premium contribution to the NHIF of the NHIMAS.

The governing principle in deducing the optimum level of contributions of each individual stakeholder is that all the identified three main stakeholders of the NHIMAS (i.e. the government, the individual and the employer) must contribute equal portions to the National Health Insurance Fund (NHIF) per capita per annum, and also for each and everyone in the national population who they are naturally responsible for including themselves as discussed earlier in this chapter under NHIMAS stakeholder identification. This means that each individual person in the country would have three different but equal portions to his or her total monthly or annual premium contributions to the NHIF. The first portion would be from government contributing for everyone as government. The next portion would be from the concerned individual himself or herself (if he or she is employed), or from his mother, father or relative (if he or she is a dependent). And the third and final portion would be from the employer (if he or she is employed). For the unemployed, government would have to pay the whole three portions all by itself as suggested before. Each contributor must be able to pay for their own portion and this is the optimum portion which we were trying to see how it could be determined here.

NHIMAS premium contributions exemplified

For example, there is this small and beautiful African country which I was once privileged to be asked to try to evaluate the feasibility of it implementing NHIMAS. Although this country was classified as a middle income country with an income rate of US$2600 per capita per annum, the income disparity or income gap on the ground was just too high. The government of this country employed about 17% of the total national workforce of whom only 3% earned above US$3000 per month and 80% earned less than US%1000 per month. The private sector employed the remaining 80 to 85% of the national workforce. Less than 1% of the private sector workforce earned more than US$3000 per month, with 90% or more earning US$100 or less per month! Here it must be pointed out that the minimum wage in government was actually US$350 per month and this was also the national lowest taxable income. This was quite a pleasant surprise considering what most governments are well known for in terms of salary differences between the private and the public sector. Anyway, what this meant was that in this country, the overwhelming majority of private sector employees who were four times more than government employees in terms of numbers were not at all contributing even a single cent to the national fiscal budget, and yet they were the biggest public service beneficiaries. But the issue is that in a country with US$2600 per capita per annum as its average national income rate, about 80% of the total workforce earned US$1200 per annum or just over 46% of the average national income per capita per annum figure. That was quite some huge income disparity gap there!

In this country, the average national expenditure per capita on health was US$260 per annum. This figure was just over four times the World Health Organisation recommended minimum of US$60 per capita per annum [4]. However, government expenditure on health was a healthy US$120 per capita per annum. So in the case of this country, and according to the recommended formula as deduced above, US$10 would have been the starting level of individual stakeholder monthly premium contributions to the National Health Insurance Fund (NHIF) under NHIMAS. But that amount would have been equal to 10% of the US$100 per month salaries of 80% of the workforce who were not even eligible to pay income tax at national level! Suddenly taxing such people 10% of their salaries for whatever good reason would definitely have caused a major political uproar in addition to pushing them further down into abject poverty among other bad consequences. For a start, that just could not be done for reasons given below.

The other thing is that with social security, certain indices apply with regards to monthly premium contributions in relationship to monthly income. The maximum individual monthly contribution to each social security scheme must not exceed 5% of the basic monthly income of that individual. This 5% cap is provided in order to prevent impoverishing the same individual while at the same time attempting to protect him or her from poverty. In case you may not have noticed it yet, social protection is all about preventing people from sliding into abject poverty. Thus, social protection must always prevent and not cause poverty, directly or indirectly, no matter what. In the case of the country under discussion here, the proposed US$10 monthly NHIF premium contribution per individual would have been 10% of the US$100 monthly income of 80% of the total workforce. As such that would not have been permissible as far as the provision of social protection without further impoverishment is concerned. The biggest question now was that how could this working poor 80% of the total workforce contribute US$10 per month to the NHIF when their monthly income of US$100 would not allow that to happen?

Under normal or natural distribution circumstances, 95% of the workforce in this country would have been earning at least 80% or more of the average national per capita income of US$2600 per annum reduced to US$216.70 per capita per month with only about 5% earning less than that figure. But in this case 80% of the workforce instead of just 5% earned far less than the national per capita per month income figure at just US$100 square per person per month. Such extremely high income disparity would normally be unimaginable but it happens sometimes.

Obviously, pegging the basic or minimum one third NHIMAS individual stakeholder portion of NHIF monthly premium contributions at US$10 per month per beneficiary would have been a big, big injustice to the majority of the working poor in this country. And yet for the proposed National Health Insurance Medical Aid Scheme (NHIMAS) and its NHIF to be sustainably viable, that was the exact and actual amount of the one third portions which every one of the identified three individual stakeholders (i.e. government, individuals and employers) had to contribute per month for each beneficiary of the scheme. And in fact that was what every individual stakeholder was going to contribute as his or her own portion. There was just no way out of this one. The only choice would be between implementing NHIMAS and not implementing it. Knowingly reducing the viability of the scheme by collecting contributions which would make the scheme none viable and therefore not sustainable and still going ahead to implement it would be like setting oneself up for obvious failure. Under such circumstances, what would be the best strategy to take considering the fact that there is absolutely no excuse whatsoever in further impoverishing people in the process of trying to alleviate the very same poverty which they are suffering from? As was said above, in providing social protection, further impoverishment would strictly be out of question. Here, it would be easier to just say that NHIMAS cannot be implemented as yet in such an unfavourable environment. But as we said before, any socioeconomic condition or situation is always suitable for the implementation of social protection schemes. And it would be the implementation of social protection schemes which would eventually drive out poverty from society as a whole. The time is always right to do what is right, or so goes the old wisdom.

Under such circumstances, the best trick would be to just focus on implementing social protection without further impoverishing anybody. In this case, considering the fact that the country deserved to be classified as a middle income country and yet it had 80% working poor people, meant that there was a disproportionately awful lot of money in the national economy which was being earned by someone somewhere, but just not by 80% of the workers. And that someone was the one who was supposed to pay for or debunk the 5% NHIF monthly premium contributions deficit of the working poor. And that person was obviously the private sector employer or the so called captains of industry! This must be pretty obvious to fathom considering the fact that it was the private sector employer who actually paid his employees the peanuts which prevented them from viably paying for their own one third portion of the proposed NHIF monthly premium contributions in full. All government or public sector employees in this country earned a minimum of US$350 per month. They were all able to pay their own one third individual stakeholder portion of US$10 monthly premium contributions to the NHIF because this amounted to just less than 3% of their monthly income. This figure was well below the allowed maximum limit of 5% of monthly basic income. This rather sad revelation shows that our poverty stricken middle income and beautiful African country was just being beautifully robbed in broad daylight by its private sector, the very same sector which, in any other country, would be expected to be the one propping up the national economy. This case could be a world first in this regard!

Anyway, after all had been considered, the calculated individual one third stakeholder responsibility portion of the

NHIF monthly premium contributions would still remain at US$10 per month as calculated in order to ensure the sustainable viability of the proposed NHIMAS. However, the actual individual person, employee or worker monthly contribution to his or her own one third portion of the total contribution per scheme beneficiary would be pegged at a maximum of 5% of basic monthly income or salary with any shortfall thereof in terms of actual amount being made good for or debunked by the underpaying employer. That way, every individual stakeholder would still contribute 100% or US$10 as their own one third monthly premium portion responsibility to the NHIF of NHIMAS as originally intended. This would make the whole scheme sustainably viable without further impoverishing anyone. This was perhaps quite a smart win-win situation one must agree.

NHIF dependent premium contributions

As far as dependent children are concerned, government and each of the responsible two parents must all contribute their full one third responsibility NHIF premium portions per month each, with shortfalls being debunked by government or employers as necessary. A child always has a mother and a father, whether married or not, it does not matter. Both parents must always be held responsible and accountable for the upkeep of their minor children. Individual employers are free to assist both parents and government with part of their portions of child monthly premium contributions to NHIF. Government must incentivise and recognise such benevolent employers with tax rebates or some other preferential treatment when dealing with them such as making them preferred suppliers of goods and services to government and the greater public sector.

NHIF unemployed premium contributions

However, as far as the unemployed adults are concerned, these people would be one hundred percent government responsibility in terms of NHIF monthly premium payments. In order to incentivise the unemployed to at least acquire some job skills of some sort, government could offer to give them free NHIMAS medical aid cards if they enrolled and continued to daily attend job skills training programmes which it would start for them if such did not already exist. Government could also offer tax rebates to parents and other relatives who would offer to partly pay NHIF monthly premium contributions for their dependent adult children and other relatives. Adult students enrolled in colleges and universities would as usual be covered by educational grants, bursaries and other scholarships in this regard. And that just about accounts for everybody under NHIMAS!

NHIMAS Management and Administration

The National Health Insurance Medical Aid Scheme (NHIMAS) would inevitably and of necessity give birth to a fund called the National Health Insurance Fund (NHIF). This is due to the fact of it being legally mandatory and contributory in nature. Legislative responsibility for NHIMAS must always belong to government. However, in terms of operations, the NHIF must be owned but not necessarily operated by the public. For the logic behind all this, refer back to Chapter 6 on the need for practical separation of both powers and people in governing and governance structures of all institutions whether in the private or public sector. Thus, NHIF must be managed and administered not necessarily by a public owned business enterprise (POBE), but by any capable and experienced private or public sector corporation with whom the public service administration (PSA) may decide to entrust their NHIMAS funds with. In fact, it is hereby recommended that the public service administration (PSA) should do just that and not try to manage the NHIF under NHIMAS all by itself under a POBE.

To start off with, no public service administration (PSA) anywhere in this world has the requisite experience or capacity to manage NHIMAS funds because that has never been the main duty or responsibility of the PSA. In countries with huge populations, managing NHIMAS funds would take more than just one organisation alone no matter how good, efficient or effective in terms of both skills and technology such an organisation may be or claim to be. Verification and payment of benefit claims from just one very large health services deliver institution such as a central hospital can be such a onerous task on its own. What about from the whole country and all its health services delivery institutions under NHIMAS? Such being the case, in an open and competitive process, any capable and experienced business organisation or entity can be called upon and contracted to collect NHIF monthly premiums and also to pay out the claims thereof just like what most private sector medical aid schemes do right now. Medical aid schemes are just the same medical aid schemes, whether privately or publicly owned. The management principles must be and are in fact just the same. As long as the guiding principles, laws, rules, regulations and other standard operating procedures of NHIMAS and its NHIF are followed by the contracted scheme and fund managers and administrators, then there must be absolutely no problem.

In terms of payment for managing and administering the NHIF, contracted fund managers and administrators would obviously be allowed to automatically retain usually not more than thirty percent of the annual premium contributions which they would have collected themselves as fund management and administration costs. Usually, there would also be an added five percent or so maximum incentive share of the annual profits or excess funds thereof. And that would be just about all in terms of fund management and administration fees. We do not need to discuss how the NHIF backed medical aid card would give everyone in the country first class access to all kinds of health services, public or private, and all kinds of freedoms which are usually restricted in all public service delivery systems because, as extensively discussed under freedom of choice in Chapter 9, that is already a given. The NHIF governing rules and regulations would ensure that such happens. The detailed principles and practices of NHIMAS and NHIF governing rules, regulations and other codes of conduct and practice constitute another entire book altogether on their own. And that would be a topic for another day or another consultancy.

The immense benefits of NHIMAS

With every citizen in possession of a high class international standard medical aid card, what else can government or anyone else in the country whish for? NHIMAS puts government squarely where it belongs. It puts government in the driver's seat and just steering instead of powering or rowing the country forward to good health. The powering or rowing bit would be done by the people themselves and their private sector organisations. And that is the beauty of it all. With NHIMAS in place government does not have to own or even run a single public or private healthcare institution in the country. In might not even have to hire a single medical doctor or nurse, except just to advise it on the rules and regulations of the profession in terms of setting the required health services delivery standards.

Although the Public Service Administration (PSA), perhaps through a public owned business enterprise (POBE) called National Health Insurance Fund Authority (NHIFA) would own the NHIF, it does not have to pay a single cent right from the start in order to operationalise that fund. The NHIFA can just be instructed through internal governing and governance policies to contract out to the experts the management and administration of the NHIF right from the word go as has already been discussed. These experts would be established private medical aid funds or schemes, insurance companies and even other private healthcare services deliver institutions. NHIF management contractors would be charged with the duties and responsibilities of recruiting and registering NHIMAS members, collecting the monthly premium contributions and paying out the medical aid claims thereof as well as was alluded to somewhere herein before. And for that, they would collect a handsome management fee of about thirty percent of the total premiums which they would have collected per annum!

With the roping in of the private sector to manage the NHIF right from the beginning, talks by many governments that instituting NHIMAS would be very expensive in terms of management and administration costs are actually very false. The truth would be that such governments would either be just unwilling to implement NHIMAS for one reason or another, or they would be absolutely lights out in terms of basic knowledge, education and training about how NHIMAS works. Sometimes simple corruption would also be at play because in terms of expenditure, the provision of public health services is usually a multibillion dollar business coming second perhaps only to education in many countries of this world. In many countries there usually would be already well established and politically entrenched health services providers who would not want to move an inch in order to give way to NHIMAS. Such providers would usually have all the influential politicians, decision makers and even professional advisors in their own pockets and eating from the palms of their own hands. This alone is the main reason why most NHIMAS programmes take ages and ages to take off the ground and yet they could actually do so almost overnight. The saying that where huge amounts of money are at play, corruption is always the dancing partner has some substance in it.

Anyway, the service standards enforcement, monitoring, evaluation, review and continuous improvement aspect of NHIMAS must always remain within the ambit and realms of government control through its national health services administration (NHSA) body as described in chapter 6 of this book. As far as the day to day enforcement of those service standards is concerned that becomes the natural duty and responsibility of the National Health Insurance Fund (NHIF) management and administration institutions which would have been contracted to manage the NHIF by the NHIFA. These contracted NHIF management and administration institutions would have to put into place their own fund management and administration systems complete with beneficiary identification and electronic medical records management which would enable them to collect monthly premiums, track as to who is being treated where, by whom and with what, and also enable them to pay benefits just like any other private medical aid fund would do. In order to induce the necessary service quality improving competition into all this, the NHIFA would be advised to award NHIF management and administration contracts to more than just one institution in the country. Several would be better and the best way would be to do it regionally or provincially or to just have an upper limit on the total number of NHIMAS beneficiaries which each contracted NHIF manager and administrator would be allowed to handle from anywhere in the whole country. In fact, the last option would be the best because it would accommodate a lot of contractors thereby allowing a lot of competition in addition to giving NHIMAS beneficiary clients the freedom of choice which they deserve. Of course, contractors who do not perform up to the required standards can always be dropped from the system at any one time, and that's the beauty of it all. With NHIMAS, service delivery standards can always be kept high up there where they belong.

NHIMAS is a real winner

NHIMAS is a real win-win proposal for any country not only because of the vast improvements which it would bring to the whole national health services sector in terms of investment, efficiency and effectiveness, but also because of the immensely positive general socioeconomic impact and benefits which it would inevitably engender. Massive capital injections into any economic sector such as would happen through the NHIF have been known to cause massively positive vibrations in any national socioeconomic system. The small African country which I had the privilege to evaluate in relationship to the feasibility of it incepting NHIMAS proved the viability of NHIMAS as a sure vehicle for socioeconomic growth and development hands down. With a population of just one million people and seventeen thousand square kilometres in land surface area, the country was just ideal for a quick and pinpoint NHIMAS feasibility and viability evaluation. And it did not disappoint either. Although 75% of the population of this country was unemployed, lived in rural areas, and on less than one United States (US) dollars a day, the country's per capita income stood at US$2600 per annum! This catapulted the country into the lower middle income group of countries as was mentioned before. That alone when taken together with the abject poverty of 75% of the rest of the population straightaway suggested that something, somewhere was not right at all. The national per capita expenditure on health of that country was a staggering US$260 per annum, or just over four times the World Health Organisation recommended minimum of US$60. This kind of expenditure matched what was happening in some middle to bottom end developed countries and yet this country was fit to be in the category of the developing of the developing nations. This glaring anomaly showed that something was seriously wrong somewhere! But then that was not my brief. My brief was to find out if it was feasible to incept NHIMAS in that country, so I just continued on that route alone.

The annual government per capita expenditure on health for that country was US$120 or just US$10 per month, remember? And this, taken together with the US$260 national per capita expenditure on health per annum worked out as calculated in some paragraphs above to mean that each individual stakeholder would contribute US$10 per month as his or her one third stakeholder portion of the three thirds (US$30) individual beneficiary monthly premium contributions to the NHIF under NHIMAS. What this meant was that each one of the country's one million people as beneficiaries would contribute a total of US$30 per month to the NHIF. This figure would be broken down thus; $10 for everyone from government as a primary stakeholder, another $10 for each and every employed person for that individual as a primary stakeholder, and also from the same person compulsorily for dependent children and voluntarily for other relatives as secondary stakeholders, and the last $10 from the employer as a primary stakeholder as well. For the unemployed, government would pay the whole $30 per month alone, but of course, from the fiscal budget. In many countries, US$30 per month is far less than the total amount (employer plus employee contributions) which is charged as monthly contributions for principal members alone by most private medical aid schemes and their funds.

As small as this US$30 per month per person NHIF premium contribution was, its projected impact was immense. First, it ensured that there was not even a single cent increase in government expenditure on health per annum. This would keep the fiscal health budget at the same level as before. But at the same time, it would also ensure that public expenditure financing for health was actually tripled from US$120 per capita per annum to a staggering US$360 per capita per annum, even well above the national expenditure on health figure of US$260 per capita per annum. Suddenly there would be an extra US$100 per capita per annum to spend on health. The socioeconomic impact of such a huge figure floating in the national economy would have moved and shaken mountains in terms of investment and other high impact socioeconomic developments. But that would not have been all in terms of benefits from NHIMAS.

Previously, no one knew exactly where, how and on what the staggering and mouth watering US$260 per capita per annum national expenditure on health was spent on. But the resultant NHIF induced US$360 per capita per annum NHIF premium contributions would all have been traceable in terms of expenditure. This is because with every social security scheme of which NHIMAS and its NHIF actually are, the expenditure of all the collected individual annual premium contributions would be strictly legislated, regulated, governed and monitored. And if the strict and standard 30 – 30 – 30 – 10% rule of expenditure allocation for social security funds management was to be adhered to or employed, then the socioeconomic benefits thereof would even be greater. This rule of thumb means that not more than 30% of the annual premium contributions would be used for administration costs, not more than 30% would be used for payment of benefit costs, at least 30% would be invested in solid assets, and at least 10% would be stashed away in reserve funds. With such expenditure allocations, there is no doubt that the socioeconomic benefits of the modest gesture of which the proposed NHI, NHIMAS and NHIF are would have been felt far beyond the scheme and the fund themselves and even for generations to come.

At the rate of US$360 per capita per annum, the NHIF alone would have raised a total of US$360 million per annum through monthly premium contributions for the one million people who constituted the whole population of the country which I assessed as discussed herein. Worth noting is the fact that at that time, the whole annual fiscal budget of that country stood at just about US$1 billion. This meant that NHIF alone would have raised a staggering 36% of the annual fiscal budget and still be able to pump 10.8% of that national budget directly back into the national economy as liquid investment funds. This would be in addition to the whooping 21.6% of the national fiscal budget which the NHIF would splash across many sectors of the national economy as payment for management, administration and health services deliver costs. And not to mention the 3.6% of the national fiscal budget in reserve funds and what that would do to the national financial and money markets as well in terms of liquid trading finance. Anyone who ever doubted that social protection, especially social security, is actually a very, very potent socioeconomic growth and development driver and not the driven vehicle itself must just look at these figures and think again about that. But since too many things behind the scenes were apparently wrong in very, very big ways in this small and very beautiful African country, the proposed NHI, NHIMAS and NHIF thereof never saw the light of day, at least for about ten years since it was first muted and still counting. One day maybe, just one day NHIMAS would be allowed to geminate in that country. That ball is always in the hands of the powerful elite and of course, also in the hands of God.

The right to education and training

The right to education and training is one of the most obvious basic human rights. However, in most societies, it is the right to basic education alone which everyone would quickly acknowledge as being a basic human need and also a basic human right without even thinking about it. When it comes to the right to training, many people seem to think or believe that it is optional, and yet as a basic human need as well, it is not at all that way. What is optional in terms of training is the career or professional path which one may choose, but not the basic need for training. Perhaps this is the major reason why people view education and training differently. Usually there are not too many options in basic education. With basic education, we all seem to go through the very same set channels of primary education followed by secondary education and then college or university education everywhere and anywhere in the world. But as far as practical job or professional job skills training is concerned, people are trained differently in different parts of the world. Anyone who has had the opportunity to undergo practical on the job training after college or university would testify to this fact. Training channels and methodologies are just different from place to place and from country to country. Perhaps this is the reason why people view basic education differently from basic training in terms of these two being basic human rights.

The purpose of basic university and college education, no matter how practical it may look, is mainly just to prepare someone for the real and practical on the job skills training in their chosen career or profession and not to make them a professional as most people erroneously think or believe. Medical doctors and engineers would be the first to tell you that. Anyway, training is a basic human need in the sense that it enables the trainee to have a career or profession which they would thereafter use to earn a living. We now live in a modern world where subsistence existence is not longer an option. In the good old days, informal home based education was all one needed to make it or survive in life. But today everyone needs much more than just that to cut it in this world. Admittedly, yes, we still need the same home based informal education, especially the kind that teaches us to be good people in terms of our individual behaviours, and also to be good citizens in terms of being able to live well with others. But that alone would not put bread and butter on the table. So, after everything has been considered, basic training stills comes out as a basic human need and consequently also as a basic human right.

Basic education and training cost money

Having thus established the basic human right nature of the need for education and training, we must then examine how government can play its role and fulfil its mandate and obligation of ensuring that people it governs access their right to basic education and training without fail. For some strange and odd reasons, many youths and other people, especially in the previously colonised Sub-Saharan African countries, have been terribly misinformed and misguided to believe that they are entitled to free basic education which is fully paid for by their governments. Some have even spiced it all up by calling it "free decolonised education" just to give it an extra taste as they clamour for it. As much as everyone has the right to and deserves to be educated, can education be absolutely for free at the point of access? The answer is definitely a very big no. Maybe in another utopian world education would perhaps be free of charge, but not in this world which we live in today, and not now, and not in the near future too. There is absolutely nothing which can ever be absolutely for free in life, just nothing at all.

Educational fees cannot fall

In one southern African country not so long ago, students from many local universities and mostly those from the previously colonised and disadvantaged racial groups, understandably took to the streets to demonstrate in what they dubbed the "fees-must-fall" campaign. Unfortunately, the demonstrations later on turned violent and nasty. A lot of property was torched and destroyed and a life or two may have been lost in the process. The concerned national government was all over the place in sixes and sevens apparently without a clue as to how it could permanently put an end to such student demonstrations for pretty much the same things year in and year out. Previously, the government had put up several commissions of enquiry into education to tackle various pertinent issues, top of which was the issue of educational fees. But such commissions did not yield the desired results as evidenced by continued student protests year after year. Even in the heat of the last demonstration, government again faithfully put into place yet another very high powered commission of enquiry into education. This time around, the result was not very kind to both government and the demonstrating students because for some strange reason perhaps better known by itself, the commission suggested such a crooked business model and approach to financing basic higher education that all students who would have been unfortunate enough to use that model would have been guaranteed to carry a very huge educational debt for the rest of their lives! Of course, all the students roundly rejected that bad proposal. Almost everyone was unanimous in condemning this commission of enquiry into basic education financing and its wayward private business beneficiating recommendations.

After their latest attempt at finding a reasonable, amicable and sustainably viable solution to the question of financing basic university education had embarrassingly failed them, no one in government seemed to have a clear-cut idea of what to do next! To make matters worse, the national academic think tanks ensconced in all universities did not even try as much as to come to the party in order to assist their own institutions, the government or the students on this matter. In the mean time, students seemed to be hell bent on making as much noise and causing as much havoc as they could about this issue, the issue of "free and decolonised education" as they aptly called it then. Various other social agitators, from business to political ones, jumped into the fray as well and they were loud, clear and vocal in their support for one side or the other. But all of them did not articulate any progressive, meaningful or tangible solution to the then onerous challenge of public education financing. Each one of these social agitators was just trying to scoop out some personal or business benefits which they could chance on and nothing else.

All in all, there did not seem to be any coherent and meaningful thought processes which were going on in that country right then in terms of attempting to shed more light on and thereby help to amicably and peacefully resolve this very important but apparently contentious issue of national basic public education financing. What was going to happen next? Where and when would all this nasty and fulminating hullaballoo end? And what would happen to the political, social and economic outlook of the country at the end of it all? No one had exact and correct answers to these very important questions. And obviously not even after the then latest commission of enquiry had released its ill-advised and ill-fated report which would have buried university students in perpetual debt as has already been revealed above. After that unhelpful report was released, it was back to square one again. Even at the time of writing this book (2018), it seemed that the question of public education financial was a pretty much insoluble one in that country which we are talking about here. But is that actually the case in reality?

Public education financing is part of social protection

The first few chapters of this book detailed what the basic obligations duties and responsibilities of any government are. One of government's most basic obligations, duties and responsibilities is to ensure access to social protection of which social security is a major component. The United Nations' (UN) Universal Declaration of Human Rights (UDHR) of 1948 states in Article 22 that "...Everyone, as a member of society, has the right to social security." Social security and social protection are therefore basic human rights as already discussed elsewhere in this book.

So far in this book, we have probably realised that social protection protects vulnerable populations in their times of need by ensuring that their basic human needs are met or financed, and that the recurrent risks thereto are reduced and perhaps even eventually eliminated. Social protection also protects vulnerable populations by ensuring that there is improved preparedness to dealing with any emerging vulnerabilities and also that there would be guaranteed individual and national resilience to such disasters if and when they occur. Finally, social protection protects populations by ensuring that there are solid environmental platforms for real and sustainably viable socio-economic growth and development for everyone. We probably have also realised that social protection does not mean free handouts, the promotion of dependency and laziness or spoon feeding people. It also does not mean over-taxation of the rich in order to pay for the needs of the poor. Under social protection, especially the social security component of it, everyone would contribute, from each according to his capacity to contribute, and everyone would also benefit, to each according to his or her own basic needs. As a basic human need and human right, public education and its financing must be social protection based.

Education is a basic physiological human need

By definition, education is the process of acquiring and mastering the skills which one requires in order to survive in the environment in which one may find himself or herself. The process can be both formal and informal. For example, there are no arguments about the fact that lions in the wild have got to impart their young ones with the appropriate hunting skills if these youngsters are to ever survive at all as adult lions and continue the natural propagation of the species. In the case of human beings, this natural process might not be quite so clear or easily understood or seen in the same way, but such in fact is what basic education also seeks to accomplish in our human societies. Basic education seeks to impart our children with survival skills in the world in which they may find themselves as and when they grow into adulthood and beyond. Without basic education and training, human beings would not even be able to work for themselves, let alone be employable. Such being the case, basic education and training are thus basic survivalistic or physiological human needs as well!

Access to basic education must be guaranteed

Going back to social protection, it therefore becomes quite clear that education, as part of social protection, is a basic human right since it is also a basic human need. Previously inn this book, it was made abundantly clear and undeniable that world governments have the duty, responsibility and obligation to ensure the provision of social protection and social security to the people they govern. This therefore means that world governments are also behoved to ensure that their people are provided with and afforded access to appropriate basic education and training at all levels from primary, secondary and tertiary education up to the on-the-job professional skills training. Note that we are not saying that governments are obliged to directly provide education to people. We are saying that governments are obliged to ensure that people are provided with and afforded access to appropriate basic education and training! This distinction is very important when considering the highly emotive issue of basic education financing at national level because it puts duties and responsibilities squarely where they belong.

Government sets national education standards

As usual, the primary role of government in ensuring universal access to education is to legislate. Legal standards and other requirements for basic education are set and monitored by government and other stakeholders so as to ensure that they are appropriate and relevant to the needs of the people and the country as a whole, while educational institutions can be owned, financed and run by anybody in both the private or public sectors. The big question is who must finance individual students at all education institutions from primary school right through secondary school and up to tertiary institutions and beyond? One thing is for sure, all minor children are naturally unable to finance themselves regardless of whether they belong to rich or poor families. Barring childhood inherited wealth, all children are born with nothing of their own and they would continue to have nothing of their own until they become independent and working adults. Unfortunately, exactly the same situation squarely applies to all dependent young adult children too. These are the people whom society thinks and believes that they are adults simply because they have reached a certain chronological age in their lives, this being the so called legal age of majority. The young adult age group is the group in which most university and college students are found. All minor children and young adults are totally dependent on their parents for upkeep and survival from birth to mature and independent adulthood. As far as basic education financing is concerned, what this means is that parents and guardians should and must continue to be responsible for ensuring that both their minor and young adult children enjoy access to basic education. But what if the parents are poverty stricken and thus cannot afford to finance the educational needs of their own children as is frequently the case in many countries? This is where government and social protection must kick in because education is a basic human need and therefore also a basic human right as has already been shown above. The next question is how must social protection come in to help out in such situations as it surely must? As the ultimate insurer of social protection, government must put in place legal means and mechanisms which would automatically ensure that where and when parent cannot afford to pay for the educational needs of their own children, social protection kicks in.

Primary education is compulsory and therefore free

We may not realise it now, but the truth of the matter is that our inborn basic and bare behavioural instincts are barbaric in nature. At birth, and as individuals, we are all naturally self-centred to the very core of our existence. Life and living are all about us and us alone. If left alone and to the vagaries of nature, we would forcibly grab whatever we need or want from whomever and wherever without even thinking or caring about what our victims would think or feel about it. Anything which would prevent us from getting what we want or need would the ruthlessly destroyed and we would not even feel bad about doing that either. On the contrary, we would feel good about getting what we want and we would even be infused with huge amounts of self-achievement, social and self-esteem. Such are the basic or natural instincts not only of all human beings but also of all living things, especially of the animal kingdom. The saying that with the birth of every newborn human child the world acquires one more barbarian is not very much misplaced. This sad observation is essentially true and correct.

The main reason why human beings nowadays do not grow up into the bad old barbarians who are now just stories from ancient times in our history books is all because of education. As each new human barbarian by nature is born into this now civilised world, it is instantaneously, inevitably and almost automatically civilised and brought up to speed with the civilised ways of the new world into which it is born through basic education, both formal and informal. It is through this basic education and civilisation that the natural inborn barbaric tendencies in all human beings are insidiously nipped in the bud. Human barbarism is thus never allowed even the smallest chance to rear its ugly head. And yet, if left alone, human beings would definitely still grow into the bad old barbarians who would again wreck untold havoc and suffering all over this planet. Now, no one wants that to happen to us all over again. And this is the main reason why even the United Nations (UN) agreed that basic primary education must be compulsory for everyone on this planet. No one wants a bunch of ruthless barbarians to be covertly or overtly cultivated by the lack of basic primary education anywhere in the world today. The historic and savage wars of the barbarians must be over and truly over for good! No one wants to get back there again. Thus, primary education must be compulsory for everyone.

The main purpose of basic primary education is to impart literacy and numeracy in all humankind. Literate and numerate people are generally easier to educate and civilise than illiterate and innumerate ones. Educated and civilised people become better citizens who could be trusted to contribute positively to human, social and economic growth and development than uneducated people. Conversely, less educated and less civilised human beings have been observed to be not very rational, logical or constructive in their personal, human, social and economic behaviours. Less educated people unfortunately always tend to want to appeal to their inborn basic bare, self-centred and rather barbaric survivalistic instincts as discussed above, much to the detriment of society as a whole. Perhaps this is the main reason why the United Nations declared basic primary education to be compulsory everywhere in this world. Primary education makes it easily possible for people to be further civilised through higher education for the benefit of everyone in terms of world peace, safety and security.

Primary education is completely government funded

If primary education is thus compulsory, what happens to those parents who cannot afford to pay for the primary education of their own children? Surely it is not a crime to be poor because nobody has ever been born rich or is poor by choice. Punishing poor parents for not sending their own children to compulsory primary school would be like punishing the victims. That would be morally and ethically wrong and unacceptable. For the reasons that basic primary education is and must be compulsory, it must of necessity also be free regardless of socioeconomic status. This means that there must not be any kind of compulsory school fees whatsoever which must be paid by those responsible for children at primary school level, be it tuition fees, book fees, building fund levy, uniform fees, or any other kind of fees for that matter. This is the only way by which every child, including the children of the poor, would be enabled to access their basic right to compulsory primary education. When primary education is for free like this, then there would be absolutely no excuse whatsoever as to why parents may not be held accountable if they do not ensure that their children are enrolled in school and that they actually attend school every day without fail.

With primary education being compulsory and free, any parent who prevents a child from going to school, and any parent who does not ensure that a child actually goes to school must be arrested and legally charged with child abuse and child neglect under child protection laws. Such a parent must even have that child forcibly taken away from them and put into foster care if only for the purposes of ensuring that the child goes to school.

Anybody who makes anything compulsory must also ensure that such a thing would always be available, affordable and accessible to anyone and everyone of whom that thing would be compulsorily required. Hence when countries unanimously agreed at the United Nations that basic primary education shall be compulsory, they also agreed that it shall be free at access point regardless of parental ability to pay or not, and also that national governments shall universally pay for all the costs involved. So even though we say that primary education is free, it is actually paid for by government, or more correctly, by all tax payers and not actually for free as if there are no costs involved. There is absolutely nothing which is for free in this world.

Secondary school education financing

Who must pay for secondary school education? Unlike basic primary education which serves to make the learner literate and numerate for the purposes of further civilisation and education, the main purpose of secondary school education is to prepare the learner for professional training and higher education while further civilisation is just but an inevitable side benefit. Secondary school education would be highly desirable but perhaps not one hundred percent mandatorily compulsory as in the case of primary school education. Such being the case, parents, guardians or relatives must pay for secondary school education in the first instance. Where these people are unable to pay, and such has been properly assessed and proved beyond reasonable doubt through set government legal standards and procedures as always, then the government itself must step in and pay since education as a whole is still a basic human need and thus also a basic human right and therefore part of the social protection duty and responsibility of government.

The rationale behind tertiary education financing

Who must fund or pay for tertiary education? Before we tackle this question, we must first of all examine a few background facts. Tertiary education students are usually young adult students. Usually, they would have reached the legal age of majority in most countries. This means that these students would have certain inalienable legal rights as adults. Legally, they can vote, marry, drive and pretty much do anything else which they may want to do without asking for permission from anyone, parents or guardians included. Adult age student are legally adults.

Being adults, college and university students are legally supposed to be responsible for themselves in terms of upkeep and everything else just like any other adult person. They can pursue whatever course or career which they may want to pursue at tertiary level without having to have the permission or agreement of their own parents or guardians first. In other words, tertiary students are free to determine their own destinies in life. In fact, this is one of the reasons why those tertiary students went toy-toying for "free and decolonised" education in the African country which we talked about earlier on. It would be surprising if those toyi-toying students asked for parental permission before they went toyi-toying. Tertiary education students are actually adult people with adult rights and responsibilities. Based on the adult status of tertiary education students, their own parents, guardians or governments are not legally obliged to pay for their education as if they were still dependent minor children. Parents must not be legally forced to maintain or support other normal adult persons even if such persons happen to be their own biological children. Support in such cases must be voluntary and capacity based. Such being the case, it is unfair for parents or guardians to be forced to pay for the tertiary education of their own grown up and adult children. In fact, such compulsion would be unconstitutional in many parts of this world. Even child maintenance is compulsorily payable only up to the adult age of majority in most countries. There is therefore no need to expect or force parents to keep on maintaining their own legally adult children throughout life. Such would be tantamount to parental abuse.

On the other hand, to demand that supposedly rich parents must maintain their adult children by financing their tertiary education while supposedly poor parents get government or any other benevolent assistance in that regard is actually unconstitutional in many counties for three reasons. And yet many governments routinely do that through what they have aptly termed "means testing." First of all, such practice is tantamount to discrimination on the grounds of perceived social or economic status. Such discrimination is normally outlawed by many national constitutions. Secondly, as has already been discussed above, it unfairly compels one legally independent adult person to maintain another legally independent adult person for absolutely no good reasons at all besides the fact that they would be related as parent and child. This is just as good as relationship based extortion. Thirdly, such compulsion might limit the freedom of choice of the so maintained adult tertiary student in terms of what course he or she may pursue at tertiary level, and yet freedom of choice is a basic human right. For example, if parents are paying university fees, they may refuse the child permission to pursue a course of the child's choice insisting that the child takes on a course which they approve of or which is chosen by them. Such parents can also actually withdraw financial assistance or support if the child refuses to comply with their demands or directives. And yet that child, as a legally adult person, has the constitutional and inalienable right to freedom of choice in deciding and determining his or her own destiny in life, especially the kind of profession he or she may want to pursue. Giving parents direct or indirect control over their children in that regard would be illegal and not right at all.

All tertiary students are poor

The other undeniable fact about all young adult tertiary students is that they are all very poor. In fact, they all have equally nothing to their own names regardless of whether they come from perceived rich or poor families. Those who are perceived to come from rich families are only perceived not to be poor because of the expected benevolence of their supposedly rich families towards them. Otherwise, if and should they fall out with their rich family benefactors for one reason or another and that expected benevolence is abruptly cut-off our supposedly rich students are in fact just as poor as any other adult students from the poorest of the poor families. Such being the case, no young adult tertiary education student is actually rich by themselves and in their own personal right! There are no rich students anywhere in this world except those who may have legally inherited something from their parents or guardians, and these are very few if ever they exist at all.

Tertiary students must fund themselves

So who must pay for the education of tertiary students? Surprise, surprise, it is the students themselves who must pay for their own tertiary education! It sounds ironic, but it is indeed very true, correct and logical as well. As much as all tertiary education students are poor by nature as has already been demonstrated above, they all must still personally pay for their own tertiary education because they are responsible adults. Adulthood does not only mean freedom to enjoy oneself whichever way one wants, but it also engenders a lot of other responsibilities, obligations and accountabilities as well. It cannot be all sweet and no sweat. Logically and rationally speaking too, there must be no argument about that. Perhaps the only question would be how could tertiary students pay for their own education when, as has already been acknowledged before, they all have absolutely nothing to their names? The fact that as adults, tertiary education students would now be totally responsible for their own upkeep, and this must include paying for their own college or university fees, is neither here nor there. It is a given.

Regardless of their inability to pay directly from their own pockets there and then, somehow, tertiary students must still be held responsible for the payment of their own education, and eventually they must indeed pay up! This is the crux of the matter which everyone must know, appreciate and understand in this case. All tertiary students must understand that the freedom of choice to pursue any course of their own liking at tertiary level comes with the responsibility to pay for that kind of freedom. Otherwise if someone pays for their tertiary education, then they may obviously have to cede that freedom of choice to the paying party. That would not be good because it may mean spending the rest of their forever stuck in professions or jobs which they may not like at all. Having the freedom to choose what one wants to professionally end up as in life is something which is well worth paying for.

Basic Education and Training Authority (BETA)

We have established the fact that first of all government is obliged to ensure that everyone has access to basic education and training, and secondly that government is responsible for directly funding primary education while parents are responsible for paying for secondary education, and that tertiary students are responsible for paying for their own education. The question now is how can all this be accomplished without government itself being directly involved in public education services provision on the ground as it should not be according to the doctrine which this book has always been preaching about right from the beginning? In other words, how can basic public education and training be accomplished without government owning or running a single basic education or training institution in the country? Remember that this is the guiding mantra in this book. Government must be able to deliver without itself doing the actual job on the ground.

We have already seen that it is very undesirable for government to be directly and intimately involved in public service provision on the ground because it is the one which is responsible for setting and enforcing service standards throughout the country and across all sectors of the economy including the education sector as well. There would be lots of cases of conflict of interests which would compromise service delivery standards if government was allowed to do that. And there is nowhere where such conflict of interest is more glaring than in the education and health services sectors, for example. We have all probably seen or come across some very pathetic cases whereby standards at government owned and operated educational institutions like schools, training colleges and universities have been allowed to deteriorate by the very same government which is supposed to enforce very high standards in that sector for reasons that government would be experiencing tough financial times and yet the private education sector would not be similarly allowed to drop those standards even when they may also be experiencing the very same financial squeeze as government. Exactly the same thing has also happened in the public health sector. The doctrine of complete and practical separation of both people and powers behoves that government as the policy decisions maker, manager and enforcer cannot also be a policy implementer on the ground. As much as it is very difficult for someone to censure himself or herself, it would also be very difficult for government to censure itself if it dabbles into public education services provision proper. Such being the case, it is recommended that government must find an outlet through which it can channel the public education funds which it is obliged to provide or ensure that they are provided.

Perhaps the best proposal would be that of establishing a public owned business enterprise (POBE) called the Basic Education and Training Authority (BETA) and its accompanying Basic Education and Training Fund (BETF) through the now famous (at least in this book) Public

Service Administration (PSA). BETF would be a public education social security fund in much the same way as the already discussed NHIF (National Health Insurance Fund) would be a public health social security fund. The job of BETA would be to do specifically in education what the PSA does in the whole of the country for and on behalf of government. BETA would on a daily basis ensure that all public education legal policy frameworks, rules, regulations, codes of practice, codes of conduct and other standards and standard operating procedures are followed and implemented to the letter and spirit of the word. Through the Basic Education and Training Fund (BETF), BETA would ensure that all registered and accredited basic education and training institutions, regardless of who owns or runs them, would be properly funded. Just like in the case of the propose National Health Insurance Medical Aid Scheme (NHIMAS) and its National Health Insurance Fund (NHIF) as already discussed in this chapter, instead of funding institutional budgets which is tantamount to just funding projected input costs as is currently the practice in most countries, the BETF would fund outputs or results. This is a best practice standard which must be adopted and followed especially by every public education system and also by every productive economic sector in general. BETF would fund results or outputs in the sense that legally registered and accredited educational institutions would only be paid for services delivered and not for services which they project that they would deliver such as projected budget expenditures. Funding institutional budgets is just like funding promises of future service delivery and yet there would be no assurance that the promised services would actually be delivered in the first place, while most retrospective budget expenditure justifications are usually just creatively and imaginatively concocted to rhyme and rhythm with the already incurred budget expenditures. They are not correct reflections of what would actually have happened on the ground. Inevitably, there are tremendous losses and wastefulness in antespective budget financing.

The proposal here is that just like with the National Health Insurance Fund (NHIF), the BETF would receive validated monthly claims from registered and accredited educational institutions reflecting the quantity and value of services which they would have delivered in the previous month and for which they would be seeking payment. BETF would pay in full for almost everything at primary school level since primary education would be compulsory and free of charge. Such being the case, all primary schools would normally not be allowed to charge any school fees at all. Any other fees which may be charged by any school at primary level must be justified by the school concerned and approved by BETA.

At secondary school level, BEFT would still pay schools for services delivered as a way of subsidising costs for parents so that most of them would afford to pay for their children as we have already realised and said that they must do so at that level of education. The BETF secondary school level education subsidy would ensure that secondary schools may not just charge whatever school fees they want. Unreasonably exorbitant school fees are practices which may be clandestinely used by some unscrupulous schools to exclude certain racial, ethnic, cultural or religious groups. Any discrimination whatsoever in admitting learners must be completely outlawed in all educational institutions.

At tertiary level, BETF would ensure that students are funded through such things as educational loans, loan guarantees, grants, bursaries, scholarships and many other instruments as necessary so that no one who would have been admitted to any registered and accredited tertiary institution would fail to attend that institution simply because they do not have the required financial muscles to pay the required educational fees. Basic education is not a privilege but a basic human need and thus also a basic human right. Everyone must be enabled and empowered to access basic education as and when needed without any excuses whatsoever. And ensuring access is the main if not the sole duty and responsibility of government as far as basic education and training services are concerned.

Basic Education and Training Fund (BETF)

The answer to the question of how tertiary students must still pay for their own tertiary education regardless of the fact that they are all poor with absolutely no penny to their names has been provided by BETF above. Actually, this was the question which university students of the "fees must fall" campaign fame, their national government, the affected universities themselves and all the other stakeholders were supposed to grapple with in terms of tertiary education financing instead of throwing stones and flames at each other and thereby destroying the very same institutions of higher education and learning which all of them desperately need for their own survival and future wellbeing. Contrary to the popular "fees must fall" slogan which tertiary students of the "free and decolonised education" campaign fame chanted as they demonstrated, educational fees cannot and must not fall because if and when educational fees fall, all educational institutions and their students would also fall together with the falling educational fees. Rather, educational fees must stand and tertiary students must pay for themselves through BETF engineered soft or interest free and long term educational loans, loan guarantees, bursaries, scholarships, grants and any other applicable financial instruments.

Tertiary students must disabuse themselves of the idea that there is anything for free anywhere in this world, least of all in education! Anything which ends up being free to the end user would have actually been fully paid for somehow and by someone somewhere along the line, otherwise it would not happen. Students, especially of the loudly protesting "free and decolonised education" variety, must be made aware of the fact that this world does not and will not give out any free handouts to anybody. Government must assist, empower and enable all tertiary students to pay for their own educational fees through social protection. BETF is just but one good example of how this can be done. There could be many others. The real bottom line here is that no one must ever be denied their inalienable right to social protection and to basic education in particular just because they personally or their parents or guardians cannot afford to directly pay for the costs involved. That would be unacceptable denial of access to basic human needs and basic human rights. The only thing that may be allowed to limit anyone's educational achievement is that person's own natural or inborn talent. Be that as it may, sponsorship does not necessarily mean that something is for free. In fact most sponsorship in life is never really for free. There would always be a payback clause somewhere, somehow!

BETF sponsorship must be paid back somehow

As a way of paying back BETF sponsorship, sponsored students may just be asked to work for the sponsor for a given period of time. During that period of time, they would get their full monthly pay with no sponsorship repayment deductions at all. The repayment would just be in the working for the sponsor itself. Such kind of sponsorship is sometimes called cadetship. In fact, this is what most sponsors, including governments, would normally do if they were looking for quality, young and dynamic labour to fill up any future gaps which may arise in their staff compliments.

Another way of paying back is to actually re-pay the sponsorship money after attaining tertiary qualifications and getting a job. Repayment can be in part or in whole, with or without interest as the case may be. This is also a very common and acceptable practice in the world of public education financing. In fact, any and every other tertiary student educational sponsorship arrangement is possible. The bottom line is that the student would be the one who would be ultimately and personally responsible for the payment for his or her own tertiary education one way or the other. The nothing for free and repayment mentality is the kind of mentality which must be ingrained in the heads of all tertiary students anywhere and everywhere in this world instead of the mentality of "fees must fall" or free tertiary education. If the free tertiary education mentality is allowed to reign supreme, this world might just go back to barbarism again! That having been said and done, the only other question about tertiary education financing would be that of the social, economic and sustainable viability of Basic Education and Training Funds (BETFs).

BETF sources of income

Education is part of social protection. The way governments normally deliver social protection services is by pooling resources together with the rest of the other beneficiary social partners and stakeholders such as working adults, parents and employers. And usually this is done through the agency of specific, well defined, well governed and well administered public owned social protection funds and institutions. A lot of examples have already been given in this book and Basic Education and Training Funds (BETFs) are just but one of such examples. BETF would be a revolving and autonomous basic education and training focused national human capital resources growth and development combined social security and social assistance fund. Such a holistic social protection fund (refer back to the definition of social protection at the beginning of this chapter) would be able to successfully, efficiently and effectively support and relieve governments, parents and students of the burden of tertiary education financing, but obviously not without their support and participation as both stakeholders and beneficiaries of the system. Such being the case, BETFs would normally collect minimally very small monthly premium contributions from stakeholder employers, working adults, parents, other individuals and any other cooperating stakeholders and social partners almost in the same manner as was described for national health insurance fund (NHIF). However, in the case of BETF, government would be the main or major contributor as it would have to redirect the usually huge education annual fiscal budget towards this noble cause. With more funds coming in from other private stakeholders and reserves accumulating, such education based and focused social protection funds as BETFs would definitely manage to also fund educational infrastructural growth and development such as the construction of schools, colleges, universities and other training institutions and then rent them out to operators to deliver educational services as necessary.

With social protection anchored BETFs in place, just as in the case of NHIFs, government would never have to own or run a single basic education and training institution, and neither would it have to employ even a single teacher or educator anywhere in the country. Even in education as well, or more especially in education, government would just have to stick to its original governing and governance obligations, duties and responsibilities to govern, legislate, serve, listen, work, deliver, empower, compete and protect. It does not have to do anything else other than just that!

BETF would improve standards of education

If there is something which service oriented social security funds do or take to the limits, it is to drastically increase the efficiency (output quantity per given input measure) and effectiveness (output quality or purpose fitness) of service delivery. BETF would do the same to education in terms of service standards improvement as NHIF would do to health.

One of the mains reason for poor service quality in many education systems is government bureaucracy. There is just too much, ineffective and inefficient decision making and process centralisation in government. With BEFT, every school, training college and university would be a stand-alone institution in terms of ownership, management and administration in much the same way as every health institution would also be a stand-alone institution under NHIF. A quick review of the proposed national education and training policy governing and governance structure discussed in Chapter 6 of this book would clearly reveal this.

Freed from direct government control and bureaucracy, individual school governing bodies would be able to hire and fire all school staff from school heads through school teachers and down to the last groundsmen. Individual school managements would run their schools almost free of the daily government interference which is very common in government owned and run schools and other government sponsored educational and training institutions. Staff supervision and accountabilities would be brought closer to home at individual schools themselves rather than being inefficiently and ineffectively directed from far removed central government head offices somewhere in the capital city or even beyond. Educators such as teachers, lecturers and trainers who would usually play truant knowing that government disciplinary processes and procedures are so long, intricately convoluted and arduous to the extent that they could always get away with murder would have absolutely no such luck or chance in an institution based and institution focused BETF educational funding system. Such miscreants would be brought to book instantaneously within the individual education or training institution itself and nowhere else since hiring and firing would be done at the same spot. This would definitely be the best thing to ever happen to education. Affected educators and other education staff members may not see it in the same light, but it is indeed the best way to run educational institutions. For example, centralised employment of educators through ministries of education means that all educators have just got one employer in the whole country. Should they be fired from one institution for whatever reason, they would have been automatically fired from all other similar institutions in the whole country. Their careers would have been doomed then. But with BETF, educators would have as many different actual and potential employers as there would be different education institutions in the country. Should one institution disengage an educator for whatever reason, unless if it would be for professional misconduct, it would be easier for that educator to get another job with another educational institution somewhere else in the same country and under the same public funded education system! Anyone who has ever been unfortunate enough to get fired from government or the public service would very much appreciate the great disadvantages of having a single and centralised public service employment system. Such a person would quickly embrace the advantages which the proposed BETF decentralised public service employment system would bring along with it without too much ado.

The advantages of BETF and the multiple employers which it would create do not just end with that alone, but there is also the added advantage of having different and perhaps even performance related remuneration packages from one institution to another. Through the Basic Education and Training Authority (BETA), government can just set the minimum remuneration packages of the various grades and types of employees in the education sector while leaving the specifics up to each and every individual institution according to its own individual capacity to pay. Under such circumstances, educators would surely have field days at the bank at the end of every month.

Government can also infuse productive competition into the education sector by linking the level of payment or funding claims re-imbursements to output in terms of performance as measured by actual results. Institutions which would have performed above certain higher levels in the previous year could be awarded their claims at certain even higher levels in the following year while the reverse would apply to poorly and decreasingly performing ones. In this way and perhaps for the very first time ever in history, learners could get the correct bang for their bucks!

The right to transport and communication

Movement is vitally important

Not many ordinary people realise how very important movement actually is until they cannot move themselves or until they cannot move any other part of their bodies. That is when they would realise how important and life giving movement actually is. In animal biology they call movement locomotion while in plant biology they call it tropism and in life in general it is referred to as transportation. Movement is actually life giving at both individual and community levels. Total body paralysis alone is as deadly as any other deadly disease even in the presence of adequate food somehow being delivered to the body. By the same token, a community which cannot engage in any meaningful human, social, economic and other activities through movement in order to sustain itself as a community would not be viable for too long. In communities and societies movement or transportation is enabled by the presence of means of transport. Such being the case, transport is therefore as essential to human life as is any other basic human need.

The transportation of messages between individuals is called communication. Communication too is an integral part of how human beings and many other animals manage to survive. Without communication, they may not live. In biology, intra-organism communication is vital for life and this kind of communication is found at all levels of the organism from intracellular, intercellular, intra-organ and inter-organ communication. Such being the case, both transport and communication are actually found in nature and therefore they are basic human needs and as such, they are also basic human rights. That is the way it is.

National Transport and Communication Authority (NTCA)

Having established the basic necessity of transport and communication, what then would be the given role of government in ensuring access to both transport and communication by the governed people? The answer is always the same as with all other basic human rights. Government does not have to directly provide any means of transport and communication to anybody or to any community under its jurisdiction. It must just ensure that the people it governs are guaranteed access to transport and communication as and when necessary. Government, as always, must just stick to its given mandate to govern, legislate, serve, listen, work, deliver, empower, compete and protect. Thus, government must govern, regulate and control the transport and communication sector through appropriate legislation. This legislation must set down the required standards and standard operating procedures which would enable people to access safe, secure and affordable means of transport and communication.

After setting down the legal standards, government must then turn over the management and implementation of those standards to the public sector through a public sector owned entity or public owned business enterprise (POBE) such as a National Transport and Communication Authority or Administration (NTCA). The NTCA itself must not be engaged in the actual implementation of the policy or the actual provision of transport and communication services. That is the job of private individuals and their private sector business enterprises. The job of NTCA would be to manage the transport and communication sector for and on behalf of government in terms of government obligations, duties and responsibilities of transport and communication standards enforcement, monitoring, evaluation, review and continuous improvement. Remember that management just involves strategic planning and pulling together of the needed resources and then putting in place the appropriate control measures which would ensure proper use of those resources before delivering the resources to those who must use them, the actual implementers on the ground. In that way, the NTCA would just ensure that those who provide public transport and communication services would do so in accordance with the laws, rules, regulations and standards which were set down by government and also that the general public in fact accesses the affordable transport and communication services which it needs or wants. The best way for the NTCA to do this is through continuous licensing, monitoring, evaluation and review of all national transport and communication services and service providers on the ground and then suggesting any needed or necessary improvements to government for legal enactment as and when necessary.

Leveraging on the private sector

All strategically important transport and communication infrastructure such as roads, railways, roadports, airports, seaports and national digital communication portals must always be owned by the public or the state and no one else, not even government. As always, ownership does not mean actually running the business operations thereof. That aspect can always be turned over to the private sector for improved efficiency and effectiveness and also for maximum economic benefits it terms of profits. Public transport and communication infrastructure ownership by the public sector does not mean that the private sector cannot help the public sector to build or develop that infrastructure. By all means it can, and in fact, the private sector must be coerced to do so by government because it is the private sector which admittedly has more of the required resources in terms of knowledge, skills, equipment and finances than the public sector. Public-private sector partnerships (PPP) such as of the build-operate-and-transfer or the so called BOT variety and many other varieties must be entered into and operationalised with the sole purpose and objective of trying to ensure that the public is adequately served with affordable and accessible transport and communication services.

However, as far as the day to day running or operation of any transport and communication services is concerned, government and the public service must not be allowed to routinely do such things as has already been advocated for again and again in this book. That must be the preserve of the private sector. And of course the public sector can always own private sector companies too as has already been pointed out elsewhere in this book. The most important thing is that there must be so much distance between government and any public owned business enterprise (POBE) that it would be almost impossible for government or anyone in government to directly influence or control that organisation in any way whatsoever. And this is very much easy to achieve if in the first instance there is such complete, practical and meaningful separation of both powers and people between government institutions themselves so much so that the PSA (Public Service Administration) the recognised actual government policy implementation structure (see Chapter 6) proper, would be more or less autonomous as it must be, being only linked to other institutions and structures of government by the common government blood which runs through them all.

For example, government must not run or operate any public road or railway transport services. Instead, it must competitively award such public service delivery tenders and licenses to private companies to provide the needed services. Such public service delivery tenders would specify every aspect of the service to be delivered by those who win them. This would include the type of vehicles to be used and their specifications down to service delivery time tables and service user fees or charges. Service user fees or charges must be such that all those people whose rate of pay is at the lowest taxable income would be able to afford them throughout the whole month as they daily travel to and from work. Such work related public transport costs must not exceed ten percent of the basic monthly salaries of the concerned individuals. Such being the case, hopefully, there is no government in the world which would allow any of its employed workforce in both the private and the public sectors to be paid monthly salaries which are below the lowest taxable income because such would be tantamount to legalising slavery (also see Chapter 21 of this book). It would also be tantamount to short changing all other workers plus the government and the country as a whole because workers who earn below the lowest taxable income do not directly contribute anything to the fiscus and yet they benefit a lot from it in terms of access to all public services and not just transport. Another thing is that work which pays below the lowest taxable income is usually not decent work at all, much against common decency and even very much against what the International Labour Organisation (ILO) would recommend for all workers. The ILO is that very important UN agency which looks out for the human rights of all workers in the world of work.

Public transport vouchers

Anyway, in the case of the unemployed and the working poor, government must also ensure that these people access their right to transport and communication as well. Instead of just handing out completely free and unconditional public transport vouchers to such people, government must make such vouchers conditional on the beneficiaries undertaking certain activities which would ensure that they would eventually be weaned from depending on government public transport vouchers. For example, in the case of school dropouts, such vouchers can be made conditional on them going back to school or enrolling and continuing to attend practical job skills training programmes which government itself would be sponsoring or funding through the private sector. Unemployed adults could get free public transport vouchers on condition that they register with employment agencies and that they are seen to be actively looking for work. Of course, school kids would also get such subsidised public transport vouchers on condition that their school class registers show that they do not miss school for no good reason at all even for just a few days per term.

The National Public Transport Fund (NPTF)

The big question could be that where would government get all the money to fund free public transport vouchers and other transport services like this, but that is not a challenge at all. This is because of the various logical and rational options which have always existed in the transport and communication sector. Transport vehicle owners and operators have always been acceptably taxed for one reason or another. There are road user fees or taxes, toll gates, fuel pollution taxes, motor vehicle accident insurance taxes, noise pollution taxes, nuisance taxes and many other similar and completely rational public taxes which owners and operators of transport vehicles must shell out. The problem here in terms of the public acceptability of such taxes is that apparently they are already just about too many. What governments must do is to consolidate all of these numerous transport vehicle taxes into at least just one grand general tax for all transport and other vehicles and their operators and owners. Such a tax would automatically become a public fund. It can then be called by whatever name it may be called as long as what it specifically covers would be known and would include all the taxes enumerated in the paragraph above or even more. This suggested social protection like fund can simply be called the National Public Transport Fund (NPTF).

The best public body which could administer such a public transport fund would be the Central Vehicle Registry (CVR), an organisation which already exists in many countries. This is because compliance with annual subscriptions to the fund would be easier to enforce if there would also be the real threat and danger of vehicle deregistration. In that case, the central vehicle registry (CVR) would collect both the once off vehicle registration fees (VRF) plus this suggested annual vehicle license to operate (VLO) fees. This vehicle licence to operate or VLO would just be authorising the vehicle to be operated just as a vehicle and not for any specific propose it may later on be approved or authorised to be used by other more relevant authorities. Such being the case, the vehicle license to operate (VLO) would be different from the vehicle operators' licence (VOL) which would be issued to the operator authorising the use of that particular vehicle in certain given operations. The vehicle operators' license (VOL) would be issued by other more relevant responsible authorities such as local authorities when authorising the operator of the vehicle to, for example, run or operate a public transport business within the locality which they govern, or for purposes which they control.

To the vehicle registration (VRF) and vehicle licence to operate (VLO) monies, the CVR could also add the now ubiquitous fuel levy which is normally piggy-banked onto the pump price of fuel by many national governments. Such and other transport related financial gymnastics would ensure that government has a lot of money at its disposal with which it would guarantee availability, affordability and accessibility to the right to transport and communication by everyone, as long as it strictly adheres to the principles of social security expenditure controls and good governance.

There must as always be meaningful, complete and practical separation of both powers and people in all governing and governance institutions, be it in the private or public sector. The relationship between government, the CVR and the NPTF would not be any different in terms of this overriding and guiding principle.

The example of public road transport which has been given here can also be applied to both railway and air transport. If any government ends up owning and running a national airline or any national railways business, for the purposes of national pride or for whatever other reason they may fancy, it must always be strictly through the aegis of public owned but privately run business enterprises (POBEs) and also as far removed as is practically possible from the direct control and influence of government and government officials, and especially far removed from government politicians. This point can never be overemphasised.

Post and telecommunication services

The case of post and telecommunication services is not very much different from that of transport services. For some traditional or nostalgic reasons, many national governments have tightly and tenaciously hung on to their post and telecommunications businesses even if and when those businesses are dismally failing to deliver on both the business and service delivery fronts. The introduction of the more dynamic, efficient and effective private postal and telecommunications services have not at all discouraged governments from just doggedly trudging on with these businesses while at the same time wasting scarce public resources. This is really inexcusable.

The only part of postal services which governments have opened up to private sector participation is the expedited mail and parcel delivery services. And the only part of telecommunication services which most governments have opened up to private sector participation is the recent and recently widespread wireless telecommunication services or the so called cellular telephones and the internet. This is definitely not the best which governments can do in terms of opening up these sectors to private sector participation. Government or public participation in any sector of the economy is not absolutely forbidden as you might have realised so far in this book. What is forbidden is direct government involvement in the day to day running of business enterprises on the ground. That is a no go area for government. If government wants to or must be involved in the business of direct service provision on the ground, there must always be POBEs with which to do that and these POBEs must always be miles away from government influence or control as usual.

The right to peace, safety and security

Without safety and security, there is no peace. Peace is the state of being free from any disturbance of any kind. Personal disturbances can be physical, psychological, social, financial or environmental. At the social environment level, disturbances can be political or armed conflict (war) in nature. Everyone has the right to live a peaceful life which is free from any sort of disturbances or stresses. Safety is the state of being free from danger, harm or risk, while security is the state of being assuredly protected from danger, harm or risk. As defined, there is no doubt that peace, safety and security are also basic human rights if perhaps not some of the most basic human rights ever. Lack of safety and security would also mean lack of peace of mind and the presence of many disturbances such as physical, social and environmental ones. Such being the case, peace, safety and security always go hand in hand. There cannot be one without the other.

Good governance secures the peace

How can government ensure that its people have access to peace, safety and security? To start with, the provision of what are called social safety nets under social protection which we have so much gone to town about in this book already, is actually part and parcel of ensuring that there is peace, safety and security all round. But the best way of providing and ensuring that peace, safety and security prevail in the country, at least as far as any internal threats to the same are concerned, is to ensure that there is always good governance being practiced at each and every level of society and service delivery, and in each and every sector of the economy as well. The social, political and military disturbances which occasionally threaten peace, safety and security in many developing and other countries of this world usually emanate from widespread and general discontentment with affected national governments, their governance systems and the way they govern their people. Such being the case, just good governance alone can be the best panacea for national peace, safety and security there ever is and ever would be! But as we all know, in any normal society, there would always be a few individuals who would want to do what they want, and to do things their own way, and thereby disturbing the peace and posing both safety and security risks to other individuals or even to the whole country at large. Such people must be stopped. And these are the people who the police and other security forces are there for. In its quest to secure the safety, security and peace of all people, government must ensure that correctly and adequately trained, equipped and funded national, regional and even local and neighbourhood police and other security forces and services are put in place and appropriately operationalised to deliver the desired results.

Safety and security forces belong to the public

The biggest issue with safety and security forces as far as government is concerned is the matter of control. Many governments want to directly control all safety and security forces such as the police, army, prisons and intelligence services. Such is very dangerous for the general public and is therefore not good at all. As advocated for in my previous book of which this one is a sequel, all public safety and security forces belong to the people or the public and not to government. This is as it must be with everything which is national in nature as has already been repeatedly pointed out in this book. Allowing government to control and influence any branch of the national safety and security forces would put government above the law and give government officials some kind of immunity which would allow them to act with impunity. No one must ever be allowed to climb above the law. Such being the case, governing bodies of all national safety and security forces such as national police and defence forces and intelligence services must always be installed directly by the voting public itself because these are all crucially important public institutions and not government institutions. Remember that governments come and go but the public or the people would always be there. The public does not come and go. Thus, all public institutions, including defence, safety and security public institutions must belong to the public or the people and not to government. If government itself, or some other misguided government officials begin to imagine that they are more important or more powerful than the general public which they are supposed to serve, then any one of the responsible arms of public safety and security forces must be able to quickly and practically call such misguided and wayward people to order and deal with them. They must be able to give such wayward people what they really deserve in terms of accountabilities without any fear or favour. The day that most countries of this world would get to such a utopian stage in the way they do the things which they do at national level would be the day that this whole world would be truly civilised. As of now, most of our national public peace, safety and security forces are just used as personal hunting and hounding dogs by those in power. This is really unfortunate and quite inexcusable in this day and age. The right to peace, safety and security is a basic human right which must be upheld and respected by everyone, and at all times too!

Chapter 11: Democratic governance of the right to justice

The right to justice

Justice refers to the upright, fair, equitable, impartial, unbiased, objective, neutral, unprejudiced, correct, decent and principled treatment of issues and people. Surely, everyone must have the inborn right to justice, both as an individual and also as part of greater mankind, humanity, community or society.

The right to human dignity

The most decent or just manner in which any person can be treated would be to accord that person the human, personal and social dignity which he or she deserves. Dignity is the simple and straight forward respect which is accorded to another person as one would like such to be accorded to oneself as well. Dignity is the kind of respectful treatment which would not leave someone feeling embarrassed or bad about being themselves or about being a human being. They might not feel good or encouraged by the treatment, but they definitely must not feel bad about it at the "human being level." That is the catch phrase about human dignity. Even our convicted criminals deserve to be treated in a dignified, respectful and humane manner as they serve their sentences in correctional facilities. The inhumane and undignified treatment of prisoners is actually forbidden by international law.

Pursuance to the right to human dignity, every human being deserves a personal identity in the form of a name, and a national identity in the form of a country of origin or of belonging. Such would make a person a given somebody from somewhere, instead of just a nobody from nowhere. And that would definitely be a dignified way of referring to somebody. Such being the case, and to start off with, as far as ensuring access to justice is concerned, government must put in place a universal national personal identity registry system which would give everyone a name, place of birth, a home or place of origin within the country and a nationality or national belonging straightaway from birth to death. In fact, the United Nations Universal Declaration of Human Rights (UDHR) in one of its articles says things to the effect that everyone has the right to a given name as given by the parents, and the right to a nationality as given naturally by the place of birth or by choice later on in life among other personal identity rights. Human dignity behoves that people cannot just be treated or looked down upon as nobodies from nowhere. That would be indecent, unfair and unjust.

The Justice Services Commission (JSC)

The realisation of the right to justice is usually served best by the creation of a politically independent national judicial or justice services commission. The latter name – justice services commission – sounds more appealing than the former name – judicial services commission – because of its proactive and preventive rather than corrective or remedial connotations. The denotation "justice services" premises a neutral situation or position whereby judgement is not as yet needed as opposed to "judicial services" which premises a situation whereby a judgement is already needed. The best way to ensure justice is not to just provide watertight judicial remediation services alone, but also to pre-empt or prevent injustices first and foremost before they can even happen. Thus, one of the most important obligations, duties, responsibilities and functions of any justice services commission (JSC) would be to pre-emptively prevent injustices throughout the whole country and even beyond. And the name "justice services commission" clearly encapsulates this pro-active and preventive approach to the delivery of justice, while the name "judicial services commission" emphasises on the meting out of just and fair judicial judgements.

JSCs must be completely independent

Complete, meaningful and practical political independence of Justice Services Commissions (JSC) is paramount. The JSC must be completely, meaningfully and practically separated from the rest of the government and its governing and governance structures in terms of both powers and people. And it must also be composed of people who are politically independent or not linked to any political party in countries which have political party based systems of government. Anyone who chooses to work for the JSC would be choosing to be politically neutral, at least publicly and also while they would still be in its employ. This requirement would apply to everyone from the Chief Justice to the last general hand on the ground. The absolute need for independence and political neutrality of the JSC automatically means that government or any government official should not, cannot and must not appoint or be able to influence in any way whatsoever, any member or workers of that commission. The top governing body of the JSC must be directly installed and uninstalled by the general public itself as usual (at least, according to this book) for such public institutions.

My previous book of which this one is a sequel goes into a lot of details about the basic minimum requirements for members of the JSC governing body in term qualifications, experience and other considerations. What would be pretty obvious to anybody would be the fact that unlike members of parliament who may not need any further qualifications and experience besides perhaps just being able to read and write, JSC members must be far more formally educated, qualified and experienced in the justice services sector than what MPs need to be. That book also talks about how the working budget of the JSC must be directly approved by parliament instead of going via the executive arm of government. The reason being that legal decisions must not be exposed to any vulnerabilities whatsoever in terms of being manipulated if the right to justice is going to be respected to the letter and spirit of the word justice itself.

The JSC must be in charge of prisons

Justice does not only end with court decisions alone. Justice also extends beyond the courts and to the correctional facilities themselves. In many African countries, prison or correctional facilities end up under the direct control and influence of government itself instead of remaining under the control and influence of Justice Services Commissions (JSCs) where they rightfully belong. Usually this is all about power and control since prison services are also part of the armed forces of any country. Government and government politicians would always want to control guns wherever they exist within government and even beyond so that these guns may not be turned against them one day. That fear is only natural, but in this case the self-centeredness of the preventive actions taken thereof is not acceptable.

Governments must not be in charge of prisons

Anyway, direct government control of prison services is bad because that is one of the biggest and main causes of political prisoners and other lack of justice related social maladies such as torture and prison deaths. Many a time courts of justice have legally cleared certain political and other prisoners of conscience from any illegality or wrong doing under the law, but governments have unilaterally and illegally kept such innocent people incarcerated until they inexplicably died at their own hands or of unknown and improvable natural causes. Others have just been illegally left to stay there in prison until they rotted. Now, that is not justice at all. And all of this happens just because it would be government which would be having the prison door keys in its pockets instead of the keys being with the JSC as they must be under normal, rational and logical considerations. Such unjust situations must be permanently corrected and prevented from ever happening again in our societies by just making sure that all prison keys are left in the hands of the Justice Services Commission (JSC) and no one else. This is most probably a new kind of thinking, but that it the way it must be and should have been all along.

Correctional facilities are public institutions

Prisons are public correctional institutions. They belong to the public and not to government. Even in the absence of government, society as a whole and different communities in particular, have always had their own different processes and mechanisms by which those amongst them who would have decided to go against societal or community rules, values, norms, practices and acceptable behavioural codes of conduct and other societal standards were dealt with, and this included incarceration of one form or another. Thus, prisons are basically public correctional institutions which must always remain in the hands of and under the control of the public itself through its public Justice Services Commission (JSC).

No one must be above the law in this world

The other major reason why the Judicial Services Commission (JSC) must be under the direct control of the general public itself is that the JSC must be able to send anyone in any and every given country, including any government official right from the Head of State at the very top and down to the last public servant on the ground, to prison and ensure that they actually stay there and fully serve their allocated time if need be. With government keeping the keys to all national detention and correctional facilities or prisons as is the case right now in most countries of this world, some highly politically connected convicted felons or criminals have somehow miraculously been given or accorded undeserved early paroles and Presidential pardons all over the show to the detriment of proper justice and the brazen and hurtful spiting of those who were wronged by such people. Such is definitely not fair or just at all and must be ended forthwith and also prevented from ever happening again. Such being the case, once the JSC is properly constituted, it must be legally handed over the keys to all national prisons and then it must immediately take complete and full charge of all correctional services personnel together with their guns, button sticks, handcuffs and all. This would be phase two of the democratisation of national justice services delivery systems after phase one which would have been the democratic installation or enthronement of the JSC itself through the direct participation of the general public as a whole and as advocated for in my previous book entitled "There is No Democracy At All in Government by Political Party Representatives" of which this is a sequel.

Preventive justice is a major responsibility of the JSC

Phase three of the complete democratisation of national justice services delivery systems and perhaps the most important phase of them all as has already been alluded to at the beginning of this discussion, would be the delicate matter of the injustice pre-emption or prevention potential or function of the JSC.

Before any law, regulation, legal standard operating procedure, code of conduct and code of practice can be passed in parliament for implementation it must first of all and always be mandatorily referred to the Justice Services Commission (JSC). This must be done not only for the JSC to sift through such new legislation in terms of identifying any illegalities therein, but to also sanitise the legislation in terms of any intrinsic and not easily noticeable hidden natural injustices which might be quietly lurking therein somewhere. And in that regard, the decisions of the JSC or any of its other structures such as the Supreme Court, the Constitutional Court or the Constitutional Court of Appeal must be legal, binding and final. Even parliament itself must never be allowed to veto any legal decisions whatsoever. In fact, in the practice of true, correct and universal justice, there must not be any room for extrajudicial pardons whatsoever. All pardons must be intra-judicial.

Justice delayed is justice denied

The most important thing to note here is that the various arms of the JSC must be able to rule on cases of preventive justice even before they are brought to court because usually, court cases are only brought to court if and when there is a complainant. And yet in the case of pre-emptive or preventive justice, as the phrase suggests, there would be no complainant as yet. Many countries wait for there to be a legal ruling after someone has challenged certain legal provisions as being unconstitutional, unjust or unfair before they can correct some injustices which would be inherent in certain laws which their governments would have passed. That practice alone is tantamount to a great injustice in itself for the reasons that by the time someone comes along to legally complain and challenge the prevailing law like that, a lot of other people without the financial muscles, capacity, courage or clout to challenge such laws in court would have already been immensely, irreparably and irreversibly prejudiced. Thus, even when such inadvertently legally inborn injustices are eventually corrected, if ever they are corrected at all in the first place, most of their victims seldom get compensated for their losses. That cannot be fair or just at all. The right to justice, personal identity and human dignity must always be respected because it is as good a basic human right as any.

Chapter 12: Right to socioeconomic development

In 1966, the United Nations (UN), as the rightful world governing body, passed the International Covenant on Economic, Social and Cultural Rights (ICESCR, 1966). This was on top of the then already passed and subsisting Universal Declaration of Human Rights (UN UDHR, 1948). Perhaps this was the UN's way of trying to re-package only those human rights which were specific to socioeconomic growth and development and which did not carry with them any political connotations like what some reluctant to ratify countries may have viewed the original UDHR of 1948 to be doing. Such being the case, even though this covenant just about restated a lot of provisions which are also found in the earlier UDHR, it is still a very important and relevant covenant by and in itself.

One thing which the International Covenant on Economic, Social and Cultural Rights (ICESCR) advocates for right from the start is the dire importance and need for legislated socioeconomic growth and development and cultural rights. It is one thing to verbally claim respect for human rights, another thing to put that claim down in writing and in law, and quite another different thing altogether too, to actually walk the talk, or to implement that claim in practice. But at least when a claim is put down in writing and in law too the chances of its practical implementation become more real than not. For example, every day we hear a lot of aspiring politicians promising the electorate heaven on earth in terms of utopian socioeconomic growth and development trajectories once they are elected into power. But because such promises are not written down and countersigned for, let alone legal in nature, no one has ever been able to legally pin down any politician for winning elections under false pretences or by making false promises, and thereby having the politician legally relieved of the political office concerned. The day such would happen would probably be the day that politicians would graduate from being the perpetual good for nothing liars whom we all know them to be today to become some sort of decent human beings after all. Apparently, that day is still a very long way off!

Anyway, some of the major provisions of the International Covenant on Economic, Social and Cultural Rights (ICESCR) include labour rights, the right to trade unionism, social security, family life, adequate living standards (food, housing and clothing), health and free primary education, the right to culture and public participation in cultural life, moral rights and the right to socioeconomic development. All these provisions touch on socioeconomic growth and development within a given cultural context.

Social rights

A society is a group of people living together in an ordered community, or an organisation or group of people formed for a particular given purpose. Social means related to or connected with society, an organisation or group of people. Social animals are animals which breed or live together in organised communities. Thus, human beings are by nature social animals. It is very hard to imagine ancient times when human beings led solitary lives if that ever happened at all. Nowadays social life is the generally acceptable way of life of all human beings. Such being the case, all human beings, both as individuals and also as communities, are entitled to social rights or the right to socialise with other human beings or other communities of human beings. Social rights are therefore basic human rights as well. Freedom of association as already discussed earlier on in Chapter 8 is actually a social right as well, while the right to happiness is also closely linked with the right or freedom to socialise. Government must ensure that people are free to socialise with whoever they may want to socialise with and do whatever they may want to do as social groups. However, as is always the case, such would be as long as such socialisation would not be for criminal purposes and also as long as it would not infringe on the social and other rights of some other people as well.

Social, religious, traditional and cultural organisations, groups and gatherings must be allowed to exist under access to social rights even though some of these things are recognised human rights in their own right. Social media groups and the electronic media platforms where such groups usually meet and socialise must also be respected under social rights. Such being the case, restrictions on access to the internet such as complete internet blackouts or the blockage of certain websites is as much a denial of social rights or freedom of association as it is also a denial of freedom of expression as well. There is usually no good or disciplined reason why any government would want to unnecessarily restrict such freedoms besides tyranny.

Socialisation can also be extended into the world of business. In fact, most business organisations are actually social groups of two or more people who would have come together and joined hands for the purposes of engaging in business enterprise. Without such business enterprises, there most probably would be no national economies worth talking about in this world. Business cooperative societies or enterprises are actually legally recognised and registered forms of private business corporations which many national governments encourage, empower and support especially for the emerging businesspeople. Some cooperative society based business enterprises such as financial credit, building, trading and other cooperative societies have grown and developed to become much recognised and respected solid cornerstones of socioeconomic growth and development. They have become an economic growth sector on their own and in their own right as well. Such positive developments testify to the great heights which countries can soar to by just upholding and respecting all basic human rights, including the social and economic rights of their people.

Of course, respecting all human rights can seem challenging under certain circumstances, especially where there might be some misguided and selfish people who might want to exploit such respect for the purposes of wrong doing. That is a common challenge. But instead of pessimistically focussing on the difficulties of observing all human rights, governments must optimistically focus on the opportunities which are presented by doing so. In life, those who always say it can't be done have done nothing while those who always say it can be done have moved mountains. As the driver and controller-in-chief of the national socioeconomic growth and development bus, government must always have a positive attitude towards everything so that the whole bus and its passengers can purposefully and positively chug forward. In fact, come to think of it, as far as social groups are concerned, the whole country itself is just one big social group, gathering or community of people whose social rights as a group, gathering or community must be respected by government. No government or outside forces must be allowed to divide and disrupt any naturally cohesive social groups including countries. This is the main reason why social or societal divisions which are engendered by political party based affiliations must be discouraged in any natural community or society as advanced in my previous book of which this one is a sequel.

Economic rights

At national level, an economy is a social system by and in which a country and all its people, social groups and communities are organised and run in terms of production, trade and consumption of goods and services. Since people must eat or consume in order to survive, individual people as well as social groups and communities which they belong to have the intrinsic right to participate in the economy or in economic activities in order for them to make a living. In other words, economic rights are basic human rights too.

Some of the economic activities which an individual person may participate in included working for or being employed by another person or registered business company, working for oneself or being self-employed, owning a business or being a shareholder in a business. Everyone has the right to earn a living or to engage in economic activities which would enable one to survive or earn a living. In fact, economic rights are as good as the right to life itself. Perhaps this is the reason why the UN in its Universal Declaration of Human Rights (UDHR, 1948), its International Covenant on Economic, Social and Cultural Rights (ICESCR, 1966) and also in its International Convention on the Protection of the Rights of All Migrant Workers and

Members of Their Families (UN ICRMW, 1990) continued to emphasise on labour rights or the intrinsic right of people to work anywhere in this world. Thus, it is just not right to prevent people, including even all migrants, from working, either for themselves or for other people in order for them to earn a living unless of course if they would be provided with that living without having to work for it.

We have repeatedly stated in this book again and again that one of the basic obligations of government is not to do anything for anybody bust just to provide an enabling social and economic environment and then empower, enable and support individual people, communities and business organisations to make a living for and by themselves. This is one of the best ways by which government can ensure access to economic rights by all people. Perhaps there is not even a better way of doing so than just this one.

Cultural rights

Culture denotes the things which we do and the way we do them today, while tradition refers to the things which we used to do and the way we used to do them then or in the past. Traditional rituals or practices are commemorative activities, practices or functions which we used to hold in remembrance or respect of certain important events in our lives either as individuals, families, communities or as the whole country. On the other hand, cultural rituals or practices are activities, practices or functions which we currently hold or do either in remembrance or respect of certain important events in our lives either as individuals, families, communities or the whole country, or as a way of life or the way we live as a cultural group. Tradition is no longer in practice while culture is currently the one which is in practice or being practiced today and going forward. These distinctions are very important because many people are frequently confused when it comes to tradition and culture. Many people are so confused that they do not know which one is which one and hence they keep on mistaking one for the other and the other for one.

Culture is inherited tradition

A lot of the things which we do today and the ways in which we do them are a continuous inheritance from the past. As would be expected, there would always be slight changes here and there, but usually the essentials would remain not that much altered from past to present practices. In fact, come to think about it, it is not only the things which we do today and the way we do them which are inheritances from the past, but everything about and around us is also an inheritance from the past. Every person boasts of a family history which chronicles his or her genetic, ethnic, tribal and racial descent among other things. However, it is not only those genetically transmitted traits which we inherit from the past, but we also intrinsically and insidiously inherit a lot of traditional ideas, beliefs, norms, values, behaviours and practices which are not genetically transmitted. Somehow, all these things just end up being part and parcel of who we are today. Thus today, in addition to our different genetic identities, we also possess unique cultural identities which are imparted to us by the different traditional histories, ideas, beliefs, norms, values, customs and practices which we inherited from our unique and different pasts. And all these things taken together are the things which give us our different and unique cultural, individual, social, community and national identities today. Hence, we are who we are today because of our different genetics, histories, traditions and cultures. And we have every right to be who we are today because that is an act of fate. We would probably not have managed to change our fate even if we tried because fate is basically an act of nature. Such being the case, everyone has the right to be what nature made them to be in the first place. And this is the main reason why cultural rights are indeed basic human rights.

Culture is not by choice

Cultural rights must be taken, considered and understood in the same context as genealogical or genetic rights. As much as it is easy to understand that no one can choose his or her own blood or genetic relatives, it must also be easy to understand that similarly, no one can chose the place and environment in which one is born or brought up, or how one is actually brought up. Apart from genetics, it is the environment in which one is born, grows and develops which imbues one with his or her unique and identifying tradition and culture. It is generally accepted that a person is a product of his genetics, experiences and surroundings. Thus, people do not choose who they are in terms of genetics, tradition and culture and therefore they must be taken and accepted just the way they are in that respect. No one, not even government, must stop people from being who they are because to be who they are is actually their natural and basic human right. "If you are not yourself, then who are you?" This culturally pertinent question was asked by one United States of America (USA) African American music singer called Brandy in one of the songs on her music album which she aptly entitled "Human."

Many governments suffer from cultural ignorance

The biggest challenge of many governments as far as the upholding and respect of the cultural rights of some of their own people lies in their cultural ignorance, judgemental and disrespectful nature as governments. As we have seen above, there usually are very good traditional reasons why certain people, either as individuals, families, groups or communities, culturally behave the way they behave today. Government's own ignorance or lack of insight, knowledge and understanding of those good reasons does not mean that the reasons become invalid and ought not to hold any water or to be respected at all, thereby implying that government could just arbitrarily ban or put a stop or end to certain cultural practices which it adjudges not to be good for one reason or another of its own as government. Government's own lack of insight simply means that it does not know or understand those good reasons as yet, or their cultural essence, meaning or significance to the concerned people. Sometimes even some of the most ardent and seasoned traditional and cultural practitioners themselves have also absolutely no clue as to why they maintain certain cultural rituals and practices besides just the fact that it would be their tradition and culture. Such being the case, instead of adopting a snobbish attitude and seeking to ban or actually going ahead to ban certain cultural rituals and practices which it might adjudge not to be good or desirable for whatever reason, government must try to just focus on and deal with the undesirable element or elements in such cultural practices or rituals while at the same time leaving the whole cultural ritual or practice itself intact. And that can and has actually been done before.

The thorny issue of cultural circumcision

For example, culture based circumcisions and other coming of age rituals which many communities routinely subject both their male and female children to at a certain ages and times in their lives are very, very topical and controversial issues around the world today. Many western countries, their international human rights groups, and other social and even economic organisations want certain third world cultural rituals and practices which they deem to be big risks to the lives, health, safety and wellbeing of affected minor children such as female genital circumcisions to be internationally banned. And to drive their point home, or to give it some kind of calculatedly scary and nerve wrecking effect, these antagonists have vociferously dubbed rather straight forward female genital circumcision "female genital mutilation" while at the same time not wanting to acknowledge the fact that even with male circumcision, a normal part of the male genitalia is also mutilated. And that has not gone down very well with some of the practitioners and proponents of the traditional and cultural practice of female genital circumcision. Rather than reconsider their cultural practice as urged by the antagonists, proponents have instead angrily dug in deeper and even further and refused to barge even an inch, much to the detriment of the affected female children and their communities at large.

What is so surprising is that the very same antagonists of culture based female genital circumcision are not calling for the ban of the essentially similar culture based male genital circumcision which in most cases would in fact be a side by side cultural practice of those who also practice female genital circumcision! In fact, and under the very same cultural environment and conditions, these self-righteous, self-appointed and self-proclaimed antagonists of female genital circumcision do not only support culture based male genital circumcision in the third world for their own good reasons, but they also actively promote and fund it! And to make it sound good and much better than what they call "female genital mutilation," they call male circumcision by the beautiful, sexy and seductive name of male medical circumcision or MMC. Such is the best way of losing the plot, causing confusion and fermenting cultural violence in any society or community. There is definitely no better way of doing so than that. Because of such blatant displays of self-centred double standards by the so called international community (just another euphemism for western culture), affected third world countries and their communities have just decided to refuse to comply. They have dug in deep and not barged a bit as far as their cultural rights to honour their cultural rituals and practices in this regard are concerned.

Both ways the innocent children are the victims

The unfortunate and prolonged stalemate between the protagonists of third world culture based female genital circumcision has now inadvertently put the whole lives and not just the genitalia of the affected female minor children at risk. These poor kids now face the greater risk of being physically, psychologically and socially assaulted or even being murdered for refusing to partake in otherwise just normal cultural rituals and practices. This would be in addition to many other nasty things like insults, family, community and social rejection and neglect and many other personal prejudices and disadvantages which they may suffer. Such is not good at all for these poor innocent kids.

Yes, it is actually true and correct that the cultural rituals of both male and female genital circumcision, if and when carried out in the same old traditional manners as they are commonly practiced by many of the affected communities today, would be risky to the safety and physical health and wellbeing of the affected children. However, not partaking in such cultural rituals and practices if and when they are expected to do so would also be very risky to the safety and physical health and social wellbeing of the very same affected minor children as well. Surely, the best rational and logical solution to this stalemate cannot and must not just be stop it and damn the consequences like the stance which has apparently been adopted by the so called international community. Perhaps, or in fact it is about time that someone somewhere realises that with regards to cultural practice disputes, there can never be only win or lose options. Such a dogmatic and negative attitude can only lead to losing both ways. There must always be the positive attitude of a win-win end result to serve the day.

Culture is such a very potent force because it is the one which unites whole communities, societies, countries and nations together, and it is also the one which gives them their unique identities, joy and pride. Refusing to obey day to day cultural practices is tantamount to refusing to be a member of that family, community or society and thereby making oneself a social outcast overnight. And supporting vulnerable and culturally ignorant children to revolt against their own cultures is akin to handing them ropes with which to hang themselves. And yet this is exactly what the so called civilised international community routinely does in third world countries! Rather than pitch very innocent, vulnerable and culturally ignorant small, and mentally immature minor children against their own very powerful societies and also against themselves through openly influencing and supporting them to deny who they actually are by nature in terms of refusing to participate in certain cultural rituals and practices, the self-appointed benevolent antagonists of such cultural practices must seriously try to find common ground and achieve a win-win solution for everyone concerned. Unless of course if they do not actually care at all about the very same minor children whom they say they care a lot about in this whole saga.

Cultural challenges need cultural solutions

Cultural challenges always need cultural solutions and not idealistic ones in order to solve them. The solution to the impasse of third world culture based female genital circumcision cannot be one sided. It has to consider and take into account the interests and concerns of both sides. Such a solution has always been there, but apparently no one has ever been really interested to find, articulate or implement it. From experience, and also from the look of things, the reason for this apparent reluctance to see or do the right or correct thing in the case of both male and female culture based genital circumcision has always been the same good old root cause of all evil – the love of money. With all due respect, many international and western based non-governmental organisations (NGOs) attract and make lots of donor monies by screaming long and loud about third world natural and man-made disasters and the way these disasters would be negatively affecting the lives of young and innocent children. But most of these NGOs do not try to do anything much or even anything at all to rectify these disasters in strategic ways which would both immediately put an end to and also prevent such things from ever happening again. This is because most of these NGOs would want to continue making more donor monies out of the continued suffering of these poor, young and innocent minor children. What a cruel thing to do!

Old and traditional methods of practicing circumcision are admittedly very hazardous to both males and females as admitted above. Many unsuspecting and innocent children have lost their lives or become permanently disabled in the process. And that cannot be acceptable in these modern times. And that must definitely change or be changed for the better. There is no argument about that. While still being respectfully allowed to keep and maintain their own preciously revered traditional and cultural practices as culturally independent communities, societies or countries, and also without belittling, despising or disrespecting the same cultural practices, affected communities must be gently and compassionately persuaded of the unacceptably high health risks which accompany both traditional male and female genital circumcision methods with the view of replacing them with safer, modern and health institution based surgical ways of doing so.

Actually, I once successfully did exactly that in one such community in my own country and achieved immediate and tremendously good results even though my case involved male cultural circumcision only and not female cultural circumcision as well. I have heard that there has not been any further male cultural circumcision related morbidities, mortalities or disabilities in that part of the world eversince that time, and that is exactly twenty-five years ago. And yet currently in some even more or better developed countries neighbouring mine, male cultural circumcision related deaths are still an expected, yearly and rising phenomenon, twenty-five years on! This is very sad and very tragic indeed.

The flip side of this is that there is absolutely no good reason at all as to why the same observed zero mortality, morbidity and disability rates cannot also be achieved with the controversial tradition and culture based female genital circumcision. No parent or guardian anywhere in this world would ever want their own child to die for whatever reason regardless of the fact that some western organisations always want to portray third world people and their cultural practices as being primitive, backwards, uncivilised or full of human rights abuses. The right to life is sacrosanct in any and every culture. As far as the preservation of life is concerned, there are no parents, communities or societies which would refuse the substitution of dangerous, unsafe and unhealthy traditional methods of female genital circumcision with safer and healthier medical institution based modern day methods of doing the same thing. What the concerned parents and societies object to is the patently apparent negation of their cultural rights which is projected by the culturally insensitive suggestion to completely ban such cultural practices altogether instead of just trying to make them safer and healthier for the involved kids. This objection is just as understandable and also as right or correct as the health and safety concerns of the antagonists of these cultural practices. Where the antagonists seem to have lost it though is that they seem to be strongly opposed to the whole cultural practice itself instead of just opposing only that component or part of the practice which posses the health risks which they want to get rid of. And yet that is quite possible to do or achieve.

Female circumcision can be made safer and healthier

I know that with culture based female genital circumcision readers would immediately and almost automatically cry out loudly that it is completely different from male genital circumcision for heaven's sake! Perhaps my response to that one would be that as if I did not know that already! However, if we take our precious time to respectfully find out why exactly those who practice culture based female genital circumcision still do so today besides the fact that it is just one of their strongly held cultural beliefs and practices which they have inherited from their own tradition, we may just be pleasantly surprised by how much easy it might be to overcome the obvious health and safety challenges which are posed by this practice. Perhaps the tradition of female genital circumcision was supposedly to protect the female minor children from sexually transmitted diseases (STDs) which would not only disable them down there, but could also possibly kill them too since there was no effective and efficacious treatment way back then as is the case today. What is worse, STDs would also make young and innocent children agents of spreading such and other related diseases in society. And perhaps in order to protect young girls from both the risk of STDs and also the risk of irresistible desire to have sex which would normally assaults adolescents of both sexes, and which desire would then expose them even more to the same risk of STDs, female genital circumcision was instituted. Come to think of it, the same reasons would also have been applied to culture based male genital circumcision. The fact that even today, common medical wisdom, although exaggerated way out of proportion in my own opinion, has supported what has been dubbed "male medical circumcision" or MMC on more or less the same STD reduction related medical grounds as espoused above for females, would lend some credence to this hypothesis. Except of course in the case of the highly personal sexual enjoyment or lack thereof part of it! However, many people who were medically circumcised later on in adult life have testified to the fact that there is actually a difference in sexual sensation and satisfaction before and after circumcision!

The other thing which may make the above supposition more likely than not is the fact that traditionally, many if not all human societies married off their female children, and sometimes their male children too, at very young and tender ages. Very good reasons for such early marriages would have been many such as ensuring that the prospective husband got a wife who was free of STDs and one whom he would nurse to maturity for himself. This would have been plausible especially considering the fact that way back then and unlike nowadays, huge dowries were almost mandatorily paid for wives (or husbands). Who back then would have wanted to pay lobola or dowry for an STD damaged wife? And what about the then extramarital sex taboo which the STD would implicitly confirm to have taken place? During those days it would have been definite that STD messed up girls would end up not being married at all considering both the absence of effective treatment and also all these cultural taboos which prevailed at that time. A lot of things which we take for granted today were probably very big issues way back then as confirmed by otherwise very small things like the way we cannot imagine life without cell phones in our pockets today and yet cell phones came about only just yesterday.

Another good example is that many normal and modern societies in today's highly permissive and liberal world still consider marrying a woman who has had even just one child, let alone several children, out of wedlock with other men, a very big no go area. What would the situation have been like in the good old or bad old traditional days if such a backward attitude, as the progressive liberals would want to call it, still prevails even today?

Hospital based female genital circumcision

Anyway, the point I am getting at here is that rather than just contemptuously and off-handedly condemning or dismissing certain cultural practices and then vigorously and actively seeking to have them completely banned, it would be much better and more prudent to devise ways and means of making such practices safer and healthier if safety and health is deemed to be their main challenge. Many communities and societies which practice culture based female genital circumcisions would not object to having the procedure carried out in hospital by qualified and trained medical doctors under safe, clean, healthy and hygienic medical conditions and using modern surgical methods and techniques which would ensure excellent prognosis in terms of physical, sexual and social health. No one will ever die, be physically disabled, sexually ruined or socially excluded after culture based female genital circumcision which would have been conducted in a hospital setting and by a qualified, trained and experienced medical doctor. During hospital based and surgically performed cultural female genital circumcision, there in fact is absolutely no need at all to cut off any part or parts of the female genitalia! This fact alone must immediately silence all those who may have screamed at me when I first suggested it above. Simple plastic surgery techniques can be employed to blanket, cover or conceal the uncut clitoris and also most of the vaginal introitus with adjacent vulval skin thereby leaving a small aperture just big enough to allow urine and menstrual blood to freely and safely flow out as usual. The end results of such a surgically and clinically precise medical procedure in terms of fitness for purpose would not be very much different or even different at all from female genital circumcision which would have been conducted using traditional surgical methods except in both outlook and the absence of mutilation or cutting off of anything. Modern surgical methods of culture based female genital circumcision would result in more or less normal looking vulvas, while traditional surgical methods have always resulted in unsightly, nasty and ugly looking vulval scars. The elastic capacity of genital skin is legendary, so there would not be any big challenges with regards to sex and parturition later on in life. After all, there can always be the normal cutting and stitching which happens at child birth and which would restore everything back to normal! Thus, cultural based female genital circumcisions can be made safer and healthier after all instead of just being banished.

If the above proposed modern surgical procedure and the safe, healthy and culturally acceptable end results thereof are properly, patiently and dignifiedly explained to the concerned communities, the possibility of enthusiastic uptake is there and probably very high too. Yes, plastic surgery or any kind of surgery no matter how apparently simple, would always be very expensive, but that is not good enough a reason to advocate for the abrupt abolition of any highly respected and cherished cultural practice, especially considering the big social and physical battles and the unnecessary innocent casualties which may be involved in trying to do so. In fact the huge expenses involved here could be used to advantage whereby, one convert at a time, these huge costs may discourage and eventually completely banish the practice altogether through natural attrition. And natural attrition is the way by which many traditional and cultural practices have slowly and insidiously become obsolete and eventually disappeared from our different societies throughout all these years.

What the opponents of cultural female genital circumcision have done so far has not helped or served the affected communities very well or at all. For purely financial reasons disguised as medical reasons, these people have vigorously championed cultural male genital circumcision and even facilitated for it to be safely conducted by qualified, trained and experienced medical doctors in healthy and hygienic modern medical facilities as also suggested above for culture based female genital circumcision. But for whatever reason, the very same people did not extend the same benevolence to culture based female genital circumcision and yet it could just as equally have been extended there too and for precisely the very same STD reduction health reasons as well as was postulated before. In fact, I am much more than just persuaded to believe that hospital conducted culture based female genital circumcision as describe above would do a much better job at preventing STDs than that which is roundly acclaimed for the same procedure in males today. Uncomfortable evidence is now beginning to emerge that the prevalence of sexually transmitted human immunodeficiency virus (HIV) infection is now rising faster in circumcised men as compared to the same or similar cohorts of uncircumcised man in many third world countries today! As someone who once cautioned about this, the urge to say I told you so would be there, but I would not say that for the sake of the victims of that most likely ill-fated public health exercise.

In one of my publications of years gone by, I once argued that as much as the medical profession seems to have convinced itself of the possible association of male medical circumcision with lower incidence rates of STDs in general, that "discovery" was purely accidental to begin with, and the extrapolated possible association thereof was purely just that – an extrapolated possible association and nothing else. The main reason for my caution was that those people who usually practice culture based male and female genital circumcision at birth, or at any other time during childhood, and in which the prevalence and incidence of STDs in general were retrospectively observed to be consistently and significantly lower than in people who did not practice the same cultural rituals in the same community, may have more important traditional, cultural, social and many other personal behavioural attributes which contributed more to this observed lower incidence and prevalence rates of STDs than just circumcision alone. And in fact, they usually do.

Traditional, religious and cultural fanatics are known to be very committed not only to their own traditions, religions, cultures and the rituals thereof, but also to their other behavioural practices, codes of conduct, ethics, morals, norms, customs and values within the set boundaries of their traditional, religious or cultural systems. And most of the set boundaries in such strict traditional, religious and cultural systems usually draw very rigid and restrictive lines around such things as casual private associations with members of the opposite sex, cavorting, premarital sex, promiscuity, prostitution, extramarital sex, drunkenness, drugs, truancy, delinquency and many other such social maladies which are usually also associated with very high incidence rates of STDs everywhere and anywhere in the world. Any transgression is usually frowned upon in ways and means which make the concerned people not want to even think about it, let alone go that way at all. Perhaps that alone, and not male genital circumcision, may be the major contributor to the observed lower STDs rates in these groups of people compared to groups which do not practice mandatory culture or religion based male and or female genital circumcision. For there to be concrete proof that only male genital circumcision alone does it, there must be valid prospective cohort studies across generations, studies which unfortunately have not yet been done.

And yet because of the availability of lots of donor money, NGOs and their donor countries persuaded many third world countries and their governments to adopt what they dubbed male medical circumcision (MMC) as a major component of their own national HIV and AIDS prevention programmes. Together, they vowed to circumcise every child and every man in every one of these third world countries as a way of stopping the spread of HIV and AIDS. For sure history will one day tell as to whether MMC was a worthwhile exercise or just an exercise in futility, or worse, a very risky and counterproductive public health venture after all. And that history may not be very kind to a whole lot of people, especially to the innocent souls who may be caught on the wrong side of it! May that day never come?

Culture is naturally always evolving

Anyway, the main point here is that government needs to empower, enable, support and allow its people and their communities to access their cultural rights without unnecessarily antagonising them. As much as all human beings have generally managed to collectively evolve and transition from the pure barbarism of the past to present day civilisation while at the same time not completely losing touch with who they really are in terms of their various traditions and cultures, we can also let and assist other traditions and cultures to make the very same evolutionary transitions without causing any nasty, unwanted and unwarranted cultural revolutions. Culture or the way we do the things which we do, is naturally always evolving. The natural way and not the forced way, is the best way to manage cultural and other social transitions. Besides circumcision, there are many other cultural rights which government ought to let its people access all the time. If there are any objectionable things therein too which may need to be changed or replaced, government and society in general can take a leaf from the suggestion which was given herein about culture based female genital circumcision.

Chapter 13: The right to natural resources

Natural resources

Natural resources are things which are found in nature, not made or caused by man, and which people and other living things need and naturally use to help them to meet their basic physiological or life giving needs. Some of the most commonly known natural resources are land, minerals, water, wildlife, air, sunshine and people themselves. All these natural resources were created or caused by nature so as to provide natural and free benefits to all those living things which would need to exploit them to meet their own basic or life needs. Basic needs are those essential needs which enable all living things to live or survive, and all basic human needs are also inevitably basic human rights as well. Such being the case, all individuals, their communities and their countries have the right to the natural resources which they were born in, with or around. In other words, the right to natural resources is a basic human right as well.

Many people do not realise the fact that natural resources are basically free creator given things or gifts. Natural resources are naturally and freely given by the creator or by nature to all the natural inhabitants of the same place in which they are also naturally found. In this case inhabitants refers to all living things and not just to human beings alone. Basically all natural resources are freely given and thus for free as well. Perhaps this is where the saying that the best things in life are for free actually comes true. The land on which we all live, the water in our rivers and underground, the air which we breathe and the wildlife all around us are all basically for free.

Natural resources are community owned [1]

As free natural gifts from nature to all communities, natural resources are therefore communally and not individually owned. No one must ever be allowed to own, think, say, pretend or act as if they actually own any natural resources anywhere in this world. What the above means is that as a natural resource, no one owns another human being, even if that person is your child, let alone your employee. No one owns land even if that land is supposedly your farm, your housing or building plot. No one owns air, even if that air is in your house, car or building. No one owns water, even if that water is in a reservoir made, built or bought by you. No one owns minerals, even if those minerals were prospected for, discovered, extracted, processed or traded by you. No one owns wildlife, even if that wildlife is in an enclosure constructed, managed or maintained by you. And obviously, no one owns sunshine.

All natural resources are naturally owned by and belong to the local people and the communities in which they are found. Such being the case, anyone who prospects for, finds, discovers, harnesses, extracts, refines, processes, trades in or exploits any natural resources in any way whatsoever must only be legally allowed to do so for and on behalf of actual owners of those natural resources, these being the local people and their communities. Local people and their communities, as bona fide owners of natural resources found in and around them, must also be the primary and final beneficiaries of the commercial business exploitation of all those natural resources in terms of the consumption of the net profits thereof and not any private individuals or organisations. This is correct even though private people and organisations would be the ones who would have carried out the actual commercial business processes involved in the exploitation of such natural resources in the first place. Business organisations which would have been involved in the commercial business exploitation of any natural resources must only be allowed to get away with fair amounts in business input costs related and some other commensurate rewards such as a reasonable share of the net profits or dividends thereof. Such businesses must not be allowed to own or to keep the whole intrinsic or natural commercial business value of the natural resources in question as if they were the true and original owners of these resources. This is because natural resources are free natural gifts from the creator to the so endowed natural communities and their people and not to any exploitative business people and their commercial businesses. Reimbursement of business input costs incurred with interest plus some reasonable share of the final net profits thereof would probably be such a fair bargain for the private individuals and private businesses which would have helped natural resources endowed communities to exploit, add value and profitably benefit from their creator given natural resources gifts.

The commercial business exploitation of natural resources principle articulated above must be applied across the board to all the eight basic natural resources which are people, land, minerals, water, wildlife, air and airspace, and finally sunshine. What this means is that commercial businesses which exploit people, land, minerals, water, wildlife, air, airspace and sunshine as their main resource or source of commercial business income cannot and must not be allowed to pocket one hundred percent of the profits from such natural resources based businesses because they do not own these natural resources in the first place. These natural resources indisputably belong to the so naturally endowed people and their communities or countries not only in terms of both their intrinsic and commercial values, but also in terms of the major share of the net benefits or profits thereof. And major in this case means not less than fifty-one percent share of net profits or even more. Payment in appreciation of expended efforts is the only rational and logical thing which commercial business exploiters of natural resources may be individually or collectively rewarded for as already stated above. The net beneficiaries of the commercial value of the business exploitation of all and any natural resources must always be the local communities themselves or the concerned collective inhabitants of the place where these natural resources are naturally found. The fact that all natural resources belong to local communities and countries as a whole, and not to individuals, businesses or organisations including even government itself, must always be respected and cannot be overemphasised.

At national level, natural resources belong to the state [1]

In today's modern world which is artificially divided up into distinct geopolitically demarcated and bounded countries, all natural resources in any given country belong to the state. A state is defined as any given country taken together with its geopolitical boundaries, all of its inhabitant people, its government, and everything else in it. Just like natural resources and in spite of artificial man-made boundaries, all states were freely put into place by the grace of the creator for the benefit of all those who live in them.

The control and governance of natural resources

Apart from the creator himself, all natural resources must also be owned, controlled and governed by the respective communities in which these resources are naturally found through both their local and their national representative governments in terms of extraction, use and beneficiation. Government permission or authority must be sought and granted before anyone can be allowed to prospect for, find, extract, process, use or trade in natural resources. Such government permission must of necessity also include natural conservation and community beneficiation oriented restrictions and controls on how the natural resources may be prospected for, found, extracted, processed, used or traded in. Such governing and governance rights as these are in fact the undisputed natural rights of the natural owners of any natural resources anywhere in this world.

Government is also a natural phenomenon

National governments are in fact also natural, intrinsically necessary and inevitable communal, societal and national centres of power, authority and control which hold all these rather fluid social organisations together and without which there would be maximum chaos and disorder therein and therefore no communities, societies, nations or countries to talk about. Just as the creator put in place immutable and unbreakable laws of nature which govern the way in which all matter, living or dead, relates and interacts with each other on planet earth so that there would be order instead of chaos, governments must also try to do the same thing with their laws of natural justice and other man-made laws.

Government is actually a creation of the creator, and the creator given role of governments would logically be to ensure that all living things under their various jurisdictions, and perhaps especially people, enjoy their right to life, liberty and happiness among many other creator given rights and liberties as previously discussed in this book. The right to life, liberty and happiness is premised on the right to all the basic human needs as invoked by Abraham Maslow. These basic human needs are food, shelter, health, education, transport, self-esteem, socialisation, social-esteem and self-actualisation among many others. So in short, all governments on earth must ensure that all the people under their jurisdiction enjoy their creator given rights to all these basic human needs. Such being the case, governed people have the right to demand exactly just that from their governments, while governments have the responsibility, duty and obligation to deliver on all these things and even much more.

Natural resources ownership must never be privatised

Community ownership and government responsibility in terms of control over all natural resources must never be privatised. As something made by nature, and naturally bestowed onto a given people, communities, countries and their respective governments for common benefit, the actual ownership and net benefits of natural resources must always accrue to the local people, their communities and their countries. And the responsibility of government is to ensure that such actually happens. Such being the case, the duty and responsibility of government to control and govern the exploitation of all natural resources in the country must, and without exception, never be privatised as well. The responsibility of government in this case refers to the powers and obligations of government to legally govern, regulate or control the prospection, finding, extraction, processing, trade, use and beneficiation of all natural resources within its jurisdiction. This intrinsic, very important and crucial government responsibility must never ever be abdicated to the private sector.

However, the governing and controlling powers, duties, obligations and responsibilities of government over all natural resources do not extend to actually doing the job of prospecting for, finding, extracting, processing, trading and use of natural resources. As this book has repeatedly stated again and again, that is not the obligation, duty and responsibility of government or the public sector but of the private sector. And as usual, the public sector can always also go in there too if it deems it absolutely necessary, but only as the private public sector through the aegis of public owned private sector business enterprises (POBEs) and not directly as the public sector itself.

Natural resources based commercial businesses

As always the economically more efficient, effective and productive private commercial business sector must be legally allowed by government, within given legal limits, and also within given legal manners or procedures of conducting business, to exploit any and all natural resources for the overall benefit of everyone else, while at the same time the sector also gets commensurate benefits for its efforts. In fact, that is how natural resources based privately owned commercial businesses must always be run. Such private businesses must never be about the commercial business exploitation of natural resources primarily or exclusively for private business or private individual benefit alone. That would be tantamount to short-changing the people who are the actual owners of these natural resources and local their communities, governments or countries.

Perhaps the question now would be how exactly can or must private businesses be allowed to participate in the exploitation of any or all natural resources for everyone's benefit in any given country? Governments need to practice an entrepreneurial approach to governance in order to adequately, efficiently and cost-effectively harness all the very good, advanced, vast and superior capabilities and potentials of the private sector so as to profitably exploit all the natural resources over which they preside for and on behalf of their people. There are of course many different ways by which each one of the different natural resources can be exploited in terms of specific business models. The rest of the chapters of this book are devoted entirely to examining how each one of the eight given basic natural resources can be profitably exploited for the maximum net benefit or profit of the people, communities and countries which own these natural resources while at the same time also ensuring that the business interests of the enabling commercial business processes and the business owners are recognised, upheld, respected, protected and adequately rewarded as necessary.

Chapter 14: Democratic governance of the right to People

People are natural resources

Why and how are people natural resources and how and why are they also the most important resources in any organisation? And how must people as natural resources be commercially exploited for public net benefit instead of for private or individual net benefit as already advocated for in this book in terms of the commercial business exploitation of all natural resources? These are some of the pertinent questions which would be answered in this chapter. A lot of people, especially politicians and political minded business people, always say that people are the most important resource or asset in any company, country, organisation or economic set up. They say so seemingly without actually knowing what they would be talking about or without much sincerity or commitment to what they would be saying as evidenced by their total lack of practical care or concern for the very same people whom they would be exalting in their public speeches. And yet it is still very true that people are the most important resource in any organisation or country.

People are absolutely essential for the economy

In any given human economy, it is people who drive the economy by producing, trading and consuming all the economic goods and services which make up that economy, or make that economy work or tick. Without people, there would simply be no economy to talk about. Simply put, people are the economy and the economy is the people. This is the main reason why people are the most important resource, asset or player in any economy.

Some people are natural resources to other people

As social animals, people need other people to survive. Of course, biologically speaking, without parents, there would definitely be no children and yet that is not all. Children also absolutely need the social care of adult people, be it their actual parents or not, for survival. As far as children are concerned, people who can feed, clothe, house and look after them in all manners of their physiological needs are by definition God given natural resources to them. In this regard, children actually need and must exploit the caring services of adult people in order to survive. To the whole world, a person may just be one other person, but to a child, that person may be the whole world. In Chapter 13, we realised that all natural resources are basic human needs. That is the reason why the right to natural resources is a basic human right. As such, if adult people are natural resources to children, it means that adult people are thus basic human needs to these minor children. And since basic human needs are also basic human rights, then adult people, especially parents, are basic human rights of all children. Perhaps this is one of the main reasons why recently, and after a very long and painful struggle for those concerned, adoptive parents and governments have come to the conclusion that indeed every person has the right to know his or her own biological parents.

Commercial business exploitation of people

Besides the fact that some people need other people for their own survival as shown in the case of minor children above, most if not all commercial businesses would never thrive, let alone exist, without people. This is because people are the only producers, traders and consumers of goods and services in many if not most commercial business enterprises. For example, banks, shops, supermarkets, food producers, processors and retailers, clothing manufacturers, traders and retailers, personal and body care products manufactures, schools, colleges and universities, hotels, bars and restaurants, health service providers, housing developers, estate agents, public transport operators, telephone, cell phone and internet service providers, professional spectator sports businesses, newspapers, radio and television services and many, many other similar people based businesses would probably not exist at all without people as both producers and consumers of their basic business services. It can therefore be confidently argued that such commercial businesses exploit people as their main commercial business resources or the resources which enable them to survive or exist as commercial businesses. This is the reason why and how people are natural resources of commercial businesses.

Business exploitation of people must benefit communities

The major component of the net benefit or profit of the commercial business exploitation of people and their needs as natural resources, as is the case with all other natural resources, must also always accrue to the people and the communities and countries which naturally own these people as their creator given natural resources and not to the exploiting businesspeople, their businesses or their countries of origin as has already been repeatedly and extensively discussed in Chapter 13 of this book. As natural resources, national governments must never allow anyone, whether local or foreign, to capture, own and commercially exploit their people in any commercial business activity entirely for private profit or private business benefit alone without giving some back to the concerned community, society or country its rightful share of what rightfully and by the grace of nature belongs to it. People, communities and countries must always share in the eventual net business profits thereof whenever and wherever their people are exploited as natural resources for commercial business purposes. Please note that the eventual net benefits which we are talking about here are the actual net business profits and not the inevitable business input costs such as the taxes, jobs, wages, salaries, goods and other services which businesses would inevitably have to pay for in the normal process of doing business. These business input costs are just the normal costs of doing or running a business and not the desired actual or eventual net profits or net benefits of the business. Net profits are the real reasons of going into any commercial business in the first place. As such, it is the full net profits of all natural resources based commercial businesses which belong to the people who own those natural resources. And it is the people who own those natural resources who must allocate a share of those net profits to the exploiting commercial business people and their businesses if they feel like doing so and not the other way round. And yet most cunning businesses and their owners tout all the above mentioned business input costs as if they were the actual and biggest benefits which they bring to any country or community which they invest in and also to its government and all its people. That is a lie! On the other hand, these cunning and crooked businessmen decidedly keep their mouths shut about the whereabouts and ownership of all the net profits which their natural resources based and exploiting businesses always reap and for nothing too. This is tantamount to robbing the people, their communities and their governments in broad daylight.

But of course, all the concerned beneficiaries without exception, from the people themselves, their communities and their governments, are eventually all to blame for such exploitation and broad daylight robbery and not the cunning businessmen and their businesses that would be telling them such white lies and diverting their attention to the nonentities of business input costs as if they were the actual benefits to the country of any business. It is these natural beneficiaries who allow clever and cunning private businesses to exploit their natural resources for their own private business benefit in the first place. Then they also allow these businesses to lie to them like this and also to eventually run away with all the net profits thereof as if the natural resources belonged to them in the first place. Given the opportunity, perhaps every one of us would also keep the profits to oneself. Such being the case, maybe we cannot absolutely condemn those who are given the opportunity to do so and then go ahead to do just that.

The stake of the people in natural resources exploitation

In order to understand the issue of the natural rights of and necessity for countries, their people and their governments to share in the eventual net profits resulting from the exploitation of their natural resources, one must consider a few basic facts of the matter. For a start, we have said that all natural resources belong to the people to whom they were given by nature, their community, their country and eventually to the state. There is no argument about that. Secondly, at national level and in real terms, the net national economic growth and development, that measurement of the real and net increase in the size and complexity of the national economy, can only happen if and when the country as a whole generates and retains more locally owned than more foreign owned business net profits, even when the foreign owned net profits may be temporarily retained locally. The eventual or final and not the temporary destination of the net economic benefits or net profits thereof is very, very key here!

For example, the only natural resources which banks and supermarkets depend on and exploit for commercial business purposes and for their survival as businesses are people or the needs of the people. Without people, there would be no banks or supermarkets. The eventual net benefit to the state as a whole from the exploitation of people as natural resources by banks and supermarkets like this is not the services produced, traded or delivered. It is not the jobs or salaries given to individual workers, the business taxes paid to the state or anything else for that matter. But it is a solid share of the eventual annual net profits which are generated by these people dependent businesses which the whole country must benefit from for there to be any real and measurable socioeconomic growth and development at national level. And yet how many third world countries or states are actually benefiting like this from the commercial business exploitation of their people as natural resources by banks and supermarkets? Definitely not any or many African countries ever benefit from such commercial exploitation of their people and their needs if at all there are any African countries which benefit from such, and yet all western countries insist on benefiting and they in fact actually benefit all the time. This is a very big shame!

Western countries benefit from their natural resources

Does anyone out there know why all western governments have always bailed out their banks during all economic and financial crises, the latest one being the 2008 to 2010 global financial crisis? Of course, western governments themselves always publicly say that they bail out their banks in order to protect the people and the country, but without going into specific details. Yes, that would be true, but specifically the real reason is because western banks of necessity belong to (as in completely or partially owned by) the state or their own citizens, and consequently, the eventual net profits of these businesses, the real building blocks of any national economy, are permanently retained in the local economy, thus causing real socioeconomic growth and development. This is the real and main reason why western governments would always bailout their banks and other businesses whenever the need arises. Any other reasons proffered by these western governments are merely added advantages being cleverly touted as the real reasons thereof.

African countries do not benefit from natural resources

But how do African countries and their governments fair with regards to benefiting from the net profits of the commercial business exploitation of their very own natural resources? What stakes do African countries, their people and governments hold in locally operating international banks, for example, for and on behalf of their own people in the same manner that western governments do as has been explained above? Are African governments not allowing their most important natural resource, their people, to be commercially owned and exploited by banks, shops, hotels, supermarkets and other related commercial businesses as their main or even only commercial business resources for private individual or private business benefit instead of for collective public benefit as must naturally be the case?

The questions posed above are not much food for thought because such exploitation of some people by other people must never be allowed to happen in the first place. But in Africa, especially sub-Saharan Africa, it sadly is the norm. Ironically, the people who advise African governments to leave their people being exploited as natural resources for private individual gains like this are the very same western governments themselves. They misadvise like this in the name of privatisation or foreign direct investment (FDI). And yet in their own backyards and in their own countries they do not practice what they preach to third world countries. All first world or western countries used the naturally resources ladder, the only viable ladder for that purpose, to climb up to the level of socioeconomic growth and development where they are sitting today [1]. But now the very same countries selfishly kick that ladder off the wall and demand that economically struggling but resource rich African countries must find alternative methods of climbing up that steep wall. In the meantime, they offer to hoist these economically struggling African countries up that wall or economic huddle using western owned elastic commercial business strings. Such strings always rebound back to the west, their business owners, every time they snap under the severe tension which is caused by the heavy economic burden which third world countries generally are. For whose and what benefit is such deleterious advice and economic assistance which is being given to third world countries by western nations? Of course, it is always for the benefit of the very same western governments and their people. Apparently, economic colonialism is still with us for a very, very long time to come.

However, the decision to continue to be economically colonised like this or not is a matter of choice. African governments have the obligation to liberate themselves from mental slavery because no one but themselves can free their own minds. Economic freedom in the lifetimes of their people is actually an achievable dream! It is just up to them to do something about it or not. And they must start doing something about it by first of all taking full charge and responsibility of their own natural resources as suggested herein and of which luckily they still have plenty. That is the only way by which third world countries can get out of the perennial and undeserved poverty which they are currently wallowing in. Most third world African countries are just like beggars sitting on beaches of gold as far as natural resources and their management is concerned.

Commercial exploitation of people must benefit people

Based on what has been discussed above, no government or country in this world must ever allow its people, the most important natural resource it has, to be commercially owned and exploited by anyone in any business venture for one hundred percent private individual or private business benefit in terms of the eventual net benefits or profits thereof. It does not matter whether or not that person or organisation is local or foreign. To let such happen is not only very heartless and disgraceful to the country and its entire population, but it is also an affront to the charitable benevolence of the creator of those natural resources.

Chapter 15: Democratic governance of the right to Land

Land is probably the only natural resource which is always on top of everyone's mind when natural resources are being discussed. The obvious reason for this is that the very idea of the existence of a country goes hand in hand with that of land. Without land, there is no country, no city, town, village or a place called home. And home is where we all belong. No one wants to imagine himself or herself homeless or without a place called home. Perhaps this is also the main reason why the land question is such a very hot and emotive topic everywhere in the world, more especially in those previously colonised countries where colonialists started off by dispossessing the colonised people of their God given land and land rights before going further to politically oppress and economically exploit them right there and then in their own countries.

Wars were fought for the right to land

Most previously colonised people had to wage armed liberation struggles or wars to gain political independence and freedom from their colonisers. Top on most agendas of such and other similar liberation struggles was the right to reclaim their stolen land and countries, closely followed by the right to vote, the right to self-rule or self-government, the right to self-determination or independence, and the right to both social and economic freedom. However, at independence, what most previously colonised countries got back was political independence only, or just the right to self-rule or self-government. This gave them the right to vote and the right to be governed by their own indigenous governments and pretty much nothing else besides that.

The right to real independence or self-determination, more especially where it pertains to the right to socioeconomic freedom, is still very much just a pipe dream in many of the previously colonised countries. Former colonisers and their descendants, companies, friends and governments still call the socioeconomic shots in almost all former colonies. For example, former colonialists still own most if not all of the commercially viable land and also all of the commercially viable national economy from primary production through secondary production and up to tertiary production. And these former colonialists also hold all the real power in terms of social, political and economic influence. Nothing much has actually changed in terms of all the important fundamentals in these former colonies except superficial and cosmetic things only such as the indigenous faces or stooges which now fill up most of the chairs and desks in government and other public administration institutions. This is the main reason why in most former colonies, the land question is still very much such a topically hot issue which even threatens to cause further civil conflicts.

There is absolutely no question about how land is a natural resource. Everyone would know the reasons why land is a natural resource without even knowing the correct definition of a natural resource. There is also absolutely no question about how land is a basic human need and therefore also a basic human right. Without land, we would simply not be here today. As far as land is concerned, the question would be how can government allow land to be economically exploited for the benefit of the bona fide owners of that land in terms of the net profits thereof? The answer to this question is actually very simple and depends on what the land in question is being used for.

The different uses of land

Land is used primarily for just four major purposes. These are building, agriculture, mining and ecoculture. Building land is used for the construction of such things as houses, other buildings, dams, roads, railway lines, airports, recreation and commercial business centres. Of course, agricultural land is used for all sorts of farming, and mining takes place most underground but on land all the same. Ecoculture is the practice of conserving and preserving land intact, undisturbed and untouched with everything else on it or in it as it naturally was at the beginning and as it would also naturally evolve. This would be done especially for the purposes of ecotourism although conservation alone is also another very good reason for doing that.

Land management obligations of government

Government does not own any piece of land in any given country. The true owners of the land are the communities of people who are naturally found on the land in question. Thus government has absolutely no right to just bulldoze people and communities off their God given land without their consent and without any compensation at all like what was done by most of the former colonialists in the then colonised countries. At national level, all land in any given country belongs to the state and we have already defined what a state is elsewhere in this book. And as the governing and controlling arm of the state, government has the natural duty and obligation to manage all the land in any given country for and on behalf of the state. Management functions include regulating and controlling, strategic planning and resource mobilisation, monitoring, evaluation, systems review and continuous improvement. These must be the only functions of government as far as land administration and management are concerned. The actual using of land or the actually conduction of operations on land, any land based operations for that matter, would not be in the purview of government. Such things would be the sole responsibilities of private individuals and their private businesses as has been repeatedly said in this book before.

As far as land is concerned, the first obligation, duty and responsibility of any government is to put into place land ownership and management laws and regulations which clearly define and spell out who can "own" or occupy what piece of land, where, when, how and why, and for what reasons, but always with the very important caveat that all land and part of the net profits thereof if that land is used for commercial business purposes, eventually belong to the state or the people as it were since the people as a collective make up and also own the state.

Land leaseholds or title deeds

Yes, all land naturally belongs to the state. Individual people can only be holders of various legally recognised land leaseholds or title-deeds which would entitle them to, or give them certain well-defined legal rights, privileges and responsibilities over the land in question. Contrary to what many people think or believe, title-deeds do not legally give or entitle the holder to the actual ownership of the land. They simply just legally entitle or give the holder the responsibility to look after that piece of land, and the right, entitlement or privilege to use that particular piece of land according to its legally designated for use or uses, and most of the time also the right to freely trade the land on the open commercial business market. And it is in this legally recognised and accepted entitlement that the much favoured name "title deeds" actually originated from. The word title here does not refer to "title to the land" as in actual ownership of the land, but it just refers to the entitlement to hold the land and to use and manage it as legally provide for. Just that and nothing more!

There are just about two main types of legally recognised land leaseholds or title-deeds. There are "tradable land leaseholds" and "untradeable" or "non-tradable" land leaseholds. Tradable land leaseholds are the very popular and common so called free title deeds or just "title deeds" which everyone seems to want for themselves erroneously believing that they entitle them to the actual ownership of the land in question. The only thing which is free about tradable title deeds is the freedom to freely trade them on the open commercial business market and nothing else. Otherwise the legally designated use of land which has tradable or "free" title deeds cannot be arbitrarily changed or altered, and neither can the land be arbitrarily surveyed or subdivided with the resultant subdivisions being privately issued with their own individual and separate title deeds. Everything must be authorised and done legally.

Tradable land leaseholds or title deeds

Most urban based land and some commercial agricultural land would normally be parcelled out under tradable title deeds. This is for obvious reasons. Land development is usually a very long and expensive process in terms of input costs. Without financial assistance, most people with the so called "titled land" (just another euphemism for land with tradable title deeds) would not be able to develop that land. Usually, they have to borrow money from banks in order for them to be able to put up any economically and commercially viable developments on their titled land. But moneylenders usually want some sort of surety for their money just in case the borrower fails to pay back for one reason or another. And the best kind of surety is something which has intrinsic, permanent and non-depreciating economic and commercial value. Besides the titled land itself, most people have no other acceptable surety to offer. Such being the case, and for exactly the very same reasons why limited liability companies had to be invented in order to enable huge public and private business investments on borrowed money, tradable land title deeds had to be invented to enable economically and commercially viable land developments to take place at both individual and organisational levels.

Tradable land leaseholds or title deeds can be accessed at either intrinsic or commercial value. For the purposes of human settlements and also coming directly from the state itself, government must always ensure that tradable title deeds are accessed at intrinsic value and not at commercial value, especially by all indigenous people. This is because basic land, or land for human habitation is a basic human right to which everyone is entitled. Such being the case, human settlement land already and by nature belongs to all indigenous people by the grace of the creator. Putting a commercial value on human settlement or housing land is tantamount to selling the land back to the owners of the same land. And that must not be done by government. It would be immoral and unethical. However, between themselves people and organisations must be allowed, empowered and enable by government to trade in their titled land and any other developments thereon at commercial value or whatever best value the market may be willing to shell out. But as must always be the case with commercial business ventures which profit from natural resources as already discussed in Chapters 13 and 14 of this book, government must always get its fair share of the net profits thereof for and on behalf of the state. Perhaps this is one of the main reasons why there are always transfer fees which are paid to Deeds Office whenever land deeds of transfer are registered in the commercial business exchange of tradable land leaseholds or title deeds.

Non-tradable land leaseholds or title deeds

The other legal type, form, or variety of land leasehold or title deeds is the non-tradable type or variety. As the name implies, non-tradable land leaseholds are legally not allowed to be freely traded on the free and open commercial business market by those who hold them. Usually, they give the holder the legal and exclusive right to use the land for very specific purposes and also for a very specific period or length of time. They also usually just make the holder pay a token fee for use of the land, which fee is usually not even of any intrinsic or commercial value. If and when the current holder no longer wishes to retain the leasehold for whatever reason that leasehold would usually automatically revert back to the state. It is only the state which would then re-allocate the leasehold to another new holder. The previous leaseholder would usually have absolutely no say in that matter.

Non-tradable land leaseholds are very common even though they are not very popular. They are not popular simply because they are not tradable and not because they are not useful. In fact, they are some of the most useful land leaseholds around. Non-tradable land leaseholds can be issued to individual people, organisations or whole communities. This is in contrast to tradable land leaseholds which can only be issued to specific individual people or to legally registered and recognised individual organisations or business entities and not to unregistered communities.

At individual and organisational levels, non-tradable land leaseholds are usually issued for such land based activities as commercial agriculture, mining and ecoculture. At community level, such land leaseholds are usually issued for the purposes of communal or rural human settlements and everything else which that entails. Most of the so called communal land is held under non-tradable land leaseholds by communities as a whole and not by individual members of those communities. As such, there would usually be no one in the community who would have in their possession the real legal papers testifying to the existence of the non-tradable land leasehold. Such a legal document, if ever it would be available in the first place, would be kept by government somewhere for and on behalf of the concerned community and the state. And such a document, if available, would also specify that the land in question directly belongs to the concerned community as a whole and not to any single or individual person, and also that eventually and at national level, that land belongs to the state just like any other land in the country. But usually it is only rural or communal land that most people know and understand to be state land or to belong to the state.

As far as the day to day management of communal land is concerned, the state may legally give certain defined and recognised community leaders and organisations such as rural district councils, traditional chiefs, village headmen and any other such civic authorities which might be in existence, very specific and well defined rights and responsibilities to administer that land for and on its behalf but always with the consent or approval of its government.

All land belongs to the state

Within certain well-defined legal confines, limitations and circumstances, the state, as the ultimate owner of all land in any and every country in this world, always has the right to withdraw or re-issue any land leasehold as and when necessary, while at the same time also meticulously paying mandatory, strict and legal attention to the natural and basic human rights of the so affected individual people and their communities. The state, through its government arm, also has the natural obligation, duty, right and responsibility to monitor, evaluate, review and continuously improve land use management countrywide as and when necessary.

Land use management obligations of government

After having examined land management from the angle of the various types of land leasehold options or entitlements which are available, it would now be prudent to examine the same issue from the point of view of land use. As what was alluded to in Chapter 10 of this book under the discussion on food security, national land use management is a very crucial matter which every government must concern itself with. Without proper and legalised land use management frameworks in place, valuable national land can be wasted, completely ruined or destroyed through inappropriate use, misuse or abuse. And to make matters worse, land is a finite and non-renewable natural resource. Destroyed land, once destroyed, can never possibly be reclaimed, recovered or reconstituted. At least not in some millennia to come! As such, it is vitally important that land must be used carefully, conservatively and appropriately or for purposes for which it is naturally best suited. The other reason why land must always be used in a "fit for purpose" approach kind of way is that it is at its most productive if and when used that way. This does not only apply to agricultural land as is obviously the case, but it also applies to all other land uses. Houses and other buildings which would be built on land which is unfit for building houses would always fall apart. Roads which would be built on land which is unsuitable for that purpose would always be unusable. And mining can never be done on unsuitable land even when that land is just rock.

Agricultural land use management

Agricultural land is land which is suitable for agriculture and which must be legally designated and reserved for that purpose alone and nothing else. Of course, there must always be some flexibility and the possibility of re-designation, but that is a thing which must never be done arbitrarily or will-nilly. What is notably very important about agricultural land in relationship to the powers, duties and responsibilities of government is that it is from this land that all the food, and especially staple food, is produced. Remember that food is one of the nine Abraham Maslow defined basic human needs. As such, government must always practically ensure that all agricultural land is profitably used strictly for that purpose alone and nothing else and also used for producing the exact agricultural products in terms of crops which it is naturally best suited for. Government must religiously do this assurance at both the commercial and subsistence levels of production. What this means is that government must continuously monitor, evaluate, review and improve agricultural land use as an ongoing exercise. Otherwise the country might just one day wake up to discover that the reason why it is no longer food secure would be that all of its prime agricultural land was now being illegally used or abused for other purposes other than agriculture or food production. This is because if and when left alone and to do as they please, human beings have this uncanny and oftentimes self-destructive aptitude to do what they want instead of what they really need or must do. They tend to want to do things which give them pleasure, especially instant pleasure or gratification, instead of doing things which they really need to do or which give them deep seated satisfaction or eternal peace, happiness, safety and security. Thus, many times, prime agricultural land best suited for staple food production has been illegally, abusively and inappropriately used for non-food commercial agricultural production with very disastrous consequences for whole countries in terms of food security. Suddenly, countries which would naturally be net exporters of staple foods have found themselves as net importers of the same at such very high cost levels as would shift their balance of trade and economic growth rates from positive to negative in an instant. Now, that is not good or healthy at all for the socioeconomic wellbeing of any country. Only under very exceptional circumstances may land which is best suited for agriculture be used for something else.

Building and construction land use management

Human settlements, both rural and urban, would normally be situated on land which would in all respects be fit for that purpose. There are a lot of things to consider in terms of building construction land use besides just the intrinsic soil types and hydrology thereof. Terrain, drainage, water supply, climate, temperature, seasonal weather patterns, natural vegetation, diseases and pests among other things are some of those very important considerations which must be taken into account when legally designating land use, but especially for human settlement.

In urban areas, human settlement land would be used primarily for the construction of urban houses, factories, shops, schools, hospitals and other individual, public and private buildings. It would also be used for road and railway line construction, water, electricity and other energy supply systems in addition to sewage, industrial and other effluent reticulation systems as well. There would be very little if any agricultural land in urban areas except for very small backyard gardens and plots which some Grandfather Greenfingers or some such other organic food fanatics may be given the leeway to partake in more for the purposes of pacifying their individual fanaticism than for anything else.

As was discussed before in Chapter 10 under the right to shelter, the job of government here is not to build anything for anybody, but to just ensure that any building construction is on designated land, up to standards and fit for purpose. Since most if not all urban land is usually held under tradable land leaseholds or title deeds as has already been explained above, it is from the management and administration of urban land more than from any other land, that the state must reap and actually reaps maximum social and economic benefits in terms of trade and commerce. Be that as it may, the day-to-day commercially profitable management, administration and development of all urban land, just as is the case with any "doing" part of anything and in any other sector of the national economy, must be entrusted into the capable hands of both the private public and private private sectors as always. The urban public sector such as city and town councils and other local government authorities must continue to just stick to their governing and governance roles of seeing to it that government land management policy is implemented to its true letter and spirit on the ground, while at the same time they continue to monitor, evaluate review and continuously recommend improvements to such public policies as and when necessary. The actual development of the land itself must be left entirely in the hands of the private sector and of course always with the usual caveat that the private public sector as represented by public owned business enterprises can also join in on that as well if they so wish.

The intrinsic state benefits from the commercial and business exploitation of urban land as a natural resource must not begin and end with just the deed of transfer fees which were pointed out above. Remember that the major recommendation in this book as far as the commercial business exploitation of all natural resources is that the state and its people as represented by government must always benefit in very big ways in terms of the net profits thereof. That philosophy must be universally applied across the board to the public management and administration of all natural resources from people up to sunshine. Such being the case, government is always entitled to the net profits of the commercial business exploitation of all land in the country, be it in urban or rural areas, and that benefit is even more so when the commercial business ventures in question also commercially exploit other natural resources such as people and their basic needs as their main commercial business trading items for their profitability and survival as business entities. Such being the case, urban based public goods and services commercial business providers such as shops, supermarkets, banks and others thus doubly owe government net profit benefits in this regard. In order to make it easy and understandable for the state to get what it is owed in such cases this due debt must always be built into the basic shareholding structures of all such commercial businesses. Come to think about it, this might apply to just about almost all commercial businesses in any and every given country of this world! Remember that paying taxes is not part of the net profits deal but just part of business input costs.

Mining land and mineral rights management

All sorts of minerals including soil itself are mined on or from land. Mineral and mining rights are usually legally managed by central government for and on behalf of the state as usual. Just like title deeds, mineral and mining rights do not entitle mine owners and their mining companies to the actual ownership of the minerals themselves in terms of intrinsic and commercial value and all. It just entitles them to mine, process and trade in the minerals and also to get commensurate compensation in terms of all input costs including management costs and that is all. The intrinsic and business commercial value of minerals always belongs to the bona fide owners of those minerals, these being the local people and their communities and their countries at large. And that value is all found only in the net profit component of any mining business. Such being the case, what is very important here is that the state must always benefit from the net profits which are made from mining and that these benefits must actually be there for everyone to see and enjoy. No one must ever be allowed to behave as if they actually own any land or the minerals thereof by claiming ownership of the net profits from any mining business. As usual, the running of mines and other mining related businesses must be left in the hands of the private sector. Local communities and the state must just have a fair share of the net profits of all mineral exploitations which take place within them.

Ecoculture land management

As was said at the beginning of this chapter, ecoculture land is land which is legally designated or set aside to be left in its original or natural wild state for the purposes of natural conservation, ecotourism or planned future use. Ecoculture land encompasses land such as nature reserves, game parks and ecological forests. Normally, there would not be any natural human communities inhabiting such land. There usually would only be neighbouring human communities which would occasionally be foraging into such land harvesting its natural resources such as wild animals, fruits, honey, firewood, timber, grass, homeopathic medicines and some such things. In fact ecoculture land must be protected from over-exploitation by local and other communities and government must ensure that it is protected.

In terms of commercial business exploitation, ecoculture land is usually sustainably viable in that regard. Barring natural disasters such as earthquakes, volcanoes, weather extremes and sometimes wild fires, ecoculture land would always be there and intact as ecoculture land. This means that the traded business commodity itself, the ecoculture land and everything else in and on it, would always be there almost free of trading capital input costs. The only input costs which are required for ecoculture would be those which are related to prevention and protection and perhaps a little bit of maintenance in terms of remediating the negative effects of such things as wildfires and soil erosion. Barring such costs, ecoculture land must just be a sitting gold mine in terms of commercial business exploitation.

As simple as that may sound, the day-to-day and profitable commercial business development and exploitation, management and administration of all ecoculture land for and on behalf of the state must always be entrusted into the capable hands of the private sector as usual, and with the usual private public sector caveat of the optional participation of public owned business enterprises (POBEs). The key factor here is capable hands and not who would be doing what. As long as optimum profits are realised, and also as long as the public has a fair share of the final net benefits or profits thereof, everything would be okay.

Chapter 16: Governance of the right to minerals

Minerals as natural resources are probably the most politically contentious natural resources of them all. This is primarily because of the natural and intimate relationship which exists between minerals and land. Land ownership is historically a very hot and hotly contentious issue especially in the colonial and post-colonial worlds. No one may want to own up to this fact today, but the real or main reason for colonialism was natural resources exploitation, especially land, minerals and wildlife. Everything else was just an added bargain or an enabling factor just as colonisation was the biggest enabling factor of them all. Unfortunately, at some point in time, indigenous human beings were also viewed just as natural resources to be commercially exploited and traded by other individual human beings for individual and commercial business gains or profits. Even though this inhuman practice of slave trade and slavery was internationally outlawed centuries ago, it still lingers on today in very many different, subtle and disguised forms. For example, if the routine payment of sub-economic wages and the rampant labour broking which most third world governments allow to happen right under their noses are not tantamount to slavery and slave trade, then perhaps nothing else is tantamount to slavery or slave trade. But then this is just a digression.

Mineral belong to indigenous people

Minerals, just like the land in and on which they are found, belong to the indigenous communities in which they are naturally found. However, with minerals, there is even another special dispensation in terms of the legal claims thereof. This is the no-claim dispensation whereby no one can claim any rights of any sort whatsoever to any minerals which may be discovered by another authorised person on the land on which they may be conducting another different business altogether other than mining or prospecting for minerals. This means that if minerals are discovered on a farm or under a house, the farm or house owner does not have any claim rights to those minerals. However, they would still hold claim rights to the land on and above the ground and the original legally designated land use thereof. But as we have said elsewhere in this book before, even that original land use designation can be legally changed with appropriate compensatory benefits being paid out.

Such being the case as it may, no one must ever be allowed to individually own or say they own minerals even if they are the ones who discovered, extracted or processed them simply because they did not make those minerals or place them into the ground to begin with. They cannot be their minerals. Like all natural resources, minerals were made by nature and placed wherever nature wanted to place them for the social, economic, political, and any other benefit of those people whom nature, in its good wisdom, placed in the same environment as the minerals. It is as simple as all that in terms of mineral rights and ownership. However, and as always, governments can legally allow any capable person or business enterprise to prospect for, extract, refine, process and commercially trade in minerals under certain appropriate and well defined conditions for the benefit of everyone concerned, more especially for the net benefit of local communities and the state as is always the case with all natural resources.

Third world countries are raped of their minerals

When looked at from the point of view of what has been discussed above, one would realise that what is happening in most third world countries in relationship to their minerals and mineral rights is very unfair and not good at all. It borders on mineral rape. Most third world countries have somehow been made to completely abdicate their mineral rights and the minerals thereof to the already super rich first world countries in exchange for so called and so much sought after foreign direct investment (FDI), jobs, taxes, socioeconomic growth and development, prestige and many other such crooked fallacies and pies in the sky. Usually, one hundred percent plus more of the intrinsic and commercial values of the so abdicated minerals are all spirited away back to the investing and already super rich first world countries. This is very, very tragic indeed. What this sad, sorry and tragic phenomenon means is that input cost benefits are the only benefits which usually remain with our naturally mineral rich third world countries after the first world foreign mineral exploiters are finished with the business of commercial exploitation of those minerals. At the end of the day, who exactly would be the benefactor and who would be the beneficiary in such a scenario? The answer to this rhetorical question must be pretty obvious to anyone who is honest and God fearing. The real beneficiary here is the one who runs away with and eats all or the biggest chunk of the net profits of the exploitation of minerals and not the supposed natural owners of these mineral resources who only get away with business input costs and nothing else much. Remember that without the permanent and local retention of the net business or investment profits within the local economy, there cannot be any socioeconomic growth and development at national level. Real socioeconomic growth and development or real expansion of the national economy can only happen or take place at the place where net business or economic benefits or profits are consumed and not where they are spirited away from. This is how the west has underdeveloped Africa!

The paradox of foreign direct investment (FDI)

As alluded to above, the building blocks of real national socioeconomic growth and development are the next profit benefits of any economic production process because it is the net profits which at the end of the day determine the direction of the bottom line in terms of the net expansion or shrinkage of the economy at national level. Economic production process input costs such as the so called foreign direct investment (FDI), jobs and their salaries, wages and any other employment related benefits, all taxes, and any other input costs, do not make any national economy grow. The main reasons for this is that all of these economic production process input costs are usually all eventually recovered in full and with interest too from the total income which would be generated by the initial investment, be it FDI or local. And as is normally the case with any cost recovery, all the recovered investment costs would accrue to the original investor. And if the original investor is foreign, it means that the much touted FDI always goes back home where it came from with some healthy and profitable interest too [1]. And to make things worse, in the sorry case of our third world mineral rich countries under discussion here, that FDI investment also goes back home with all the net profits thereof, thereby leaving our poor but mineral rich third world countries even poorer than before because they would no longer be mineral rich anymore. If this is not a tragic phenomenon, then perhaps nothing else would be tragic in this world. What many third world and particularly African countries do not seem to know is that there is not a single country in this world which has ever economically grown or developed through foreign direct investment (FDI). Excessive foreign ownership of a national economy can in fact be harmful [2].

Reclamation of mineral rights

But it is always right to look at the bright side of things. And the bright side of things here is that all mineral rich third world countries may not always remain oblivious forever to the uncalled for minerals bleeding which happens to them courtesy of FDI. As they wise saying goes, one may be able to fool all the people sometimes, but one would never be able to fool all the people all the times.

However, as sad as this situation may be right now, the possibility of redress in third world mineral bleeding to the first world is very remote, but the possibility of cessation of that bleeding is always there, sooner or later. Sooner or later, someone in the third world will wake up to the fact that minerals, as is the case with all natural resources, rightfully belong to those to whom they were given by nature or by the creator. These are the indigenous people and their respective communities. And sooner or later, someone will know that foreign direct investment (FDI) is not an economic production process benefit but an economic production process cost which must and is always eventually paid for. And sooner or later someone will also know that the real economic benefits from and of the commercial business exploitation of any natural resources at national level, minerals included, are the net production or commercial business profits thereof and not the business input costs as represented by the so much loved new jobs and expanded tax bases regardless of what the politicians and their business allies say. And sooner or later, someone will know that it is the final destination of these net profits which really matter in terms of real economic growth or the net shrinkage or expansion of the national economy. And when that day arrives, third world countries will stop haemorrhaging minerals to the west. They will harness all of their natural and creator given wealth for their own human, social and economic development as it must have been all these years. That day is coming and it will arrive one day.

As much as the day of resurrection or reckoning, the day on which poor third world countries shall wake up to re-claim what is rightfully theirs in terms of taking back direct charge of their own mineral rights and all other natural resources is coming, a word of caution is very much needed here. It is one thing to redress a historical injustice or imbalance and quite another to perpetrate a worse injustice in the name of redressing a previous one. That must never be allowed to happen. There are many just and fair ways and means by which any historical injustices can be redressed without committing more or even worse injustices in the process. And those ways and means must be found and used. For example, most historical injustices cannot be redressed at individual levels. They can only be redressed at national or government to government level. Such being the case, it is only governments which can and must compensate other governments and their people at national level in redress of historical injustices and not individual people or businesses.

Chapter 17: Democratic governance of the right to water

Water is vital for life

Water is a well recognised, vital and very important natural resource which is usually only remembered as such when it becomes scare for one reason or another. There is no question about water being a natural resource because no one manufactures the bulk of the water which we access and use every day. Purification is not the same thing as manufacturing *de novo* or from scratch. There is also no question about the basic necessity of water to all life on earth. This makes water one of the most important basic human needs perhaps only coming behind oxygen. Such being the case, everyone's natural right to water is a given.

A person can go on for weeks without eating any food on hunger strike, but if that person does not also drink water, he or she would not last for a couple of days maximum. Death from dehydration would be a sure thing. That is how vital water is to life. Maybe this is one of the main reasons why in many cultures on this planet if there is just one thing which is apt to be handed out for free and immediately on request, it is drinking water. No one refuses a request for drinking water and no one asks for any payment thereof either. If you ask for drinking water even from a total stranger and it is available, you get it, no questions asked.

Because of its vital importance, one of the most basic and critical considerations when positioning human settlements is the availability of reliable sources of water for drinking and other uses. Human settlements do not thrive where there are no permanent and reliable sources of water. From history, water supply based community and national wars have been fought with one community wanting to own one natural water source or body to the exclusion of another community. At the end of such tug-of-wars, people have usually come to their senses and realised that water, as a gift from the creator, belongs to everyone.

Water is a shared natural resource

In today's world people have come to their senses and realised that water is a shared natural resource, especially the water which is found in natural water bodies such as underground, rivers, seas, natural lakes and oceans. Even the water which may be found in artificial water bodies such as man-made dams and lakes does not exactly belong to anyone in particular but to everybody in the sense that such bodies only harness water which is already there in natural water bodies such as rivers or underground water.

The realisation of the shared character of water and natural water bodies has made people appreciate the fact that one community or country cannot just do as it pleases with that portion of a natural water body such as a river or lake which happens to be on its side without considering the interests of other communities or countries with which it shares such natural or even artificial water bodies. The international community has come together on this issue and put in place binding international water laws which may not just be overlooked willy-nilly because there would be dire international consequences for doing that. Thus, as far as very large natural water bodies such as seas and oceans are concerned, demarcations have been made delineating boundaries between international waters where no one can lay any claim rights to, and national territorial waters where countries can and are allowed to lay national claim rights to. But even territorial waters are not one hundred percent territorial in that any country cannot just do whatever it pleases with its own territorial waters. Water and water bodies are shared resources which must always remain shared, be they international or territorial. For example, no one may refuse a distressed ship and its sailors anchorage in any port and for whatever reason.

Anyway, at national level, no one must ever be allowed to privately and completely own water, water bodies or any waterways such as rivers, dams, oceans and seas. All these things belong to the state and the state must as usual have a sizeable stake in the final net profits thereof should such natural resources be exploited for commercial business purposes. But as usual, the profitable economic exploitation and management of water and water bodies can be placed in the hands of the most capable enterprises, whether private public or completely private. There can also be an entrepreneurial collaboration between the public and private sectors in this regard. As long as the state reaps maximum net profit benefits at the end of the day, in most cases it does not really matter as to who exploits or administers which natural resource.

Management and administration of essential services

Water together with electricity and other energy supplies deserve special consideration in terms of management and administration at local community level. Without constant, continuous and completely reliable supplies of water and energy there would not be any households or communities to talk about, let alone household or community economies at all. No home or household can endure a day or two without any water whatsoever or without any form of energy at all. As far as household energy is concerned, we shall just use electricity as an example although in some countries natural gas and coal generated heat also play very important roles as essential energy services as well.

The special consideration as far as water and electricity supply are concerned is that while government must ensure that people have access to these basic human needs and therefore also basic human rights, government would not be the preferred producer or supplier of these services as has been repeatedly said in this book. And yet because of the vital nature of these essential services, governance issues in terms of service production and availability, service delivery and accessibility, and service costs and affordability thereof must be so carefully and closely attended to and monitored by government to the extent that government inevitably also becomes part and parcel of the entire service delivery exercise or process itself.

Double exploitation of natural resources

The other special consideration in the case of water and energy is that the biggest customers of water and electricity supply services in terms of aggregate service consumption are people or the public at individual household level. Thus, water and electricity supply services, in addition to also being products of natural resources themselves, also exploit the natural resources which people actually are, and their basic human needs which are also their basic human rights, for commercial business purposes and benefits or profits.

And yet to begin with, water, as in direct household use water, is also a natural resource as is also the water, coal, sunshine or nuclear reactive minerals which may be used to generate the electricity which is supplied to the very same households. What this means is that as services which are produced from natural resources, the state must benefit from the commercial business exploitation of water and electricity at the production level first and foremost, and also benefit from the same at the consumption level as well because of the commercial business exploitation of yet another natural resource in the form of people at that level.

Water and electricity supply leverage

Local governments can strategically leverage on water and electricity supply services to manage and administer certain important aspects of land development, more especially with regards to human settlements, housing and building legal standards and practices. One thing which is a big and unsightly blot on the faces of many urban settlements in sub-Saharan Africa and other third world countries is the huge problem of unauthorised or illegal buildings and settlements or squatter camps. For such illegal settlements to thrive, they obviously need constant supplies of water and electricity. Leaving the supply of water and electricity entirely in the hands of the private sector under such circumstances may mean the mushrooming of even more illegal buildings and squatter camps all over the show. This is because even in the presence of legal prohibitions, completely private suppliers of water and electricity would always put profits ahead of any other considerations. And once an illegal community of people has thus been illegally connected to water and electricity supplies, disconnecting them from such illegal supplies would definitely have such political fallouts as no government politician would ever want to fathom, let alone have on his or her own hands.

POBEs are the best option for essential services delivery

Such being the case as described above, the best way to approach the supply and delivery of very basic and absolutely essential public services such as water, electricity, transport and others may be through the use of private public business enterprises such as public owned business enterprises (POBEs). As long as the doctrine of the complete and practical separation of both powers and people is strictly adhered to as detailed in Chapter 6 and many other chapters of this book, there would be absolutely no challenge in the use of POBEs to provide certain very basic and essential public services such as the ones enumerated herein and above. And the use of such POBEs would actually kill several birds with just one stone.

First of all, the use of POBEs in the delivery of certain essential pubic services would guarantee and not just ensure that people access their basic human needs as well as their basic human rights without fail. Secondly, it would also ensure that the state benefits in full and not just in the form of a share of the commercial business profits thereof, from the exploitation of all the natural resources which are involved in these kinds of service delivery right from service production and down to service delivery itself. Thirdly, the use of POBEs would also mean that the state can use the supply, delivery and consumption of such essential public services to manage and enforce legal compliance with certain public service standards, rules, regulations and codes of practice such as settlements, building and housing standards as has already been alluded to above. Fourth, POBEs would guarantee that those who cannot afford paying for essential services may still access them in the sense that government can always subsidise such costs through the POBEs themselves. Government can prohibit the concerned POBEs from denying such essential services to those who cannot pay, and to bill government directly instead, but of course always with the necessary verifications being done in order to prevent any corruption or fraud. POBEs would be a real quadruple catch here!

All essential services must be guaranteed

Access to essential services must be guaranteed and not just ensured or assured. Essential services are those human needs or services which are absolutely necessary for both physiological and social wellbeing. All basic human needs supply services, public safety and security services, all public and environmental health services and public emergency response services are some of the most obvious essential services which may easily come to mind. The best way to guarantee access to and the delivery of all essential services would be to entrust them in the hands of private sector public owned commercial business companies dubbed public owned business enterprises (POBEs).

As was discussed elsewhere in this book, POBEs must always be efficiency, effectiveness and profit oriented as well just like any other private sector commercial business enterprises if they are going to survive or make it in the world of business. But as public owned entities, they must also be equally focussed on service delivery itself in terms of availability, affordability and accessibility. In their service delivery pricing models, POBEs would not be expected to remain completely fixated on exacting maximum profit gains at each and every turn of the business, and at all costs as well. But they would be expected to only ensure such profits as would simultaneously guarantee both their survival as commercial business entities while at the same time also guaranteeing service availability, affordability and accessibility to all those in need of the essential services which they offer.

Thus POBEs would not be expected to conduct business for the sake of business alone in terms of service delivery, but business for the sake of the general public good as well. This would mean that sometimes just breaking even would be good enough for POBEs if such would be the level of business operations which would guarantee the accessibility of their services to everyone who might need them. This inborn human business spirit or attitude of POBEs is the one thing which sets them apart from the privately owned, privately operated and privately beneficiating commercial business enterprises.

POBEs must do business more with their hearts than with their heads. Their profit margins must just be enough to ensure business survival and not so much as to make their services unaffordable and hence inaccessible to the majority of the people who may need them. In fact, the basic and essential services which POBEs would provide must remain accessible to almost everyone if not actually to everyone in need regardless of capacity to pay. This is what social protection is all about and POBEs are there to ensure that everyone is guaranteed access to social protection.

Access to essential services may not be denied

And what is more, the supply of basic or essential services must not be arbitrarily denied for whatever reasons, and this includes even for the reasons of incapacity to pay. Denial of basic or essential services when they are needed may actually be more than just a death sentence in itself. It may be the same as the actual process of execution itself! If and when left completely in the hands of purely private business enterprises, the delivery of some very basic and essential services such as medical ambulance services may lead to daily and multiple such executions for reasons of incapacity to pay. And that would be very inhuman, cruel and unacceptable for any government of the people by the people for the people to do. This is perhaps the main reason why POBEs are the best delivery vehicles for all basic and essential services in any country.

Chapter 18: Democratic governance of the right to wildlife

Wildlife as natural resources

Wildlife refers to wild plants and animals as opposed to domestic plants and animals. Apparently, everyone knows and understands why and how wild things are natural resources. No one seems to need to be reminded that wild things were not created or caused by man but by nature. Perhaps the main reason for this natural awareness of wildlife as natural resources emanates from the fact that these resources are already in the wild and also the fact that that is where all human beings came from, or how all of us as human beings came through to be where we are today. Never mind the fact that some people now want to see other people, especially of the *Homo sapiens var negroid* variety, as still being more wildlife or more in the wild than them. That is called racism and it is uncalled for.

Wildlife belongs to the state

With everyone being that very much aware of the naturalness of wildlife, it therefore goes without saying that wildlife first and foremost belongs to the community in which it is found, and eventually to the state as a whole. No one must ever be allowed to own or say that they own wildlife even when such may be found in an enclosure built by that person around such natural wildlife. For that reason, nature reserves and natural game parks should never and can never be privatised. They always belong to the people or the state. But the state, through its government, can legally give concessions to private commercial businesses to exploit, manage and administer wildlife based economic and other business ventures. However, that does not mean that the wildlife now belongs to the private business person or people concerned. Wildlife remains the property of the state at all material times. And as usual, the state must always enjoy the lion's share of the net benefits of the commercial business exploitation of all of its natural resources including wildlife as has repeatedly been said in this book. That must not change.

The right to wildlife

Although wildlife based commercial business ventures cannot be said to offer essential services by definition, local or indigenous people must not be prevented from enjoying their creator given wildlife by prohibitive service charges such as exorbitant entry fees to national parks and game reserves. The temptation here would be to say that such entry fees must be waivered for locals, but as is the dictum in this book, there is absolutely nothing which is for free or must be for free in this world. Even the air which we freely breathe in and out all the time is not exactly for free if one comes to think of it because without the physiological effort of breathing it in and out, the free air would never freely enter and exit anyone's lungs. Thus, service fees at wildlife sanctuaries such as national parks and game parks must be generally affordable to all locals, but first of all, such fees must at least be enough to run and maintain such facilities as sustainable and viable commercial business entities without destroying them or bankrupting the business aspect of doing that. This would be the correct approach which every concerned stakeholder must be encouraged to take and not just the doctrine or stance of free things.

In the same vein as alluded to above in terms of availability, accessibility and affordability of services, where wildlife exploitation for the purposes of pleasure and not for commercial business purposes may be allowed such as in recreational fishing and game hunting, the same nominal charges must apply. But where wildlife exploitation would be for business or commercial purposes, then the full commercial value of the exploited wildlife must be charged and recovered. Such an entrepreneurial approach must be possible to implement with such things as commercial business logging, fishing and game hunting among others. However, the recovery of the full commercial value does not mean leaving the other business person with absolutely no profit margin at all. That would not make business sense. Just about enough money must be charged to pay for the maintenance of the park plus just a little bit more to put on the side for a rainy day and not much more so as to get rich out of it or so as to put the other party out of business.

The best wildlife management entities

The need to keep profit margins at nominal levels in the case of wildlife resources exploitation gives rise to a special dispensation in the way in which wildlife must be managed at national level. As we have already said before in this book, although private private sector commercial business enterprises would probably be the best to manage wild life resources in terms of both quality of service delivery and the profits thereof, such business enterprises may not be very appropriate here or even voluntarily willing to do so themselves because of the nominal profit margins involved. Where the private private sector has been roped in to manage wildlife resources based commercial business services, such services have become completely inaccessible to the poor, and especially to the local indigenous people who usually and correctly so too, view access to such wildlife as their God given right. What that inaccessibility has done in most cases is to pit local communities, who usually know better about the concerned wildlife than any non-local wildlife expert may care to claim, against the designated commercial business mangers of that wildlife. Instead of normal, controlled and conservative wildlife harvesting, such contested wildlife has unfortunately always been the victim of rampant, reckless and destructive poaching and some such other undesirable happenings. In such conflicts, the aggrieved locals would always win hands down for obvious reasons (they always know their wildlife better than anyone else) and the wildlife would always lose both ways. Thus, the private private sector probably has very little role to play in wildlife management unless, of course, if it would be willing to be more service delivery oriented than profit oriented as the private public sector (POBEs) would be under such circumstances.

Community based wildlife management

In order to prevent wildlife poaching and also in order to bring in the vitally important local community participation in that respect, it would be prudent for mangers of wildlife to practically demonstrate the tangible socioeconomic benefits of proper wildlife conservation and management to local and surround communities. Without local and surrounding communities' participation and buy-in, wildlife management and conservation would remain very problematic for everyone concerned. Local communities must always be consulted and involved in decision making and sometimes even in operations too. That would be the best way to ensure that they understand and appreciate why things must be done the way wildlife management experts would usually insist that they must be done. Sometimes, management ends up being taught one or two correct or good things by locals in that regard, even as uneducated as they may seem to be at first. Everyone must remember that unrestricted wildlife exploitation is second nature to all human beings. That is how all human beings were like during their nomadic days. People would just plunder all the available wildlife in their area and then relocate to another fresh area once the other one had been "finished" in terms of wildlife exploitation.

The days of nomadic life may be well and truly behind us, but ardent nomads still exist in all of us in terms of our basic and natural instinctive predispositions as human beings. The thought, idea and practice of wildlife conservation are not the sort of things which come naturally to us as human beings. They are things which we really need to and must be constantly reminded of and also convinced about. Just watch out how when people are gathering wild fruits they don't just gather the fruits alone but sometimes needlessly gather the branches as well or even the whole fruit trees themselves too! It is really amazing, but that is what we are like as natural or wild human beings. We do not seem to be naturally awake to the immense value of the trees and grass which we did not plant, for example, or of animals which we did not rear, domesticate or look after. Such being the case, wildlife management experts have the duty, responsibility and task of explaining, educating and demonstrating to local communities both the values and benefits of good wildlife conservation, management and harvesting techniques.

Local communities must visibly benefit from wildlife

The best way to practically demonstrate the value of good wildlife conservation and management would be to also let local communities share in the profits thereof at both individual and community levels. Local individual and community participation in wildlife management and conservation as already suggested above would be superb, but it must not just end at doing the work without also realising the profit benefits thereof. Without the enjoyment of the benefits thereof, there would be no confirmation of the validity of the claim that wildlife conservation pays. It is as simple as all that. Such being the case, once in a while when wildlife is being harvested, local communities must be given small but significant individual family portions of it or the net business profits thereof so that they too could see for themselves and with their very own eyes that it actually pays to appropriately conserve and manage wildlife. If such is done, there would be no telling how much useful information, knowledge and wisdom these local people would be willing to come forth with in terms of managing and conserving wildlife even much better than any trained college or even university graduate in wildlife conservation and management could ever dream of.

Chapter 19: The right to air and airspace

Air and airspace are obvious natural resources and also obvious basic human needs and therefore obvious basic human rights as well. And yet the right to air and airspace are basic human rights which not many people are usually aware of. The reason for this could be that under normal circumstances air is freely available to everyone in the free and open space around them, so no one ever thinks of the possibility of someone denying them that air or airspace. The only time when someone may become aware of the need to ensure that there is always clean and respirable air all around them is perhaps when there happens to be massive, persistent and respiratory airways irritating air pollution from one cause or another so much so that normal breathing is adversely affected. Otherwise most of the time, nobody cares that much about the air which freely moves around them or the air which they breathe. And yet breathing air is so vital that without it there would be no life in less than five minutes flat! Without air there would be no plant or animal life on earth as we know it today. Even the plants and animals which live in water need breathing air in order for them to survive.

The right to free air and free airspace for free

Air and airspace are unique natural resources in that unlike other natural resources they are not only for free (i.e. no payment is needed) but they are also freely available. Air and airspace are freely available everywhere and as such there is no need to look for or gather them from the wild. All natural resources are for free, but they are not as freely available as air and airspace. For example, one has to go out there and fetch water in order to have it, mine and process minerals in order to have them, hunt for and gather wildlife in order to have it, look for and settle on land in order to have it. But with air and airspace, one does not have to do anything of that sort because these things are already there all around us since we live in and around them at all times. This is just as it is by the grace of God, and perhaps also as it should be. What this means is that the right to air and airspace must not just be the right to air and airspace, but it must be far more than that. It must be the right to free air and free airspace and for free as well with emphasis on the word free because naturally free, un-trapped, unrestricted and uncontrolled is the way in which air and airspace are and were made to be accessible and available to man for free. So in reality, people have the right to free air and free airspace and for free as well, and not just the right to air and airspace. The distinction and emphasis on free air and free airspace for free as well is very significant as we shall see later on in a moment.

The right to clean free air

As a vital requirement for life, the right to free air and for free as well is a foregone conclusion. Of course, people do not just have the right to free air for free, but they also have the right to clean free air for free. The reason for this is that un-free or enclosed air is unnatural air in that it is not the state or way in which air is natural available. And un-free or enclosed air is more often than not unclean air as well because of that unnatural presentation. Unclean air is unhealthy air to breathe or live in. Unhealthy air causes diseases and death. These are the reasons why people must have the right to clean free air and airspace and not just the right to air and airspace. The reason why naturally available air and airspaces are unrestricted, unconfined or free is that it is that freedom which makes natural air and airspaces healthy or disease free. Confined air in confined airspaces would quickly become unhealthy once used if it was not already unhealthy in the first place just because of that confinement alone. Such being the case, and as far as the right to clean free air and airspaces for free is concerned, government must ensure that people access clean and healthy free air for free anywhere, everywhere and at all times. The only pertinent question here is how government does that and not why it must do it.

Legally mandatory natural ventilation

Of course and as always, legislation is the answer to how government must ensure that people access their right to clean free air and for free. Starting at household level, government must put in place and enforce such housing and building legal and other standards which would ensure the continuous unrestricted or free movement of clean free air in and out of all residential homes, houses, buildings and any other confined spaces or places where people may stay, sleep or work. Natural air, the freely moving and usually clean air which is available all around us, must be enabled to continuously and freely move in and out of all buildings and any other confined spaces and places even when all the doors, windows and other closable inlets or outlets of such buildings, places and spaces are air-tightly closed because natural ventilation is the only way by which the constant availability of clean, fresh and healthy free air inside such buildings and confined spaces can be ensured. Artificial ventilation cannot always be trusted or relied upon to provide fresh, clean and healthy free air inside any building or confined space whether residential or workplace. Such being the case, there must be legal requirements that in every building or confined space or place where people live, reside, stay or work, natural ventilation must always be enabled, ensured and practically functional at optimum levels and at all material times too. And that legal requirement must be strictly enforced, adhered to and monitored at all times.

Building ventilation standards

In Chapter 10 and under the right to shelter, we talked a bit about building and housing standards. We said that one of the major drivers of airborne and other diseases was poor building standards, particularly poor housing standards. This is absolutely very true and especially very true where such standards do not include the enablement of constant and adequate natural ventilation in each and every building which houses people. Artificial ventilation such as closable doors and windows or even blow in and blow out extractor fans would never be good enough at continuously supplying clean free air into buildings and other confined spaces. The reason is that in very cold weather conditions, the natural tendency for everyone would be to tightly close all windows and doors through which the cold may supposedly enter without even thinking about it or any other consequences thereof besides the locking out of the biting cold. Such being the case, building legal standards must ensure that all buildings and places where people are found would have appropriate, appropriately positioned, properly inserted, adequate and fixed, built-in and un-closable continuous natural ventilation devices such as louvers, permavents, ventilation sieves, holes and some such other gadgets. Such permanent ventilation devices would ensure that air can freely move in and out of confined spaces at all times.

Poor building ventilation standards

Many third world countries always seem to neglect the proper enforcement of their own building standards and usually pay very heavy prices in airborne disease tolls for that kind of behaviour. I have the habit of checking on the availability of adequate natural ventilation in every building which I enter. This habit has left me heart broken in most instances, especially in third world countries. For example, the spare bedroom in which I am sitting right now as I am writing this book has absolutely no natural ventilation at all, just like all the other rooms in this supposedly high end (by local standards) and spacious three bed-roomed rented apartment of mine. There is just one window on one of the four walls and a standard door on the other wall leading into the corridor and that's it. In fact, all the rooms in this apartment just boast of one window and one door on an opposite wall each and no any other openings whatsoever! When both the door and the window are closed with just one person inside, this spare bedroom starts to smell of breathed air in just a few minutes. What about if there were two or more people, and what about for the whole night? Just what kind of air in terms of quality would prevail in this room under such circumstances? And what if we add just one other person with open tuberculosis (TB) into the room for example, what would be the chances of the other roommates avoiding to contract TB in just one night of sharing this bedroom with such a person? I will tell you what those chances are. They are nil. Anyone who would be unfortunate enough to spend just a few hours, let alone one whole night with an open TB sufferer in this bedroom would be guaranteed to contract the disease there and then and there is no doubt about it. And yet this is supposed to be a high end apartment!

I can go on and also tell you that if you spray perfume in any part of, or in any room in this high end rented apartment of mine, the smell of that perfume would always end up in the main bedroom upstairs for some reason perhaps known only to or by seasoned architects and building construction engineers! It does not matter whether all the doors and windows would be open or closed; the destination of the perfume would always be the same – the main bedroom upstairs! What this alarming phenomenon means is that the TB buggies from our open TB sufferer in this downstairs spare bedroom would also always end up in the main bedroom upstairs! And I have not even started telling you about the perpetually soggy and mouldy atmosphere in the bathrooms and the total absence of any sound proofing whatsoever which allows me to hear everything which would be happening in the adjacent apartment. And by everything I mean every little thing including the opening squeaks of a door, let alone its closing bang. I am sure the neighbours hear a lot of noises from my side too!

If such is the state of my high end rented apartment in terms of building standards, what about the rest of the other apartments, houses, industrial and commercial buildings and rooms in town and in the whole country at large? Would other less than high end building structures be in much better or worse state than my revered place of abode? The correct answer would be perhaps not much better at all and maybe even worse than my place. Would you then wonder why if I also told you that this country in which I am sitting right now as I write this book has the unenviable position of being one of the countries with the highest rates of TB and HIV infections in the whole world? These are the sort of things which poor building standards can do to any country!

Comprehensive and holistic building standards

Of course, there is more to and bout building standards than just natural ventilation alone. Natural lighting, temperature and humidity control standards are also and equally very important considerations among many other things. A comprehensive and holistic approach is the best approach to take as far as building standards are concerned. This would ensure that all other important issues are not overlooked while too much attention would be lavished on just one aspect alone. Natural and other ventilation standards are particularly very important in buildings, rooms or confined places which are occupied or used by many people at the same time such as classrooms, lecture rooms, churches and public halls. They are also very important in public transport vehicles such as kombis, buses and trains. Such standards are also vital in industrial workplaces such as stores, supermarkets, offices, factories, and underground mines.

Perhaps underground mines and similar confined places deserve special mention here. This is because although natural ventilation must also be ensured in underground mines, it is usually not enough and must therefore always be properly, adequately and appropriately augmented by artificial ventilation and also because air quality control is very paramount in such places. Air quality in the mines must be closely controlled, monitored and appropriately adjusted almost on the go in terms of dust content, humidity, temperature and any other impurities thereof, otherwise the health, safety and wellbeing of miners would be compromised in very big and very bad ways.

If there is one place which clearly brings out the real value of freely moving clean free air, it is the mines. Pneumoconioses are permanently disabling dusty lung diseases which mostly afflict miners just because of poor ventilation and poor air quality control standards which sometimes prevail in certain mines, especially illegal mines. Thousands and thousands of miners have been adversely affected by pneumoconioses, especially of the silicosis variety over the years and most of them have not even been compensated as they should have been. This is really unfortunate. However, prevention is the correct answer here and not compensation. Compensation would not bring back dust damaged lungs and neither would it prolong life.

Prevention of airborne diseases

The disease pulmonary tuberculosis (TB) is not the only airborne disease there is although it is one of the most well known airborne disease. Airborne diseases are many. There are other airborne diseases such as pneumonia, pneumonic plague, influenza, coryza, pneumocystis carinii pneumonitis, brucellosis, measles and many, many others. Ventilation control, among many other measures goes a very long way towards prevention of airborne diseases. The bigger portion of the pulmonary TB which we have seen in this world comes about as a result of poor ventilation standards alone especially in residential buildings. Even in the presence of human immunodeficiency virus (HIV) infection, one still needs to be infected with TB bacteria from breathing in TB infested air in order for one to suffer from HIV related pulmonary TB. In the absence of such infection, then there would be no contraction of pulmonary TB even if HIV still persists in the blood. It is not as if once one has HIV then one also gets pulmonary TB from out of the blues.

In fact, as far as disease control through the improvement of living standards alone is concerned, TB presents a very special and classic case as an example. TB infection rates in the United Kingdom (UK) declined to almost their present day levels starting from the mid nineteenth century because of improvements in the general standards of living alone and without much use of any medicinal drugs at all. And building standards alone, especially ventilation control, played a very crucial role in that decline. Of course, there were a myriad of other improved living standards which helped out as well such as nutritional, personal and environmental hygiene standards among others, but building standards, especially residential building standards of the Victorian era, prominently stood out amongst them.

Air traffic rights

Atmospheric air and the general airspace around the world and over all countries are exploited as natural resources in commercial business enterprises dealing with air transport and radio and telecommunication operations. All these things or activities would probably constitute what should be called the air traffic industry, but whenever air traffic is mentioned people are apt to think of air transport as in human beings travelling by air and not of any other things such as radio and other electromagnetic waves sharing the very same airspace as well in terms of travelling or being trafficked, but not necessarily travelling by air as in being supported by air as they travel or get transmitted. Electromagnetic and radio waves do not travel by air but travel or are trafficked or transmitted in the empty space or vacuum in which the air is also housed or found. Without this empty space or vacuum, there would probably be nowhere where the air which we breathe and use for transport purposes would be contained in the atmosphere around us. Such being the case, air traffic rights would refer to the rights to both the air filled space and the empty airspace or vacuum for the purposes of trafficking either aeroplanes and other air transport devices, or for trafficking radio and other electromagnetic waves.

Air transport rights

As has just been pointed out above, besides being vital for life to exist, natural atmospheric air is also used for transport purposes not only by birds and other flying animals, but also by human beings. Air transport is a very recent phenomenon as compared to other modes of transport such as road and railway transport, but it has quickly become almost essential because of the long distances it can cover in very short periods of time. Unless if it is purely for the fun of it, no one today can ever contemplate an overseas trip or journey by road or railway transport interconnected by sea. Such a journey has got to be strictly by air and nothing else. That is how essential air transport has become.

Countries naturally own the atmospheric airspace in and around them. International laws and treaties have also confirmed this natural right of countries and their people. Such being the case, unauthorised intrusions into another country's airspace would be illegal and appropriately frowned upon. In air travel, airlines have to get permission in the form of licences in order for them to be allowed to use the airspace at both national and international levels. No one can start an airline business and just fly to wherever and whenever they want. Airline licensing would normally be done by a state agency and not government because the airspace, just like any other natural resources, belongs to the state and not to government as we have repeatedly pointed out in this book. Such being the case, it is the state as a whole which must also exact maximum benefits from the exploitation of its airspace for commercial business purposes such as airline businesses. And as usual, the state through its government would be very much discouraged from also directly partaking in airline commercial business operations unless if it does so through the usual private public business corporations called public owned business enterprises (POBEs) or corporations (POBCs) as previously discussed at length in other chapters of this book.

Communication rights

As human beings, we just do not live on earth only, but we also live in the airspace or atmosphere around the earth as well. Of course as already discussed above, without the natural air in that space we would not live. But for there to be air in that space, the empty space itself must first of all exist as an empty space. And this is the space which we are referring to here as airspace in terms of communication rights. Such space which is devoid of air is called a vacuum. Radio and other electromagnetic waves which we use for our daily telecommunications through so called cell phones are trafficked, transported or transmitted in that vacuum or empty space. In fact, the presence of solid objects or other solid particles other than just pure natural air actually interferes with the transportation and transmission of these radio and electromagnetic waves. This is the reason why cloudy weather is usually not so good for internet services especially narrow bandwidth services.

Even though the radio and electromagnetic space in and around a country cannot be physically defined, it would be necessary to somehow define that space in order to prevent the chaos and disorder which would arise from any and every country doing whatever it pleases with any and every radio and electromagnetic waves it fancies. Such chaos and disorder would make both radio and telecommunications completely impossible. Anyone who was ever caught up in crossed radio frequencies or crossed telephone lines would understand this very well. As a result of this need for law and order, and through the agency of an international body called the International Telecommunications Union (ITU), the world saw it fit to even ensure that each and every country has been allocated its very own radio and other electromagnetic waves bandwidth or space which it owns and controls as much as it owns and controls the actual atmospheric airspace which surrounds it. This space is earmarked by each and every country's given international standard dialling code. These international standard dialling codes actually denote given wavelength bandwidths in terms of radio and other electromagnetic waves which bandwidths are strictly reserved for ownership, control and access by those specific and individual countries alone. The international standard dialling codes also define the relationship between countries all over the world in terms of interconnectivity through radio and electromagnetic waves. Countries are thus supposed to generate, transmit and receive radio and other electromagnetic waves for the purposes of communication only within their own given international standard dialling code bandwidths both within and outside of their borders. Countries can also allocate subdivisions of these radio and telecommunications wave bandwidths to any commercial business ventures for commercial business exploitation such as the provision of internet and cell phone services. But just like any other natural resources, these allocated electromagnetic wave bandwidths still belong to the state and the state must always reap its fair share of the final profits thereof as always. Internet and telecommunications businesses owe the state doubly in this regard because at local or national level, such commercial business ventures actually exploit another natural resource in the form of people and their internet and telecommunications needs for commercial business purposes. Remembers that both transport and communication are basic human needs and as such they are also basic human rights as well, while air and airspace are natural resources, basic human needs and also basic human rights as well. Thus, the state has quite some stake in commercial internet and telecommunications businesses! Consequently, apart from collecting licence and other fees, national governments must also collect a good share of the net profit cheques from all air and airspace based transport and communication businesses such as airline, cell-phone and internet service businesses.

Chapter 20: Right to sunshine

The sun is vital for life on earth

The sun provides us with two things, sunlight and sunheat. Besides enabling photosynthesis to take place and thereby giving life to everything on earth from plants to animals, sunlight itself gives rise to the phenomenon which we call day and night and our diurnal lifestyles. Sunheat ensures that we all do not freeze to death on this earth. I cannot imagine what kind of a day it would be if the sun never came out one day! But then if there is something which human beings are so sure of to the point of overconfidence, it is sunrise. They have even coined a phrase for it – as sure as sunrise, they always say. One just wonders what would happen should for whatever reason that overconfidence about sunrise gets shattered one day. But of course, and as always, the religious amongst us would say that they know what would happen. And you would never win an argument against these religious people even if you tried. The best which mere mortals like us can do is to just hope that such a day never comes while we are still here.

Sunlight and sunheat are natural resources

The sun is perhaps the only one thing which most people, religious or not, are agreed that it must have been created. Apparently, there are no alternative plausible theories as yet about how the sun came about, religious or scientific. But which is our natural resource here, the sun or the sunlight and sunheat which it provides? Of course, natural resources are the things which we benefit from the sun here on earth and not the sun itself since it is too far away from us. The sun is the source of those natural resources. Thus our natural resources here are sunlight and sunheat. As natural resources, sunlight and sunheat are as free and also as freely available as both the air we breathe and the "empty" atmospheric space which we live in. Under normal circumstances, no one ever dreams of the possibility of someone denying another person his or her right to sunlight. And yet it happens every day somewhere in some dark corner of this world. Even though no government would today ever admit to doing it, subjecting perceived security risk suspects to continuous darkness until they become hopelessly disoriented is part of torture techniques which some governments still authorise for use in certain instances. The infamous USA Guantanamo Bay comes to mind in this regard. Torture itself is inhuman no matter how and why it is administered so there would be no need to go into the merits or demerits of denying someone their natural right to sunlight while being tortured.

Commercial business exploitation of sunlight and sunheat

Sunlight and sunheat are exploited for commercial business purposes everyday and everywhere too. We just do not see or realise it because we have so totally accepted and gotten accustomed to it as the normal way things happen that our brains are now blind to that fact. All the time we plant our crops for both commercial and subsistence purposes we just plant them and leave the rest up to the sun (and the rain of course) to complete the process of maturation. We only come back to cultivate or weed-out, tender for and harvest. Without sunlight and sunheat, there would be no harvesting of anything at all from our cultivated crops. No one anywhere in this world has yet viably produced any agricultural products from the sole and exclusive use of artificial light and heat alone. And no one has even tried it for it is not worthwhile not only because there is plenty of free and freely available natural sunlight and sunheat anyway, but also because for some reason, there is nothing which is better than the natural sun in supporting healthy plant growth, development, maturation or productivity. So first and foremost, we use sunlight and sunheat everyday for both subsistence and commercial farming in agriculture.

The only natural resource which belongs to no one

The biggest questions of them all in relationship to the sun as a natural resource is that can it be treated in the same territorial way in which other natural resources such as land, people, water, minerals, wildlife, and air and airspace can be treated? The answer is a definite no. The same or even similar territorial logic does not apply with the sun. The sun is not territorial but global in nature. And there is no one who can prevent the sun from shining over any one or any country as yet. No country can claim exclusive rights to the sun or any share in the final commercial business profit benefits arising from the use of the sun's energy. Thus commercial business solar energy projects would only owe the state for the commercial business use of the land on which such projects would be built and not for the sunlight which they would use for generating electricity. This is just in much the same way as all commercial business agricultural projects would also only owe the state for the land used in agriculture and not for the sunlight and sunheat which naturally and automatically power all agricultural crops to growth, maturation and productivity.

Chapter 21: The right to the public purse

The public purse

If there is one basic human right which many people are completely unaware of, it is the right to the public purse. The public purse is made up of all the monies which all public owned entities and governments generate or collect directly or indirectly from all those various businesses, taxes, fees, levies, duties, premiums, contributions and whatever other terminology which governments usually come up with when they just want to collect more taxes. The main reason why most law abiding citizens would ready pay taxes and not seek to dodge is the knowledge and belief that after all the tax money belongs to everybody and that it would be used by government and other public agencies for the public good or for the benefit of the general public. This expectation of government to govern for and in the best interests of the governed people or general public is the sort of psychological contract between government and the governed citizenry which makes the people concede to be governed by their government and also which keeps them faithfully paying their tax dues. And this is also the very same sort of psychological contract which makes the right to the public purse a basic human right which everyone must be enabled, empowered and allowed to access and enjoy by their government.

In Chapter 2 of this book we said that government was the custodian-in-chief of the public purse and in that regard the duty and obligation of government was to ensure that everyone contributed to the public purse, each according to his or her own capacity to contribute, and also to ensure that everyone benefited from the public purse, each according to his or her own needs. In terms of access to the public purse, what this means is that whenever and wherever government spends public money, it must always ensure that the bulk of that money, if not all of it, would always end up benefiting the general public or the people, either directly or indirectly. That must indeed be the rule of thumb for each and every government in this world as far as public expenditure is concerned. Governments must never spend public monies in ways which would benefit other people or businesses more than it would benefit the generality of the governed people themselves. That would be a violation of the right of the taxpaying governed people to the public purse which is in fact their basic human right.

Right to the public purse is routinely violated

The sad fact about the right to the public purse is that this right is routinely violated by most governments especially in developing countries. If you do the mathematics of it all, you will discover that this assertion is sadly very true even for your very own beloved government and country. For example, what proportion of the annual public expenditure in your own country in the past few years has actually ended up directly and indirectly benefiting the general public in exact monetary terms? In other words what proportion of public expenditure was directly paid out to the general public in monetary benefits (salaries, etc), and what proportion was indirectly paid out to the general public in non-monetary benefits?

The rule of thumb here is that at least one third of public expenditure must be paid out directly to the general public in monetary benefits of one sort or the other, and at least another one third must be paid out to the same general public in non-monetary but solid material goods benefits, also of one sort or the other, while the remaining one third would be paid out in non-tangible service goods, or non-material and non-monetary benefits of one sort or the other as well.

For example, as far as public health expenditure is concerned, the first one third could be paid out in salaries and other employment benefits to say employees of both the public and private healthcare sectors, the next one third could be paid out in material benefits to patients such as drugs and other medical supplies, and the last one third could be paid out in non-tangible service goods benefits such as the medical consultation fees thereof. It would be quite anomalous and also very scandalous for, say, the costs of non-tangible medical consultation service fees alone to absorb the bulk of the public expenditure on health services delivery with very little going into drugs and salaries. And it would also be quite absurd for salaries and other employment benefits to devour the bulk of this expenditure to the detriment of all the other costs as well. And yet public service delivery systems are littered with examples where sometimes as high as even eighty percent or more of total public expenditure has been spent on salaries or on non-material service costs alone. At the end of such scandalous and skewed public expenditure, there would usually be nothing to show for it because non-material service costs do not leave behind any tangible evidence.

The one third rule of thumb in public expenditure is not new but just a derivative of the one third rule of thumb which is normally employed when allocating expenditure costs for any project or programme, be it in the public or private sector. In any project or programme, expenditure costs allocation must be such that not more than one third of the total project costs may be spent on labour costs alone, not more than one third may be spent on material goods costs alone, and also not more than one third may be spent on non-material or service goods costs alone as well. National public expenditure must also follow the same one third rule because every public expenditure on any public project or programme is exactly as good as any other project budget expenditure. In both cases, there are labour costs, material goods costs and non-material goods or service costs involved. As far as public expenditure goes, labour costs would be represented by the monetary benefits which would directly go into the hands or pockets of individual members of the public, material goods costs would be represented by the non-monetary but material goods benefits which would directly benefit members of the public, while non-material goods or service costs would be represented by the costs which would be spent on professional service fees for example.

If you do the maths for your own country, you would most probably be disappointed to realise that maybe even less than twenty percent of public expenditure ends up directly in the hands of the general public as salaries and other non-monetary but also material goods benefits, while eighty percent or more ends up in the hands of very few private business people in the invisible and intangible form of non-material goods or service costs! In many of our developing world countries, the biggest chunk of public expenditure always ends up in the hands of a very, very small number of politically connected business people in the form of these invisible and intangible non-material goods or service costs! What this actually means is that the bulk of our public expenditure ends up being used to pay for virtually nothing since at the end of the day there would be nothing to show for it except stories about how and what the money was used for! This is definitely not the right or correct way to expend the public purse in terms of ensuring that people access their natural and basic human right to that public purse, and yet it happens all the time.

A holistic look at public expenditure

A word of caution is needed here in terms of calculating the proportional distribution of public expenditure with regards to the right to the public purse. Many people may not realise that it would not be as simple as just looking at the government's national annual fiscal budget and saying proportionately, how much of that budget is paid out in civil or public servants' salaries, how much is paid out in non-monetary material goods, and finally, how much is paid out in non-material and non-monetary service goods? If one looks at the issue of public expenditure in such simplistic terms, one may be tempted to quickly and mistakenly point out that in fact, most if not all developing world national governments spend more than fifty, sixty, seventy or even eighty percent of their annual fiscal budgets directly in the form of civil or public servants' salaries and other employment benefits alone, and the remainder in the form of material and non-material service costs thereof. But first of all, national public expenditure is not made up only of the national or central government's annual fiscal budget expenditure alone. National public expenditure is made up of all of that, plus all the expenditures of all the other decentralised public government structures such as state, provincial and district governments, local authorities and municipalities, other public services administration bodies and also all the public owned private commercial business enterprises (POBEs). National public expenditure is the aggregate or sum total of all the expenditures of all public institutions in the country from all public owned and public administered institutions up to all privately administered but public owned institutions such as POBEs. And the public here in terms of public expenditure does not just refer to government employees, public or civil servants, but to all members of the general public, young and old, both employed and unemployed, and in both the public and private sectors of the national economy. Public here means everyone because public expenditure must benefit just about almost everyone in the whole country.

Short changing the public

Without confusing ourselves with the global picture of public expenditure, let us focus on a few cases of how the general public is usually short changed as far as their right to the public purse in concerned. One day I watched a large group of grass cutters cutting the grass along a public road which served the place where I stayed. I felt very sad and also very sorry for the grass cutters and the whole country in general with regards to that particular grass cutting public expenditure in terms of its proportional distribution amongst its beneficiaries. As someone who had worked for a whole decade in that country and also who had stayed for the same period of time in that particular city, I had very good knowledge about the financial facts surrounding that grass cutting operation. This is the knowledge which made me feel so sad about how the grass cutters were being so unfairly and unjustly short changed by their own municipal and national governments in this grass cutting exercise as far as the final distribution and actual beneficiation of that particular public expenditure was concerned.

The municipality which had the responsibility of cutting grass along all the roads in that city would always contract that job out to private sector contractors almost every year. Annual municipal grass cutting contracts would always be advertised in the local press once a year during the grass cutting season. The adverts would state what the grass cutting contract would be worth that year in terms of the total amount which the city council would be willing to spend on that job. The contract advert would also state the exact duration of the contract in terms of the calendar dates and actual number of working days which would be allowable from start to finish. The advert would also state the minimum number of grass cutting workers and grass cutting machines which would be needed for the job. Proof of possession of the required grass cutting machines and the grass cutting workers was always part of the contract evaluation process. Of course, the winning private sector contractors would always hire casual workers and the grass cutting machines for the job because of the seasonal nature of that job. And that was allowed too.

Here is what always made me feel sad about this whole scenario. I knew that private sector contractors always did things at the basic bare minimum legal requirement level. From the total value or worth of the contract, the maximum allowable length or period of time, and from the minimum number of workers which the city council insisted on for the grass cutting job, I deduced that the contract would pay about US$500 per month per worker together with his or her grass cutting machine. As someone who had worked for eight consecutive years for the Department of Labour in that country, I also knew that the gazetted legal minimum wage for grass cutters was just US$100 per month and that was exactly what the winning contractor would pay the hired casual workers and not even one cent more. I also knew that the grass cutting machines themselves could be hired for just US$3O per month or just one dollar per day.

What all this meant was that in this grass cutting public expenditure, the city council, a public government entity, was directly benefiting the hired casual workers, the real citizens of the city and the country, to the tune of only twenty percent (US$100) while it benefited the involved private sector business contractors (i.e. the winning contractor and the one who rented out the grass cutting machines) to the staggering tune of exactly eighty percent (US$400) of the concerned grass cutting public expenditure. Such skewed public expenditure must never be allowed to happen in terms of the right of the people to the public purse. What was worse in this case was the fact that as far as the actual numbers of the individual beneficiaries was concerned, the involved casual workers were a minimum of one hundred individuals while there were probably only two or even just one winning contractor because most of the time, those who usually rented out grass cutting machines would routinely hold them back in order for them to win these seasonal grass cutting jobs when the grass cutting time came.

How on earth could a city council be allowed to spend eighty percent of public money on just one business person, and in just one extremely very short period grass cutting contract while at the same time it spent just a mere twenty percent of the same public money on one hundred of its desperately in need poverty stricken citizens? As far as fairness and natural justice are concerned, this would be grossly unjust and unfair. How would poverty end then if the minority rich would thus continue to be enabled, empowered and allowed by government to directly pocket eighty percent of public expenditure while the majority poor would continue to be made to scramble for the remaining twenty percent or less? This is the crux of the matter here and this is where all the fight about the right to the public purse is also located!

Governments are obliged to ensure that the lion's share of public expenditure in any and all public expenditure based or financed programmes, projects or contracts, big or small, public or private, always benefits the general public at large, both directly and also indirectly, and in very big ways too in terms of proportionalities as has already been strictly calculated, discussed and argued above. When national governments and all other public institutions, organisations and bodies go out there to purchase goods and services from whoever they may want to purchase them, they must always ensure that the general public benefits from that expenditure in the same big way. There would be absolutely no excuse for anything less than that because that is what the right to the public purse is all about. The public has got the right to its own money. And yet, how many national governments in the third world for example routinely ensure that the general public are the major beneficiaries of any public expenditure in their respective countries? Most probably none and this is not good at all!

Multi-million and multi-billion dollar public expenditure supported contracts are always awarded to the rich and famous all the time and everywhere in this world by national governments and other public institutions while the general public itself continues to be fleeced in terms of any monetary and material benefits thereof. Consequently, the rich continue to get richer, while the poor continue to get poorer each every day which passes by. There definitely needs to be a very big paradigm shift in this matter of public expenditure beneficiation, otherwise the general public would remain impoverished forever while their money, the very public purse to which they are all entitled, goes on to enriched just a few private individual. A government of the people by the people for the people would always want to ensure that the people themselves are the first and also the biggest beneficiaries of any public expenditure no matter what. That is what truly democratic governments would do.

Public expenditure and private participation

The need for prioritisation of public beneficiation in all public expenditure is not at all at odds with the doctrine of government not having to actually do anything on the ground directly or all by itself which this book has all along been preaching about. In fact, it is just part of that doctrine. For example, there was nothing which stopped the grass cutting contract awarding city council which was discussed above to also stipulate in its grass cutting contract the requirement that the winning contractor would have to pay the hired casual workers at a minimum of at least the legally gazetted lowest taxable income rate which stood at US$350 per month per person at that point in time. After all, no self-respecting and people centred government or any other public entity or institution in this world for that matter, must ever spend public monies on businesses which pay even just one of their workers at a rate which is below the legally gazetted lowest taxable income because lowest taxable incomes are usually pegged right at the poverty line. Doing business with organisations which pay their workers below the lowest taxable income would be tantamount to entrenching poverty and legalising slavery which is just unacceptable. Underpayment of labour as exemplified by wages which are below the lowest taxable income is actually the biggest source of the working poor and the general abject poverty which pervades many countries today. The promotion of routine underpayment of labour by government through the awarding of public service delivery contracts to companies which pay their employees below the lowest taxable income is just unacceptable.

Governments must only do business with businesses all of whose workers are positive instead of negative contributors to the fiscus in terms of payment of monthly income tax. Such being the case, the requirement that any business contractor who would want to win a public sponsored business contract must always pay his or her workers at the minimum wage rate which is equivalent to or above the legally gazetted national lowest taxable income would be quite a very good, reasonable and logical requirement. This requirement would still be quite good, fair, reasonable and logical if it were also applied to dealings between private sector businesses themselves!

By simply requiring that its seasonal grass cutting contractor must pay the grass cutters at or above the rate of the lowest taxable income which at that time stood at US$350 per month, the city council which we discussed above would have instantaneously put seventy percent of that particular public expenditure directly into the hands of one hundred individual members of its general citizenry instead of putting eighty percent thereof directly into the hands of just one businessman as it did! Just imagine the difference between one hundred individual households which the seventy percent public expenditure on grass cutting by the city council would have economically helped as compared to just the solitary household which the eighty percent expenditure actually benefited! In terms of positively impacting on socioeconomic growth and poverty reduction at national level, which one of these two scenarios would be more effective than the other? There is no price for getting that one correctly because it is so obvious.

To conclude this discussion, there is absolutely no good reason why government cannot ensure that the biggest chunk of all public expenditure in the country both directly and also indirectly benefits the general public as a whole. Absolutely none at all! Perhaps the only reason for any government not wanting to ensure that such is actually the case would be the ever present scourge of human corruption, and of course, also the ever present sickening apathy of the concerned general public itself in terms of standing up and demanding access to their inalienable right to the public purse and all other rights. What a pity this is! What would it take for the general public to one day wake up to the fact that the world is in a bad place today not because of the misdeeds of a few bad guys amongst us, but because of the inaction of the many good guys of who the majority of us actually are? This is the million dollar question in public government and governance issues.

Corruption is not a basic human right

Corruption is an inborn psychosocial behavioural malady which is naturally found in all human beings but just waiting to rear its ugly head if and when given the opportunity to do so. By nature, every human being without exception has got the capacity to be corrupt. The best way to prevent corruption is not to give it any chance to surface, and for that to be possible, one needs to know and understand what corruption is and also what it is all about.

Corruption is a crime of conscience. It is the act of obtaining material advantages, gains or favours by morally or ethically wrong or unfair means. Unlike cases of fraud and theft, corruption cases are not that obvious or straightforward, and they are usually very difficult to pin-point or prove due to lack of factual or solid evidence. And yet it is obvious that cases of corruption are far more rampant than those of fraud and theft, and that corruption actually costs more in terms of wasted resources. This is tragic for governments, businesses and the general population. Tragic in the sense that corruption turns out to be the biggest drain on resources for everyone from individuals, communities, businesses and up to governments alike.

The common factor in all corruption cases is human beings, or rather human behaviour [1]. To be able to effectively deal with corruption, we must first of all be able to thoroughly understand and accept the intrinsic attributes of human behaviour inside out, otherwise we shall never be able to get on top of this game. Human intrinsic and survivalistic behaviour, by nature and also just like the intrinsic and survivalistic behaviours of all other living things, especially of the animal kingdom, is governed by the Darwinian theory of the survival of the fittest and the dog-eat-dog, one man for himself and God for us all kind of attitude. This is very true no matter whatever protestations to the contrary some pretentious holier-than-thou people amongst us may try to proffer. In fact, anyone who denies this fact would actually be acting corruptly right there and then. Those who say that they are not corrupt would actually be trying to corruptly lowering your own guard against corruption so that they could easily take advantage of you somehow once your guard against corruption is down.

Every honest person knows that they are always apt to want to take advantage, fairly or unfairly, of any and every situation which would somehow benefit themselves, and that the only thing which would normally stop them from always doing so would be some kind of inborn self-restraint and not because of the lack of the natural desire to do so, or to be corrupt. The desire to be corrupt is always there in every one of us. It is only this self-restraint and not the lack of desire which keeps individual corruption at bay in most cases. Unfortunately, a few amongst us do not have enough of that kind of self-restraint, or at least their self-restraint threshold is very low. Such corruption prone people actually need to be restrained somehow.

Anyway, we really have to accept the fact that human beings are intrinsically inclined to be corrupt by nature and there is absolutely nothing we can do about that regardless of what religious priests or anybody else for that matter may preach about it. We are all corrupt, full stop. Or maybe let us be a little bit kind to ourselves and say that we all can be corrupt or can be corrupted sometimes. It is only if and when we accept this fact that we can then begin to deal with corruption effectively.

When we completely accept, know and understand the naturalness of corruption, we would realise that punitive anti-corruption laws and anti-corruption watchdogs are not and would not be as efficient and as effective at tackling corruption as preventive anti-corruption operating systems are or would be. Corruption is actually a systemic issue because it is deeply and firmly engrained in the human psyche, thinking, behaviour and way of life. In fact, corruption is a natural system of human behaviour. Such being the case as it is, corruption can only be successfully tackled both systematically and systemically as well.

The first step to tackling corruption systemically is to expect and anticipate corruption in every human business and social transaction. We must accept the fact that corruption is inborn, highly secretive, intimate, very private and stubbornly persistent too. And yet because of its secretive nature, corruption also naturally hates openness and publicity. Such being the case, any public or government business must be transacted very openly and publicly too in order to prevent, avoid and beat corruption. Public business must be open to public scrutiny and public examination, and it must also pass this public scrutiny and public examination test every time. Without public openness, public scrutiny and public examination, corruption would be very difficult to see, detect and root out.

Government tender processes and procedures must not only be open and known to the general public like the back of their hands, but the processes and procedures must also garner the support and endorsement of the majority of the very same general public as well. Likewise, bidding for public and government tenders must also be very open, public and truly competitive with absolutely no chance of insider trading or manipulation. All public tender processes and procedures right from conceptualisation, drafting, advertising, adjudication, monitoring, evaluation, review and administration must also be very open and public. These processes and procedures must also be based on well publicised hard and factual considerations, and they must be presided upon by totally independent and non-conflicted professionals of publicly proven competencies in that field who would have also publicly declared their interests beforehand or who would have recused themselves from all the tender administration processes as necessary.

It is absolute and rampant secretiveness, the non-disclosure of personal interests and relationships, and the failure to recuse oneself from certain specific public business tender administration and management processes as and when necessary which give rise not only to the possibility of corruption, but also to the actual fact of corruption itself. Almost in the same vein, laws which prohibit certain people or businesses from partaking in tendering for government or public contracts more often than not promote corruption rather than help to expose, prevent, stop or eradicate it. This is because such mistaken and misguided laws would obviously force people to operate from underground with hidden identities which can only make corruption far worse and far more difficult to see, recognise, prevent, detect, find or eradicate than otherwise. It is far better to allow everybody, and this includes registered private companies owned by workers, public or civil servants, to do business with government and the whole public service business sector at large as long as there would be full and public disclosures of any and all conflicting business interests and complete recusal of all interested and related parties from all and any tender contract conceptualisation, drafting, advertising, tendering, adjudication, management and administration processes.

Public openness tends to help to eradicate corruption while privacy or secrecy tends to promote it. Preventing and fighting corruption is as easy as all that. But believe me, the most difficult decision to make for every politician in this world is to go public or to be open about anything. With politicians, the political process of being open or going public would itself be so riddled with corruption that the results thereof would actually be corrupted results! And that has been the fate of most of the window dressing mandatory asset disclosures which politicians have always hoodwinked the general public with every time they assume public office in an effort to show that they were not and would not be corrupt while in office. Such pretentious acts are just corruption in motion!

The role of Central Banks in managing the public purse

The Central Bank plays some very crucial roles in managing the public purse. Eversince money was invented and Central Banks then became necessary, the main duty and obligation of any Central Bank, Reserve Bank or by whatever names such an institution may be called from country to country, is just one thing and one thing alone. It is to absolutely ensure that the perceived value of the national monetary currency which it owns and also issues would always be as close to the actual or real material value of that money or currency as is practically possible, while also simultaneously ensuring that the general public would not be unduly cheated out of that material value or worth of the money by anybody and in any way whatsoever. Thus, the Central Bank must always ensure that the perceived value of the local currency must not be highly inflated or deflated, and that any monetary currency value based transactions must be free, just and fair to everyone concerned. This is the main role of the Central Bank. Everything else which Central Banks do would just be complimentary or incidental to this main role.

Many people think that the main role of the central bank is to just print and issue out local currency. Yes, this is partly true in the sense that soon after it was invented, the need to centralise the control, management and administration of national monetary currencies in terms of production, storage, issuance, legal exchange, monitoring, evaluation, review and continuous improvement became inevitable. But printing money and everything else which is related to that would just be monetary administrative or operational issues and not monetary governing policy issues of which we are talking about here. Monetary currency governing and governance policies are the ones which give money its day to day perceived and actual values. Commensurate with this central role, it therefore means that as far as managing the public purse is concerned, the Central Bank must ensure that the perceived value of the public purse is as close to its real or actual material value as is practically possible so as to give the public real value for their money.

What is Money?

This brings us to the question of money. What exactly is money? If this question was posed to university students and their professors, one would get answers which would be laced with phrases like money is a medium of exchange, trade or doing business, all of which correctly describe what money may be used for, but not exactly what it is in itself. On its own, money is just a token representation of wealth and nothing else! This is because money does not have to be exchanged for anything in order for it to become money. Money is just money or just a token representation of wealth whether it is being actively exchanged for anything at that particular point in time or not. And money on its own, by itself and in itself as just a token representation of wealth is actually and intrinsically completely worthless or valueless! Many people do not realise this, but it is actually very true and also very correct. The only value which money has is its perceived commercial business value and not its real, intrinsic or material value because it does not have any intrinsic or material value at all in the first place. This is the main reason why local currencies of many if not most countries have absolutely no commercial business value whatsoever outside their own borders. Both locals and outsiders would normally not accord any commercial business value to currencies of other countries other than their own, so they would not use such foreign currency in their own countries. There are only very few foreign currencies in this world whose perceived commercial business value is now almost universally acceptable on the international global money market. Such currencies as exemplified by the United States dollar can be used in almost any and every country of this world in terms of being exchanged for the local currency but usually not in terms of being exchanged for over the counter goods and other services. But such is an exception rather than the norm, and this fact alone also proves the point that monetary currency or money only has perceived commercial business value and not any real, actual or intrinsic material value by and in itself. In other words, without this perceived commercial business value, any money or currency is actually valueless or of absolutely no value at all! Are you surprised by this? Of course, may people would be surprised by this audacious revelation because usually, people equate having a lot of money or cash to being rich. And yet there actually is a very big difference between being moneyed and being rich or wealthy. Money is not wealth because it does not have any material or intrinsic value on its own unlike real wealth such as food, clothes, land, buildings and other material things which have material or intrinsic value all by themselves as they are just sitting there.

Paper money is intrinsically valueless

Anybody who thinks that a piece of paper called money is worth anything on its own or by itself has never been in a hyperinflationary environment. When inflation hit the five hundred trillion percent mark in Zimbabwe in 2008, money which could buy a loaf of bread early in the morning had absolutely no value at all and would not buy anything, and I mean nothing at all, by mid-morning of the very same day! At that time in Zimbabwe, prices of commodities where no longer being displayed in the shops because as Professor Ha-Joon Chang (23 Things they don't tell you about capitalism) would say, they had become meaningless noises! At one point in time, the physical size in terms of volume of paper money which one needed to buy a loaf of bread was several times bigger than the physical volume or size of the loaf of bread itself. That is when the Zimbabwean Central Bank came up with one hundred trillion dollar notes (Of course the then Zimbabwean dollar). Unbelievable, but it is actually true. The Zimbabwean Central Bank had by then utterly failed in its main duty and obligation to ensure that the perceived commercial value of the local currency which it issued was as close to the currency's real or actual material value as is practically possible. The resultant inflation actually inflated the then Zimbabwean dollar out of existence! I think this phenomenon deserves a place in the Guinness Book of World Records.

In 2008, after the national Central Bank had slashed a total of twenty-six zeros from the currency on two consecutive but separate occasions in a very desperate attempt to control the supersonic inflation, the Zimbabwean dollar finally took a bow and spontaneously left the scene on its own accord. There was no official declaration of the death of the official national currency. The official national currency just insidiously and automatically disappeared from circulation only to be insidiously and automatically replaced by the United States dollar. No one ever mourned the loss of the Zimbabwean national currency at that time perhaps with the exception of government politicians and their relatives and friends who had by then developed the bad and selfish habit of printing the local currency on cheap bond paper and then exchanging it for real US dollars in the black market. These heartlessly cruel guys were creating money from nothing and thereby adding on to the already wild monetary hyperinflation which finally burnt the country to the ground.

Determining the perceived commercial value of money

The above sordid description of the 2008 Zimbabwean hyperinflationary and very sad monetary currency situation aptly demonstrates the absolute lack of any intrinsic value whatsoever of money and the crucial role of the Central Bank in managing the public purse. How does the Central Bank ensure that the perceived commercial value, or in fact, the tradable value of which the perceived commercial value actually is, of the local currency is as close to its real or actual material value as it practically possible? There are actually not very many ways of doing this because such ways would have to be related to how the commercial value of money or currency is perceived by the general public, and those public perception modalities are not infinitesimal.

First of all, people perceive the commercial value of money through how easily tradable as a currency that money is both internally and externally. High commercial value currency or money in terms of perception is the one which is universally tradable everywhere and anywhere in the world. If the Central Banks allows the local currency to freely move in and out of banks, in and out of the pockets of the people, and also in and out of the country, such currency would eventually be highly tradable anywhere and everywhere in the world and consequently it would also be of very high perceived commercial value. Such being the case, the first step in increasing the perceived commercial value of any national currency is actually less and not more monetary control measures by the concerned Central Banks. Less monetary control measures would not only increase the perceived commercial value of the money or currency through the ease of movement of the money, but also through keeping the bulk of that money and all its movements within the legal monetary channels as well. Too strict and too stringent monetary control measures have the tendency not only to inhibit capital flows to the point of paralysis, but to also drive that money into the dark and deep underworld of the black market where only illegality is the winner and no one else.

After freeing the currency or money from any unnecessary and actually counterproductive controls, the Central Bank would just then just sit back and watch amazing things unfolding in front of it in terms of the perceived commercial value of its own currency. That value would just shoot up spontaneously! Of course, this is provided that one other very important aspect holds true and remains constant. This is the aspect of the amount of money in circulation. The Central Bank is the one which determines the amount of money in circulation in terms or releasing that money into the circulation. The question is that how does the Central Bank know or determine the correct amount of money which must be in circulation at any one given time? A bit of history is needed to answer this very pertinent question.

Most of the paper money which was issued by different countries in the past used to correctly reflect and attest to the fact that the money was just a token representation of wealth by bearing the following words in the name of the governor of the Central Bank and also supported by his or her own personal signature below them: *"I promise to pay the bearer on demand to the value of .e.g. ten dollars."* And ten dollars would be the face value or the value written on the face of that particular bank note as issued. Of course, the perceived commercial value of the bank note would be the actual or material value of what that bank note can buy or be traded for and not the ten dollars written on it. If that ten dollar bank note cannot buy anything at all, then not only would its perceived commercial value be nothing at all, but so would also be its real or actual material value. The double job of the Central Bank here is to make sure that the face values of the banks notes which it issues would be as close to both their actual or material and perceived commercial values as is practically possible, and both at the same time too, and then also to go ahead and ensure that these values remained that way at all material times too.

The Central Bank does the above mentioned currency value protection and assurance first and foremost not by freeing the money from any unnecessary and counterproductive controls as it eventually must, but by first of all giving our intrinsically valueless currency some kind of intrinsic value of its own. And this takes us back to the caption *"I promise to pay the bearer on demand to the value of .e.g. ten dollars"* which was mentioned above. What exactly would the Central Bank governor be promising to pay the bearer on demand here? That is exactly where the answer to the Central Bank given intrinsic value of any national currency lies. And that answer must be there somewhere. Any currency which is worthy anything at all is and must always be supported by real or material wealth which has got tangible intrinsic and un-diminishing value all by itself. The promise by the Central Bank governor to pay the bearer on demand some kind of material value to the tune of a given figure as used to be written on the face value of many currencies meant that if anyone walked up to the governor and demanded to trade in the monetary currency in his or her possession in exchange for what that currency would be worth in material terms, then the Central Bank governor was obliged to be able to cough up the material value equivalent of the monetary currency there and then, and hand it over to the demanding fellow in exchange for that monetary currency. What object of equivalent material value would our promising to pay the bearer Central Bank governor hand out in such cases? Whatever that thing or object was or would be, it would be the thing which gives money both its real and perceived commercial values as a token representation of real or material wealth.

The value of monetary currency needs material backing

In the real world, money or currency which is not supported or backed up by real material wealth is of no value at all. In the good old days, it was rumoured that the real material wealth which backed up all monetary currencies which Central Bank governors thus promised to pay the bearer on demand was actually solid gold which was reportedly kept in very secure vaults at all Central Banks. Nowadays no one really knows what Central Banks keep as security or surety for the paper money or currencies which they issue out into circulation. But whatever it is, the principle must perhaps still be just the same good old principle of real material wealth surety or security. And this principle behoves that Central Banks cannot issue out into public circulation amounts of paper money whose total face value would exceed the actual material value of the surety or security which they hold in their possession somewhere and somehow in lieu of that money. Whether or not that surety or security is still in the form of gold, not a single Central Bank governor is talking. But that is besides the point because the point here is that in order for the Central Bank to ensure that the perceived commercial value of the currency which it issues is as close as is practically possible to its actual or real value in material terms, the bank must first of all ensure that the totality of the issued currency does not exceed, and neither must it fall below, the real or material value of the surety which the Central Bank holds in lieu of that currency. Too much money in circulation would mean inflation while too little would mean deflation. That surely must be the real starting point of Central Banks in terms of their obligation to manage the public purse. Freeing money from unnecessary and counterproductive control measures would just be auxiliary to this initial and main role of all national Central Banks.

The above enumerated two major steps would just about do it for Central Banks in terms of what they must do and how they must do it. The business of tweaking with interest rates and currency exchange rates is not the mandate or prerogative of Central Banks but that of the free market. And yet many Central Banks, especially in the third world, are almost exclusively submerged in such private sector business operations with very dire and counterproductive repercussions for their already very poor countries. Last but not least, Central Banks must always be state or public owned business enterprises (POBEs) and not government or privately owned and privately operated businesses as already defined and discussed elsewhere in this book. Central Banks have the crucial role of issuing out and managing the value of national currencies in a manner which would enable the general public to extract real and material value for their money and the public purse as well.

Conclusion

What is wrong with government? After reading this book, this must no longer be a rhetorical question but a real one. And why do people love to hate government? The answer to this second question is very simple. People love to hate government because there usually is something wrong with government. So what exactly is wrong with government?

To start at the beginning, the first thing which is wrong with some governments is that they come into power the wrong way. Besides the undeniably bad and unacceptable military *coup de tat* method of coming into power, there are other more subtle but equally bad ways by which many world governments usher themselves into power.

The best way for any government to come into power is to be ushered into power by the voluntary, free and fairly expressed will of the governed people themselves. There must be no coercion, no forced matters. There must be a whole lot of freedom and fairness about it all in the way people must express their will to be governed by their own government. The habit of bribing, forcing, threatening and cheating people into expressing the will to be governed by a particular government is not at all the way to go about it. And yet, short of military *coup de tats*, may governments routinely do exactly just that at each and every election. They always unfairly bride, threaten, force and cheat people to usher them into governing power and still claim that as governments they would be there as the result of the freely and fairly expressed will of the governed people! This is very bad and also very unfortunate as well.

For example, one of the biggest but unfortunately generally acceptable bribery or coercion of the will of the people is the use of political manifestos to garner votes during public elections. Most pre-election political manifestos are, by and large, just a bunch of pure lies and false promises. Most politicians never intend to actually deliver on the things which they promise in political manifestos but they just say and promise such things so that they could capture the public votes which they need to win elections. Such must surely be wrong, corrupt, unethical and immoral!

The other funny thing about political manifestos is that they are unidirectional in a completely wrong way. Manifestos usually originate from politicians and are aimed at the voters instead of the other way round. As has been argued in this book before, one of the major duties or obligations of government is to listen to the people and not to just talk to them in a unilateral or unidirectional way or manner. Government does not know what people want, but it is the people themselves who know what they want, so it is them, the people, who must tell the government what they want and not the other way round. And yet political manifestos play the whole equation in reverse gear. Surely this must be the wrong way of doing it!

In political manifestos, it is always the politicians who tell the electorate what the electorate wants instead of the electorate telling politicians what they want from them. Perhaps this gives credence to the saying by Allan Coren that democracy consists of choosing your dictators after they have told you what you think it is you want to hear! Political manifestos which originate from politicians going to the electorate are nothing but just a bunch of legalised falsehoods and coercive bribes. For manifestos not to be tantamount to legalised bribes, they must come from the people going to politicians instead of from politicians to the people. For example, politicians must just go to the people and ask them: "What do you want the government to do for you?" After asking this question, aspirant politicians must then just shut up, sit down and listen while people freely and fairly speak out their own minds. After listening very carefully and perhaps even asking for further elucidations, politicians must then come back to the podium and tell the people the truth. They must tell people which ones of the things which the people would have asked for they think they could successfully deliver in the given period of time, and which ones they may not be able to deliver. They must also tell the truth about who would do what, when, where, how and why in that promised public service delivery exercise. After such a frank, truthful, non-coercive and non-bribery exchange of ideas, it would then be up to the electorate to vote for the politician or not. Surely this sounds very much like the right way to do it! The rampant practice of politicians promising to build bridges where there are no rivers must stop. Perhaps it is about time that politicians are criminally charged for garnering votes under false pretences when they fail to live up to all those juicy promises which they always lavishly adorn their manifestos with. All countries in this world must not accept the fact that the will of the people to be governed can just be bought by legalised false promises, open bribery, blue lies and coercion through manifestos because that is the wrong way of coming into government power. And that - the way it came into power - is what would be wrong with government right from the start!

Usually when all sorts of coercion and bribery have failed to garner the will of the people, politicians don't shirk at using brute force to get what they want. Unfortunately, the forced will of the people is the method by which most governments which are already in power retain the power to continue to govern. Usually, such governments do not physically force the electorate to vote for them, although such has actually been done before and also continues to be done in some unfortunate countries. They force the will of the people through credible and real threats of one kind or another and which threats are usually sprinkled with practical examples or demonstrations when and if necessary. Thus, some people have been badly beaten up and some lives have even been lost as such threats are practically demonstrated on the ground. After such practical demonstrations of threats, most of the electorate usually just falls in line and delivers the will to be governed by the threatening government. Such evil tactics are so common in many world governments that it is sickening. There is absolutely no need to wonder as to what would be wrong with government when such government would have obtained the will of the people to govern through brute force or threats of force. Governments which come into power like that always govern forcefully and that is what would be wrong with them right from the beginning.

The really crooked governments just cheat their way into power, no bribery, coercion, threats or force used. Just simple, straight forward and plain cheating and that is all. Such cheating or thieving governments usually start with gerrymandering whereby electoral constituencies or voting mechanism are intrinsically and strategically manipulated so as to give them subtle but real advantages over their political opponents. One of the biggest and most commonly employed gerrymandering tactics is the use of the so called Electoral College votes instead of normal individual or popular votes. Electoral College voting systems have on many occasions crowned popular vote losers as election winners at the end of the day. The latest example is when President Donald Trump of the United States of America (USA) walked away with the presidency despite losing the national popular vote to the aspiring Hillary Clinton by more than two million votes in the 2016 US presidential elections! Such would be broad daylight cheating or stealing of the elections, whether it is legalised or not, especially in a country which says that all people are equal. If all people are equal, how come some people's votes do not count as much as other people's votes do in Electoral College based voting systems? That is a lie!

Anyway, besides the legalised chicanery of gerrymandering as described above, some governments just resort to real streetwise cheating and broad daylight theft in order to grab the will of the people so as to govern them. They rig elections in one way or the other. Ballot box stuffing is the most blatant one of them all. Some simply cook the election results and also cook explanations thereof as well and just damn the consequences. Others have elections where there would only be just one candidate or one option. One then wonders what the point of choosing would be if there would only be one thing to choose from! And yet others find reasons to postpone elections indefinitely so that they remain in power indefinitely as well but all the time claiming to represent the will of the people without the participation of those people. Some more blatant cheats just do not announce the results of the elections forever and ever sighting a lot of incomprehensible reasons one after another and year after year until people give up as far as expecting election results would be concerned. And then we ask what is wrong with government? Can we not see it for ourselves that the way government comes into power is one of the root causes if not the sole cause of what is wrong with government?

Besides the fault being in the making of government as described in the above paragraphs, one of the things which can also be very wrong with government and which was extensively covered in this book is the basic functional structure or framework of government itself. Structure is very important because it is the structure which determines functionality. Wrong or inappropriate structures would definitely not work or function properly while correct or appropriate structures would work or function properly. It is as simple as that and this book has tried to show the basic functional structures of government which are needed to make government work or function properly so that there would be nothing wrong with government. These structures from the top to the bottom are the government oversight structure, government policy decision making structure, government policy implementation management structure, government policy implementation structure and finally the government policy implementation audit structure. As advocated for in this book, each basic functional structure of government must be completely and practically separate from all the other structures of government but remain connected to them only through the government blood which must run and floor through them all. The question which readers must now be asking themselves would be that do their governments have all these necessary and much needed basic functional structures in place in their own countries right now? If the answer to this question is no, then that is exactly what is wrong with government!

The fault or wrong in government can also be in the function of government itself. In terms of functions each one of the basic functional structures of government must be given its own practically separate and distinct functions in addition to its own practically separate and distinct workers or staff members as well. The doctrine of true, meaningful, complete and practically separation of both powers and people is more applicable to the functional aspect of all the basic structures of government than anywhere else in government. After reading this book, readers must ask themselves if their governments adhere to this doctrine down it its last letter and spirit or not, and that could provide them with answers as to what would be wrong with their own governments. As we have probably already discerned from this book, the biggest thing about function which could be wrong with government is actually in terms of what it does. This is not in terms of allocation of duties between all the relevant structures of government, but it is in terms of the exact nature of those duties and responsibilities thereof. Most governments are simply doing the wrong things or doing what they are not supposed to do while neglecting those things which are their true and correct mandate and which they must do. This book points out the fact that even though governments must not descend to actually doing things for the people and their communities on the ground, they still have natural or intrinsic obligations, duties and responsibilities to govern, legislate, serve, listen, work, deliver, empower, compete and protect. Governments must accomplish all of these obligations, duties and responsibilities without actually putting on their overalls and sweating it out together with the crowds in terms of actual policy implementation on the ground. Government policy implementation is the business of the private sector, which sector also includes each and every person as an individual. Governments must just enable these people and the private sector to implement government policies by first of all making sure that all government policies are squarely aligned to the wills, needs and aspirations of the people whom they govern, legislate for, serve, listen to, work for, deliver to, empower, enable to compete and protect through those very same policies. That is the correct function of government anywhere and everywhere in this world.

Besides just doing the wrong things as explained above, the other thing which could be wrong with government in terms of function would be focusing on the wrong things. The biggest and perhaps only mandate of government is to ensure that people access all their basic human needs and human rights and it would have finished its job right there and then. It does not have to focus on anything else after that. In fact, the only thing which government would have to focus on after that would be to govern, legislate, serve, listen, work, deliver, empower, compete and protect with regards to ensuring that people access all their basic human needs and human rights and its job would be done and dusted. And this book is all about that if nothing else.

Now the big question here is that are all our current governments doing the right things in terms of their obligations, duties and responsibilities, and are they also focussing on the correct or right things in terms of ensuring access to basic human needs and basic human rights by the people whom they govern? If our governments are not doing the right things or focusing on the right things, then that is what may be wrong with government!

Of course, there could also just be something intrinsically wrong with government as in the character of government itself in general no matter where government may be found, what it would be doing, or how it would be doing it. And there are many things which could be characteristically wrong with government in that regard. For example, everyone wants a true democracy and every government claims to be a true democracy no matter how mickey-mouse or autocratic it may in fact be. This is because everyone knows that the best government ever is a true democracy and that most people want just that, so every government just claims to be a true democracy. Of course, true democracy is government of the people by the people for the people as Abraham Lincoln said centuries ago. Being a true democracy is actually an inborn, basic and natural characteristic which many if not most governments cannot and do not measure up to for various reasons. And that is what is usually wrong with the character of government!

With the burial of outright or open colonialism, very few governments in this world are now not governments of the people, meaning governments made up of representatives of the majority governed people themselves and not foreigners. Only in a few cases do we still have some kind of colonial Heads of State. And where such things still happen, then that would be something definitely wrong with the basic inborn character of government itself in that regard.

The tenet of democracy which says government by the people is more problematic in terms of fulfilment than the one which says government of the people. The way governments come into being by the will of their people can be very problematic as we have already seen here. There is a lot of coercion, bribery, force, cheating and stealing of the will of the people going on in there and that is the big problem in terms of what is wrong with the basic character of government. Because of the untoward ways in which they come into power, sometimes governments just take on the conniving, cheating, thieving, corrupt, fraudulent, dictatorial, forceful or even murderous complexions or characteristics of their leaders. And that is what would be wrong with such governments.

The last tenet of democracy whereby it says government for the people is even more problematic than everything else. For any government to be there for the people or to govern in the best interests of the people, such government must not only be made up of the governed people themselves as in being truly of the people, but it must also have come into power through the unfettered will of the people as well. There is absolutely no way by which governments which come into power through all sorts of conniving, cheating, thieving, corrupt, fraudulent, dictatorial, forceful or even murderous means can then be governments for the people. You can't be for them if you are already against them. It is as simple as all that. And that is one big thing which could also be wrong with the natural, basic or intrinsic character of any such government.

The last thing which could be wrong with government could just be that everything about government would be wrong.

And in this case, the government which we are referring to here would be central government. How far possible and credible would it be for any central government of any country to be truly democratic if the country is a federation of multiple states or regions composed of many different people of different races, tribes, ethnicities, languages, histories, cultures, traditions, norms, values and practices? In such a scenario, would it not be better to let real governing power reside in the hands of local governments where the governed people are a bit more homogenous? Food for thought!

References

Chapter 1: Our expectations of government are wrong

1. Sibanda, C. 2017; Chapter 3: Political parties always tend to mislead people. There is No Democracy At All in Government by Political Party Representatives. pp36 – 58. AFROHD Publications

2. Ha-Joon Chang. 2011; Thing 17: More education in itself is not going to make a country richer. 23 Things they don't tell you about capitalism. pp 178 – 189. Penguin Books

3. Jack Ma Quotes – BrainyQuotes.
https://www.brainquote.com/authors/jack_ma
 Retrieved 17 June, 2018.

Chapter 2: The actual mandate of government

1. David Osborne and Ted Gaebler; 1992. Reinventing Government. Chapter 1: Catalytic Government: Steering Rather Than Rowing. pp 24 – 48. Addison-Wesley Publishing Company, Inc. USA

2. David Osborne and Ted Gaebler; 1992. Reinventing Government. Chapter 7: Enterprising Government: Earning Rather Than Spending. pp 195 – 218. Addison-Wesley Publishing Company, Inc. USA

Chapter 3: Government must not do anything for anybody

1. Sumerian King List. Wikipedia, the free encyclopaedia. http://en.wikipedia.org. Retrieved 07 April 2018.

2. David Osborne and Ted Gaebler; 1992. Reinventing Government. Chapter 2: Community Owned Government: Empowering Rather Than Serving. pp 49 – 75. Addison-Wesley Publishing Company, Inc. USA.

3. Ha-Joon Chang. 2011; Thing 5: Assume the worst about people and you get the worst. 23 Things they don't tell you about capitalism. pp 41 – 50. Penguin Books, 2011.

Chapter 4: Government can deliver without doing

1. David Osborne and Ted Gaebler; 1992. Reinventing Government. Preface. pp xxi. Addison-Wesley Publishing Company, Inc. USA.

Chapter 5: The correct governance strategy

1. What's the difference between publicly and privately held companies? https://en.m.wikipedia.org. 15 June, 2018.

Chapter 8: Democratic governance of the right to freedom

1. United States Constitution.
http://www.archives.gov/exhibits/characters/constitution
Retrieved 16 February, 2009.

2. Ha-Joon Chang. 2011; Thing 4: The washing machine has changed the world more than the internet has. 23 Things they don't tell you about capitalism. pp 31 – 40. Penguin Books, 2011.

Chapter 10: The right to social protection

1. 10 Facts About Hunger, WFP, 2015. www1.wfp.org
Retrieved 10 June, 2018

2. State of Food Security in the World, FAO, 2015.
https://www.fao.org/3.a-i4646e.pdf
Retrieved 10 June, 2018

3. ILO, 2011. Social Protection Floor for a Fair and Inclusive Globalisation: Report of the advisory group chaired by Michelle Bachelet convened by the ILO with the collaboration of WHO. ILO, Geneva.

4. How Much Should Countries Spend on Health? Discussion Paper Number 2 – 2003. WHO.
Https:www,who.int/health_financing/en/how_much_shoul d_dp_03_2pdf. Retrieved 17 June, 2018

Chapter 13: The right to natural resources

1. Ha-Joon Chang; Thing 8: Capital has a nationality. 23 Things they don't tell you about capitalism. pp 74 – 87. Penguin Books, 2011.

Chapter 14: Democratic governance of the right to people

1. Ha-Joon Chang; Thing 7: Free market policies rarely make poor countries rich. 23 Things they don't tell you about capitalism. pp 62 – 73. Penguin Books, 2011.

Chapter 16: Governance of the right to minerals

1. Ha-Joon Chang; Thing 8: Capital has a nationality. 23 Things they don't tell you about capitalism. pp 74 – 87. Penguin Books, 2011.

2. Ha-Joon Chang; "– excessive foreign ownership of a national economy can be harmful." Thing 8: Capital has a nationality. 23 Things they don't tell you about capitalism pp 83. Penguin Books, 2011.

Chapter 21: The right to the public purse

1. Ha-Joon Chang. 2011; Thing 5: Assume the worst about people and you get the worst. 23 Things they don't tell you about capitalism. pp 41 – 50. Penguin Books, 2011.

Our political storylines must change for the better

A political paradigm shift is needed

Chapter 2: The actual mandate of government

The basic mandate of government

Government must do without doing

Human rights

Ensuring access to basic human rights

What government must do and not do

Government has the duty and obligation to govern

Government has the duty and obligation to legislate

Government has the duty and obligation to serve

Government has the duty and obligation to listen

Government has the duty and obligation to work

Government has the duty and obligation to deliver

Government has the duty and obligation to empower

Government has the duty and obligation to compete

Government has the duty and obligation to protect

Chapter 3: Government must not do anything for anybody

Government must just meet people half way

Government is not born to do things for people

Government is not born to do things for people

Government does not have adequate resources

Government does not know what people want

Government has no motivation

Spoon feeding people is counterproductive

Good governments are unneeded governments

Good governments are unnoticeable governments

Personal accomplishment synergises itself

Spoon feeding communities destroys social cohesion

Communities govern themselves better than government

Communities are more committed than government

Communities know better than government

Community governments solve community problems

Communities are more enterprising than government

Government must not dictate but listen

Government must not do but just enable

Government must let people ask for help, not offer it

Help when approached, do not dictate helpers

Government must not capture but free talent

Make laws which free people and not enslave them

Just focus on governing and nothing else

Government must strategically deliver through SOEs

Chapter 6: Democratic governing structures

Complete and practical separation of powers and people

Community based government

The five basic governing structures of government

Government policy oversight structure

Government policy decision making structure

Government policy implementation management structure

Government policy implementation structures

The private sector as government policy implementer

There are two different types of private sectors

The private private sector

The private public sector

Government policy performance audit structure

The principle of separation of powers revisited

Separation of powers must start in government

Head of State and Cabinet must be two separate people

Separate Heads of Cabinet and Parliament

Separate Heads of Cabinet and the Public Service

The non-existent public service administration (PSA)

Government minister interfere with the public service

Public service delivery must be devoid of politics

The befuddled role of the Secretary to Cabinet

Separation of powers vital the private sector too

Private sector governing and governance structures

Typical private sector institution or company level hierarchy
of policy governing and governance structures

Typical local government institution level hierarchy of policy governing and governance structures

Typical national schools administration authority level hierarchy of policy governing and governance structures

Typical national health services governing authority level hierarchy of policy governing and governance structures

Typical national water governing authority level hierarchy of policy governing and governance structures

Typical national electricity governing authority level hierarchy of policy governing and governance structures

No matter how far gone down the wrong road, turn back

Chapter 7: Democratic governance of the right to life

The intricacies of the right to life

Further implications of the right to life

Basic human rights are not absolute

The right to life is the right to basic human needs

Chapter 8: Democratic governance of the right to freedom

Governments always restrict freedom
Freedom and independence are not mutually exclusive

Freedom is a basic human right

Food security

National staple foods

Who produces foods?

Where is food produced in the country?

When is food produced?

How is food produced?

Why is food produced?

Augmented food security

Wrong kind of support for food security

Correct kind of support for food security

The right to shelter

Government must empower people to access shelter

Everyone must be sheltered

The right to health

The best possible solution to health services delivery

National Health Insurance

National Health Insurance Medical Aid Scheme (NHIMAS)

Safety and security forces belong to the public

Chapter 11: Democratic governance of the right to justice

The right to justice

The right to human dignity

The Justice Services Commission (JSC)

JSCs must be completely independent

The JSC must be in charge of prisons

Governments must not be in charge of prisons

Correctional facilities are public institutions

No one must be above the law in this world

Preventive justice is a major responsibility of the JSC

Justice delayed is justice denied

Chapter 12: Right to socioeconomic development

Social rights

Economic right

Cultural rights

Culture is inherited tradition

Chapter 14: Democratic governance of the right to People

People are natural resources

People are absolutely essential for the economy

Some people are natural resources to other people

Commercial business exploitation of people

Business exploitation of people must benefit communities

The stake of the people in natural resources exploitation

Western countries benefit from their natural resources

African countries do not benefit from natural resources

Commercial exploitation of people must benefit people

Chapter 15: Democratic governance of the right to Land

Wars were fought for the right to land

The different uses of land

Land management obligations of government

Land leaseholds or title deeds

Tradable land leaseholds or title deeds

Non-tradable land leaseholds or title deeds

What is money?

Paper money is intrinsically valueless

Determining the perceived commercial value of money

The value of monetary currency needs material backing

Quotable quotes about government

1. The government is us; we are the government, you and I. *Theodore Roosevelt.*

2. To lead people, walk behind them. *Lao Tzu.*

3. Patriotism is supporting your country all the time and government when it deserves it. *Mark Twain.*

4. Mankind, when left to themselves, are unfit for their own government. *George Washington.*

5. An oppressive government is more to be feared than a tiger. *Confucius.*

6. Every decent man is ashamed of the government he lives under. *H .L Mencken*

7. A patriot must always be ready to defend his country against his government. *Edward Abbey.*

8. There can be no faith in government if our highest offices are excused from scrutiny – they should be setting the example of transparency. *Edward Snowden.*

9. If men were angels, no government would be necessary. *James Madison.*

10. Governing a great nation is like cooking a small fish – too much handling will spoil it. *Lao Tzu.*

Astounding! This is the only way to describe this book. There is definitely something which is seriously wrong with government! Governments must change the way they do the things they do both as a matter of priority and also as a matter of urgency. This is the inevitable double conclusion which one would make after reading this wonderful and wisdom laden book. People must change their own patently misguided and obsolete perceptions and views about government. In fact, the general public must start taking themselves seriously in terms of their knowledge and understanding of the world around them if they do not want politicians to continue to take them for a ride. This book is a deserved but terrible indictment of people and their governments. Read this book today!